Owsley County, Kentucky,
and the Perpetuation of Poverty

CONTRIBUTIONS TO SOUTHERN APPALACHIAN STUDIES

Owsley County, Kentucky, and the Perpetuation of Poverty

JOHN R. BURCH, JR.

CONTRIBUTIONS TO SOUTHERN APPALACHIAN STUDIES, 18

McFarland & Company, Inc., Publishers
Jefferson, North Carolina, and London

LIBRARY OF CONGRESS CATALOGUING-IN-PUBLICATION DATA

Burch, John R., Jr., 1968–
    Owsley County, Kentucky, and the perpetuation of poverty /
John R. Burch, Jr.
       p.   cm. — (Contributions to Southern Appalachian studies ; 18)
    Includes bibliographical references and index.

    ISBN-13: 978-0-7864-3264-6
    softcover : 50# alkaline paper ∞

    1. Poverty — Kentucky — Owsley County. 2. Rural poor —
Kentucky — Owsley County. 3. Sociology, Rural — Kentucky —
Owsley County. 4. Owsley County (Ky.) — History. 5. Owsley
County (Ky.) — Economic conditions. 6. Owsley County (Ky.) —
Rural conditions. I. Title.
HC79.P6B85   2008
339.4'609769176 — dc22   2007031835

British Library cataloguing data are available

Cover photograph: Jasper and Rhoda Burch sit with their son
Charlie and his family in front of their home in Owsley County
during the early 1900s (Burch Family Papers, Southern Appalachian
Archives, Berea College, Berea, KY)

Manufactured in the United States of America

*McFarland & Company, Inc., Publishers
  Box 611, Jefferson, North Carolina 28640
  www.mcfarlandpub.com*

For Idalia, Sami Jo, Morgan, Alexandra, Christopher, and Kayleigh

Acknowledgments

One cannot complete a project of this scale without a significant amount of assistance; therefore, I must express my sincere gratitude to all those individuals and institutions that made this endeavor possible. First, I must acknowledge the great contribution to this work by Ronald D Eller. Dr. Eller is the person I credit, and my wife blames, for steering my research towards Owsley County. While serving as the chair for both my thesis and dissertation committees, he always found more questions for me to answer every time I thought I had completed my work. While the process was extremely frustrating at times, there is no doubt that it resulted in a more detailed study than I had ever envisioned. Thanks are also due the many scholars at the University of Kentucky who served on my dissertation committee: Joanne Pope Melish, Daniel B. Smith, Francie Chassen-Lopez, Dwight Billings, Robert Ireland, and Evelyn Knight. Since this list includes the names of the people who traumatized me during my qualifying exam for the Ph.D., those individuals can now assume that, after the passage of several years, I have finally forgiven them.

An expression of gratitude is also due to James C. Klotter, an Owsley Countian who also happens to be the State Historian of the Commonwealth of Kentucky. From the very beginning of my research, Dr. Klotter has made himself available to me as a resource. He has read several versions of this work over the years, and has given me invaluable leads over the course of my research that have led me to the resting places of pertinent resources that I would have never discovered on my own. Thanks is also extended to an anonymous scholar who read an earlier draft of this manuscript. Once I got over the harsh comments, I discovered that the individual was completely correct. As a result of the individual's suggestions, this manuscript was greatly improved.

A number of libraries and institutions have graciously allowed me access to a wide variety of research materials: W.T. Young Library at the University of Kentucky, University of Kentucky Special Collections and Archives, Thomas D. Clark Library at the Kentucky Historical Society, Kentucky Department of Libraries and Archives, Filson Historical Society, Kentucky Heritage Council, Hutchins Library at Berea College, Eastern Kentucky University's Special Collections and Archives, Western Kentucky University Library and Special Collections, and Montgomery Library at Campbellsville University. I would be remiss if I did not single out the contributions of the Interlibrary Loan Department at Hutchins Library, Berea College. For years, Patty Tarter and her staff have patiently filled the inordinate number of interlibrary loan requests originating from Campbellsville University. Thanks are also due to Mike Turner, John C. Zimmerman, and Jan Hemberger for assisting me in using the documentation at the offices of the Planning Division of the United States Army Corps of Engineers, Louisville District. All of the people I met in the Planning Division were extremely generous as they shared their valuable time and expertise with me.

Financial assistance while I was a graduate student at the University of Kentucky was provided by both the University of Kentucky and the Appalachian College Association. The University of Kentucky graciously provided me with several Commonwealth Incentive Awards that paid for my tuition and some of my textbooks. I was also extremely fortunate, and honored, to receive the Alice F. Emerson Librarian Fellowship from the Appalachian College Association in both 2003-2004 and 2004-2005. From the Appalachian College Association, I especially need to thank Alice Brown, Tony Krug, Alice F. Emerson, and the Mellon Foundation.

My interest in both history and Appalachia was cultivated during my undergraduate years at Berea College. Among those who helped provide me an excellent education at the institution were Paul David Nelson, Warren Lambert, Richard Drake, Loyal Jones, Shannon Wilson, and Gerald Roberts. While at Berea College, I also incurred a huge debt to the entire professional staff at Hutchins Library, especially Tom Kirk, Phyllis Hughes, Edith Hansen, and Catherine (Kit) Roberts. If not for their mentoring, I would not be a librarian today.

At Campbellsville University, I cannot offer enough thanks to Michael V. Carter, Frank Cheatham, and Mary Wilgus for all of the support they have provided me since I arrived at the institution. While I pursued my graduate studies at the University of Kentucky, I depended greatly on my excellent library staff at Montgomery Library, which includes, or has included, Timothy Hooper, Patty McDowell, Sandra Riggs, Ted Schulz, Mary Street, Keith Lewis, and Regina Thompson. Their efficiency made it easy for me to immerse myself in my research without having to worry about the day to day operation of the library. Further thanks are also due to Tim Hooper for sharing so many hours on the road and in archives with me.

Many thanks also go to my family and dear friends. John Sr., Elza, and Leroy Burch have endeavored for years to ensure that our branch of the Burch family would not forget its Owsley County roots. Eustacia O'Malley, Sean O'Malley, Lauren O'Malley, Danielle O'Malley, Donna Crawford, Andy Crawford, Annaliese Crawford, Amber Rich, Pam Tuttle, Francis Burch, Betsy Burch, and my father, John Russell Burch, Sr., have all provided much more support and love as I have labored to turn my dissertation into a monograph. William, Cassandra, and Tyler Stephens are to be thanked for giving my family a life without me while I obsessively pursued my research. They turned my family into farmers and introduced them to horseback riding. The Stephenses also provided me two new mouths to feed, namely our twin horses. Most importantly, I need to thank Idalia, Samantha, Morgan, Alexandra, Christopher, and Kayleigh Burch. My mother, Idalia, made it possible for both my wife and me to attend school and work without having to worry about who was caring for the children. Thus my wife and I are to blame for "Nini" spoiling the kids rotten. Samantha, my wife, has been extremely encouraging of this entire venture, although she is personally tired of hearing all about Owsley County and my myriad theories concerning its history. Finally, thanks to my children, Morgan, Alex, Chris, and Kayleigh, who provide me with the inspiration needed to keep me juggling all of the tasks that I deal with each day.

Table of Contents

Introduction

Within any American community, there are many differing visions of an amorphous idea popularly known as "The American Dream." While the specifics of each version of the dream may differ, one constant is that there tends to be an underlying sense of optimism that the future will usually be better than one's present circumstances. The question that inevitably has to be addressed when there are competing visions of the American dream present within a community is whose future will be better? Is it the future of the community at large? Is it the future of individuals who are positioned to hoard community assets to improve their political, economic, or social standing? Why is one version of the dream privileged over another? These questions helped shape the initial stages of this study of Owsley County, Kentucky, as I sought to examine how the dreams and aspirations of Owsley's predominantly rural populace interacted with the visions of the local elites who controlled the county's political structure. Political power also obviously translated to economic power since county politicians in charge of either the courthouse or the local school system also controlled access to most of the paying jobs available within the poverty stricken county.

Curiously, Owsley County's poverty is well known within certain circles. National journalists and academics frequently offer up Owsley County as one of the quintessential examples of all that ails the Appalachian region. Within its borders, the presence of poverty is unmistakable. According to the United States Census Bureau (in data from 1999) 45.4 percent of Owsley's population of 4,856 survives on an income that falls below the federally defined poverty line. Its per capita income is only $10,742, which is significantly less than the $18,093 average income for the Commonwealth of Kentucky. Part of Owsley County's difficulties comes from not having a diversified economy. For instance, Owsley is largely devoid of nonfarm business establishments. Only 44 nonfarming business entities existed within the county in 1999, and between them they employed only 269 individuals. It is sobering to note that the afore-mentioned employment figure represents a drop of 34.1 percent over the previous decade. In contrast, the Commonwealth of Kentucky showed an overall increase in nonfarm employment of 23.9 percent for the same period. Many writers from outside of Owsley County have seized on this type of data to use Owsley County in order to dramatize poverty, laced with Appalachian stereotypes, to a national middle class audience.[1]

While outsiders have proven to be much too eager to sensationalize Owsley County's misery, local historians have instead opted to ignore the poverty that has surrounded them. Two of the published histories of Owsley County, namely Joyce Wilson's *This Was Yesterday: A Romantic History of Owsley County* and G. L. Bailey's *Early History of Owsley County, Kentucky*, are replete with stories celebrating the early white inhabitants of the region who determinedly conquered a rich wilderness teeming with wildlife on abundant lands. Both of the aforementioned works examined specific episodes in the county's history. There was no attempt on the part of the respective authors to write a continuous narrative concerning Ows-ley's history. As those Owsley County authors knew, and I quickly learned, it is extremely difficult to research the history of Owsley County because much of the documentary evidence of its past was destroyed on January 29, 1929, when a fire consumed the county's courthouse.

Other histories written about Owsley have focused on institutions located within the county. Joe Powlas's *The Church with the Golden Roof* chronicled his tenure at the Cow Creek Presbyterian Church during the latter half of the twentieth century. Powlas did provide brief glimpses of the county's persistent poverty through his discussions of his religious work. Dr. James C. Klotter and Henry C. Mayer, in *A Century of Bank-ing: The Story of Farmers State Bank and Banking in Owsley County 1890–1990*, did touch upon some of the economic challenges faced by the county throughout its history. They documented a number of failed attempts to establish a bank within the county before one actually succeeded. Klotter and Mayer also identified the limitations of the county's resources for economic growth, including an observation that Owsley's transportation systems were historically woefully inadequate. Still, this was a minor portion of the book since their primary aim was to celebrate the accomplishments of one of the few successful nonagricultural businesses in Owsley County.[2]

One factor that is evident in all of the previously mentioned published histories on Owsley County is the love that the authors have for their subject. This is not surprising when one considers that all are, or were, residents of the county. While I technically bring an outsider's perspective to the subject matter, it must be acknowledged that some of my ancestors resided in Owsley County during much of the period that I document in the narrative. William Burch and his wife, Malinda Mays Burch, immigrated with their family to Owsley County in 1858 from Barren Creek in Claiborne County, Tennessee. William and his sons, Jasper (my great-great-grandfather) and Newton (Newt), all served in Company "D" of the Seventh Kentucky Volunteer Infantry fighting alongside their Union brethren in the Union army. My great-grandfather, John G. Matthew Burch, left Owsley County sometime during the second decade of the twentieth century. Like many residents of the county, he was forced to migrate from his home in order to find employment. Although I have assiduously attempted to separate my biases from the narrative, I must admit that I am extremely sympathetic to the plight of the people who reside in Owsley County today.[3]

The literature on the Appalachian region is replete with theories for the poverty that pervades the region. Yet, it is important to note that these theories were not necessarily initially developed as a response to poverty within Appalachia. For example, in 1959 anthropologist Oscar Lewis said of his culture-of-poverty concept that it could be found "in lower-class settlements in London, in Puerto Rico, in Mexico City slums and Mexican villages, and among lower class Negroes in the United States." Lewis was particularly interested in specific psychological and behavioral traits, such as resignation, that he identified within data collected from families residing in Mexico and Puerto Rico. After a minor semantic change from resignation to fatalism, Lewis's theory is subsequently applied to describe Appalachia's ills.[4]

The literature on Appalachia began to develop in the 1870s when elites from the northern portion of the United States discovered what they believed to be a population of pure-blooded Anglo-Saxons that were living in a highly uncivilized fashion. This was difficult for the intelligentsia of the day to understand because they believed that the privileged and civilized lifestyle that they enjoyed was due to the supposedly superior Anglo-Saxon genetic traits that they had inherited from their forefathers. Either they were mistaken about their genetic superiority or there was another explanation to describe the individuals they had discovered within the mountainous environs of Appalachia. Berea College's President William G. Frost found an explanation to the conundrum that proved satisfying to the northern elites. Frost posited that the reason for the substandard economic and cultural development in the mountains was its geographic isolation. It should be noted that this explanation also conveniently aided Frost's fundraising efforts on behalf of his educational institution since northern elites felt bound to aid in the uplifting of their "contemporary ancestors." Although self-serving, William G. Frost's theory found support in the writings of academics such as Ellen Churchill Semple and George E. Vincent.[5]

By the early years of the 1960s, national attention was once again drawn to Appalachian poverty by John F. Kennedy's presidential primary campaign in West Virginia and by the publication of Michael Harrington's monograph entitled *The Other America: Poverty in the United States*. For such poverty to exist at a time when most of the United States of America was enjoying significant economic growth was distressing to many people across the nation. Appalachia thus came to symbolize the failure of the American dream. National shame over conditions within Appalachia led to the region becoming a major battleground during President Lyndon Baines Johnson's War on Poverty. Over the course of the 1960s, several models arose to explain Appalachia's poverty and lack of economic development.[6]

The culture-of-poverty theorists blamed the poverty within Appalachia on traits found within the subculture of the region. They contended that cultural deficiencies had developed over time within the subculture of the mountains and had been passed to subsequent generations. In an article entitled "The Passing of Provincialism," Thomas R. Ford attempted to identify the deficient traits that were stifling the development of the inhabitants of the Appalachian region. Alas, as argued by Dwight Billings, Ford's survey instrument was fundamentally flawed since its design had been strongly influenced by the literature on Appalachia that existed at the time. Due to the survey instrument, Appalachians were bound to be found deficient since they were being compared to the supposedly superior values of white, middle-class America. Another flaw was that the survey results were not compared to the non–Appalachian regions of the United States to determine whether the results were truly unique or could be readily applied to other locales within the country. Surprisingly for Ford, his survey results did not yield the conclusions that he expected. Ford concluded among other things that the denizens of Appalachia were "progressive-minded" and "achievement oriented." This success orientation led Ford to initially reject fatalism as a core cultural trait of the region. Yet, despite the data from his own survey instrument, Ford still found a way to identify fatalism as one of the defects found within inhabitants of Appalachia. He determined that fatalism was "psychological insurance against failure that he half anticipates and half fears will shatter hopes and ambitions raised too high."[7]

Jack Weller, a missionary stationed in West Virginia, built on Ford's study in *Yesterday's People: Life in Contemporary Appalachia*. The monograph served to crystallize the image of the stereotypical Appalachian as a relic of the past. Among the negative character traits that Weller held responsible for Appalachian poverty were individualism, traditionalism, and fatalism. He blamed the origination of these traits on isolation, fundamentalism, and close-knit families. In the "Comparative Summary" that served as the appendix to his book, Weller compared the traits of middle-class Americans with those he identified among Appalachians. Among Weller's observations were that middle-class Americans were "oriented to progress" while Appalachians were "oriented to existence." In virtually all of his comparisons, the people of Appalachia did not meet the ideal middle-class values that supposedly existed in the rest of the United States of America. Weller ultimately determined that the cultural deficiencies he observed within Appalachians would prove to be the biggest hurdle that would have to be overcome if the nation was to address Appalachia's persistent poverty problem.[8]

Sociologist Richard Ball echoed Weller's sentiments in blaming mountain folk for their plight. Ball identified the existence of what he termed an "analgesic subculture," which he defined as "the institutionalization of frustration-instigated behavior." It is important to note that Ball's insights into frustration-instigated behavior were gleaned from a series of experiments that were conducted on rats. Ball was particularly troubled by the presence of two major regressive traits that he identified as "welfare syndrome" and "extreme familism." Welfare syndrome manifested itself as a willingness among people from Appalachia to make social dependency an

acceptable means of making a living. His description of "extreme familism" was a "neurotic dependence on kin." Ball's final conclusion was that
the primary reason that middle-class Americans could not understand the
Appalachian way of life was that the people inhabiting Appalachia tended
to act in irrational ways.[9]

John Fetterman's contribution to culture-of-poverty theory differed
from that of many of his contemporaries. Rather than attempting to identify deficient or regressive traits among his subjects, Fetterman opted to
simply interview a number of "hillbillies" in Knox County, Kentucky, during the middle portion of the 1960s. Although he seemed sympathetic to
the plight of those he interviewed, the author was nonetheless condescend-
ing towards the subjects of his interviews. Fetterman acknowledged that
while the commencement of President Johnson's War on Poverty provided
hope for a brighter future for the residents of Stinking Creek, he personally was pessimistic as to the conflict's chances for ultimate success. Fetterman believed that the best that could be hoped for was that the War
on Poverty would succeed in making "poverty more comfortable."[10]

A recent application of culture-of-poverty theory can be found in
Robert D. Hawkins Jr.'s doctoral dissertation from Sam Houston State
University entitled "Social Control in the Eastern Kentucky Subculture of
Violence." Hawkins' research on "hillbilly psychology" determined that
Eastern Kentucky was a place where shooting individuals perceived of
wrongdoing was a socially acceptable manner of solving problems. According to Hawkins, this rampant lawlessness was a legacy left their descen-
dants by the Scots-Irish immigrants that first settled the region. Since these
Scots-Irish pioneers supposedly had no interest in farming or acquiring
wealth, they instead relied on their guns to provide them the sustenance
that they required. Over generations, the tendency to use a gun to acquire
all that was needed developed into a violent subculture that received rein-
forcement from poverty.[11]

For those who did not want to blame the mountaineers as the cause
for the poverty that surrounded them, modernization offered another
explanation. The proponents of modernization posited that poverty was
simply the result of economic underdevelopment. The Appalachian region
could not compete in the marketplace on an equal basis with other portions of the United States because it lacked economic capital, social infrastructure, an educated populace, and privately owned industries. The
solution to this problem was to provide educational opportunities, access

to technical expertise, improved transportation systems, and other forms of economic infrastructure.

David E. Whisnant, in *Modernizing the Mountaineer: People, Power, and Planning in Appalachia*, argued that, although well-intentioned, most of the modernization projects achieved very little, with many being outright failures. Unfortunately, some of these failures created consequences that dwarfed the original problem. One such example was the decision by the Tennessee Valley Authority to utilize coal fired steam generators in order to produce cheap electricity. The coal required to run the generators encouraged the strip mining of coal that subsequently proved catastrophic both economically and ecologically within the region.[12]

Whisnant posited that one of the primary reasons that the modernization efforts had limited, if any, successes was the relationship between those doing the modernizing and their "target population." Although ostensibly not blaming mountaineers for their impoverished state, these proponents of modernization still believed that the people of Appalachia needed to adopt the middle-class values found within the nation as a whole, along with its associated lifestyle. Not surprisingly, individuals imbued with notions of superiority had extensive difficulties working with the local populace and their leaders. Another reason for the failure of many modernization efforts was the models used to identify and correct problems within Appalachia. As stated by Whisnant, "the history of development efforts and agencies in Appalachia as I have come to understand it teaches me the nearly surreal durability of bad models and the essential superficiality of analysis that undergirds them."[13]

Whisnant did identify some limited successes within his monograph. Among the success stories were the jobs created to support antipoverty programs. Unfortunately, the end of the War on Poverty also marked the end of those particular jobs. Whisnant pointed out that in 1973 alone more than 3,085 jobs were lost. One thousand of those jobs were located in Kentucky's four poorest counties, one of which was Owsley. While the influx of jobs had to have alleviated at least some of the poverty in Owsley County, it ultimately proved short-lived.[14]

Ada Haynes' *Poverty in Central Appalachia: Underdevelopment and Exploitation* set out to undermine modernization theory by utilizing neo–Marxist development theory. Using a statistical model, Haynes determined the surplus value of labor utilized within Appalachian counties located in Tennessee, Kentucky, Virginia, and West Virginia between 1963 and 1982.

Haynes argued that the surplus value number represented the level of exploitation of employees. Through the manipulation of census data the author ultimately came to the conclusion that Appalachia was already integrated into the world economy by the 1960s. She also claimed that the rates of surplus value in manufacturing indicated that the region was susceptible to political and economic events occurring locally, nationally, or internationally. In truth, there are not many places in the entire world that would not be impacted by political or economic problems in the local to international spheres. Despite the author's claims, there did not seem to be a clear correlation between the statistics she produced and the poverty she was supposedly studying.[15]

Glen Taul provided a much more sympathetic assessment of modernization efforts in his account of the creation of the Appalachian Regional Commission (ARC). In his doctoral dissertation entitled "Poverty, Development, and Government in Appalachia: Origins of the Appalachian Regional Commission," Taul lauded the commission for its emphasis on building roads within the area it defined as Appalachia. He argued that the roads not only diversified the economic base of the region but also eventually significantly reduced the number of counties within the region that were classified as distressed.[16]

Elgin Mannion conducted a study on the impact of modernization efforts in the Appalachian portions of Kentucky from 1969 to 2003. His findings supported Whisnant's contention that the modernization efforts achieved limited success. Mannion found that during the early period covered by his study there was progress made in reducing the rate of income inequality between the Appalachian counties and the rest of the state. This trend was reversed in the 1980s when the income inequality grew to a point that it exceeded the initial 1969 figure. In terms of specific counties, Mannion demonstrates that Elliot, McCreary, Morgan, Lewis, Clay, Magoffin, Menifee, Jackson, Owsley, Wolfe, Wayne, Clinton, Leslie, Knott and Martin had the lowest amount of income growth in the entire state. It is no coincidence that many of those very counties also had the lowest number of people participating in the labor force.[17]

Mannion charged that models based on modernization theories were flawed due to the assumptions that were used for their construction. Those models focused on providing what the Appalachian counties did not have, namely the capitalist infrastructure required to develop sustainable economic growth. Mannion persuasively argued that those models mistakenly ignored an agricultural sector that did exist and should have been developed aggressively.[18]

Modernization theory was not attractive to many individuals writing about Appalachia during the 1960s and 1970s because of the existence of coal companies in the region. If the solution to Appalachia's problems were capital and industry then why had the coal industry not lifted Appalachia out of its poverty? The industry was highly capitalized and technologically advanced. It certainly was extracting a rich natural resource that was valued throughout the world. Although many Appalachians worked within the industry, the wealth it was generating was obviously not filtering down to the inhabitants of the region in great amounts. A number of critics of modernization theory determined that the poverty was not necessarily due to underdevelopment. The problems within the region were those economic and political entities that shaped and profited from the development of the region.

Harry Caudill's *Night Comes to the Cumberlands: A Biography of a Depressed Area* marked a turning point in the bibliographic literature on Appalachia because it articulated a more complex explanation for Appalachian poverty. While he embraced the genetic deficiencies identified by culture-of-poverty theorists, he also pointed to existing structural problems within the Appalachian social, political, and economic spheres. In particular he addressed the role of economic and political entities in exploiting the region's wealth. He exposed the coal, timber, and railroad industries as the primary culprits for the poverty in Appalachia. His account of the economic exploitation of Eastern Kentucky was jarring for the mass audiences that read his monograph.[19]

One of those inspired by Caudill was David Cattell-Gordon. Cattell-Gordon contended that generations of job loss had left the people of Appalachia suffering from "culturally transmitted traumatic stress syndrome." Chronic unemployment and exploitation had created cultural traits within Appalachians, such as resignation, depression, and dependency, that Cattell-Gordon concluded were clinical manifestations of the illness. The author differentiated his work from culture-of-poverty theorists by blaming the creation of cultural traits not on mountain folk but rather on those who had economically exploited them.[20]

Caudill's monograph in 1963 foreshadowed some of the themes that would in a few short years be developed into the colonialism model. According to the proponents of colonialism, Appalachian poverty was not caused by geographic isolation or deficiencies in a folk subculture. Their explanation was that outside capitalists had seized economic and political control of the region.

Helen Lewis and Edward Knipe helped define the colonialism model by identifying four stages of colonization. The first stage consisted of forced entry by outsiders. Secondly, there would be changes in values and lifestyle caused by the outside influences. Thirdly, the colonizers would assume political and social control over the natives. Finally, notions of superiority would justify mistreating and dominating the colonized. Helen Lewis, in the article "Fatalism or the Coal Industry," subsequently applied the four stages of colonialism to the history of the coal industry in order to demonstrate the model's applicability.[21]

The Appalachian Land Ownership Task Force reinforced the colonialism model by showing that much of the region was controlled by outside forces. In their publication, *Who Owns Appalachia?*, they examined the relationship between land ownership and socioeconomic conditions. Through the examination of land ownership in eighty counties located in Appalachia it was determined that "ownership of the land is concentrated in relatively few hands, dominated by absentee and corporate holders, with little available for local families to work, farm, or otherwise enjoy." The Appalachian Land Ownership Task Force also demonstrated that there was a clear correlation between absentee ownership and the socioeconomic conditions within the Appalachia region. The absentee owners paid only a small fraction of the property taxes that were collected by the respective counties, although they owned a vast majority of the land. The consequences of having a small tax base within the respective counties included poorly funded schools and an inability to construct needed infrastructure improvements such as roads.[22]

In *Power and Powerlessness*, John Gaventa attempted to explain why mountaineers did not rebel against the coal companies that repressed them in the latter decades of the nineteenth century into the twentieth. His explanation was that they simply did not have the power to overcome their oppressors. The corporations thoroughly controlled the economic, political, and legal mechanisms that existed throughout the region. They even had the ability to utilize force against the mountaineers if it proved necessary, as evidenced by the "Battle of Evarts" in 1931. It was this total domination that Gaventa credited with the development of the quiescence and fatalism that so enthralled culture-of-poverty theorists.[23]

One group of scholars took exception to the colonial model because it provided too simplistic an explanation of how outside capitalists came to dominate the region. The colonial model, they argued, ignored other critical factors such as the role of local elites in aiding and abetting the outside capitalists in entering and later subduing the region. Scholars such as David S. Walls and Douglas O'Neil Arnett began to turn towards emerging world systems theory to address the issue of poverty in Appalachia.

Arnett took exception to the image of Appalachia as a colony because it was no different from any other part of the United States. Its inhabitants were guaranteed all the rights granted to other citizens of the country by the Constitution of the United States. He instead posited that it was inevitable that the same market forces that industrialized the rest of the country would eventually have done the same in Appalachia. Arnett credited internal elites within Appalachia with both encouraging the entrance of outside capitalists to the region and helping them to establish and maintain control. These internal elites controlled the counties politically and economically on behalf of the outside capitalists who rewarded them. It was these entrenched local power brokers that blunted the efforts of reformers during the 1960s to effectively assist the poor in Appalachia. Arnett suggested that these internal power structures would have to be dismantled if the underdevelopment of the region were to be effectively addressed.[24]

Walls' "Internal Colony or Internal Periphery? A Critique of Current Models and an Alternative Formulation" argued that one would have to exaggerate historical realities in order to apply Lewis and Knipe's four-stage model of colonization to Appalachia. For example, one could not equate the entry of outside capitalists to Appalachia to the conquest of Native American lands. He also noted that the outside corporate interests did not establish government structures in order to control Appalachia. They instead worked within a system that predated their entry into the region. Walls identified the primary weakness of the internal colonization model as having too simplistic a solution for a complex problem. He viewed the colonial model as essentially calling for a takeover by the populace of the offending industry and its affiliated support structure. In order to get at the causes of Appalachian dependency, Walls suggested turning to the world systems framework that Immanuel Wallerstein was developing in his writings.[25]

Ronald D Eller's *Miners, Millhands, and Mountaineers: Industrializa-*

tion of the Appalachian South, 1880–1930 was an important transitional
work between the colonial model and its successors. Like proponents of
the colonial model, Eller posited that the socioeconomic conditions present in twentieth-century Appalachia were in large part due to the region's
transformation from an agricultural folk culture to an industrialized society. Eller portrayed Appalachia in the nineteenth century as a region comprised primarily of farms and scattered villages. It was a way of life where
familism was valued as an integral part of the culture. Its people lived a
tranquil lifestyle. The outside corporate capitalists who industrialized the
region corrupted this idyllic way of life.

Unlike most works grounded in colonial theory, Eller's demonstrated
that the change from an agricultural to industrial economy did not hap-
pen suddenly. Eller instead demonstrated that the exploitive industrialization efforts gradually altered the ethical lifestyle previously enjoyed in the
region, including the breakdown of traditional family structures. Traditions that strengthened agricultural communities, such as cooperative work,
were replaced by dependence on national bureaucracies.

Breaking from the colonial model, Eller briefly pointed to the role of
internal elites in the industrialization of the region. He showed how individuals such as Colonel Fess Whitaker and John C. Mayo were able to
amass large fortunes serving as middlemen for outside corporate interests.
Eller persuasively argued that it was internal elites such as Whitaker and
Mayo that "spread the gospel of 'progress through industrial growth' into
most of the hamlets and villages of the region."[26]

Recent scholars have turned their attention more to the role of internal elites. Mary Beth Pudup disagreed with Eller's contention that
Appalachia's suffering in the twentieth century was due to the industrialization of the region. In "The Limits of Subsistence: Agriculture and
Industry in Central Appalachia" she argued that it was subsistence agriculture that sowed the seeds of poverty. Due to subsistence agriculture,
the region failed after 1850 to develop any general manufacturing entities.
Most individuals were also not developing trades outside of farming. The
net result was that there was no capital in local hands to exploit the bitu-
minous coal deposits throughout the region. Pudup, like Arnett, argued
that it was inevitable those resources would be eventually exploited. Since
Appalachians didn't have the means to exploit their natural wealth due to
the limitations of their agricultural economy, outside capitalists merely
took advantage of the opportunities available to them.[27]

In *Feud: Hatfields, McCoys, and Social Change in Appalachia, 1860–1900*, Altina L. Waller examined the actions of internal elites in the Tug Valley that straddled the states of West Virginia and Kentucky. Through the use of land, legal, and business records, Waller was able to reconstruct the notorious feud. She concluded that the feud consisted of two phases. The first phase definitely involved violence between a faction allied with Devil Anse Hatfield and one loyal to Randolph McCoy. Waller demonstrates that the second phase had little to do with the McCoys. They were merely the excuse used by Pikeville, Kentucky, elites, such as Perry Cline and John Dils, to eliminate a local timber baron, namely Devil Anse Hatfield, who stood in the way of "progress." Led by Cline, a lawyer, these elites hoped to develop Pikeville into a center of industry. Key to their efforts was attracting railroad lines to Pikeville. Devil Anse Hatfield interfered with their plans because he happened to own land over which the railroad would pass. By prosecuting the Hatfields, Cline and his business associates not only cleared the way for railroads for Pikeville but also endeared themselves to outside capitalists by showing that law and order reigned in their corner of Kentucky. Supporting Eller's contention about local elites during this era, Waller demonstrated that Pikeville elites interested in assisting with the industrialization of the region helped pave the way, and in essence invited, the corporate interests that exploited both the region's populace and its natural resources.[28]

David C. Hsiung found a similar phenomenon at work in East Tennessee. He identified two types of individuals residing in the mountains. One group of individuals endeavored to connect itself to the market economy of the United States through infrastructure improvements such as the construction of railroads. These were individuals such as those described by Arnett, Eller, and Waller. Others remained largely isolated on mountain farms. Hsiung argued that it was this creation of these two societies that led to the stereotyping that continues to define the region. Those individuals advocating economic connections to the rest of the country differentiated themselves from their isolated neighbors by commenting on their "backwardness." It was this creation of the "other" in the mountains that was one of the common threads linking the writings of local-color authors, President Frost and his contemporaries, culture-of-poverty theorists, and even some proponents of modernization theory.[29]

Like Eller, Ronald L. Lewis, in *Transforming the Appalachian Countryside*, identified the timber industry as the agent for change. While Eller looked at this change throughout Appalachia, Lewis focused on West Virginia. He showed how the timber industry, with the cooperation of railroad companies, deforested much of the state between 1880 and 1910. They were aided by a political and legal system that favored the interests of the capitalists over that of the general populace. Lewis clearly demonstrated that the timber industry was just as ecologically harmful to Appalachia as the coal industry.

Elites figured prominently in Lewis's monograph as supporters of industrialization. They reaped the profits of their association with the timber and railroad companies. Lewis did show that these elites were not in lockstep with each other. He detailed "wars" between competing groups of elites over the location of county seats. Initially county seats in West Virginia were centrally located since they served as economic centers for the county's populace. Self-interested elites moved the county seats to peripheral areas of their counties that were located at railroad junctions. This served to separate a majority of the inhabitants of the individual counties from the economic center of their community.[30]

Other scholars challenged Eller by pointing out that internal elites in Western North Carolina were connected to outside economic interests long before the era of industrialization. John C. Inscoe's *Mountain Masters: Slavery and the Sectional Crisis in Western North Carolina* illuminated the economic connections between a powerful group of slaveholding elites in the mountains with markets located in South Carolina and Georgia prior to the Civil War. It was these economic connections to the plantation South that led North Carolinians, under the influence of these local elites, to cast their lot with the Confederacy when the secession crisis erupted.[31]

Ashe County's Civil War, by Martin Crawford, examined one county within Western North Carolina from the eve of the Civil War to the conclusion of the conflict. Prior to the Civil War, Ashe County's elite class remarkably resembled that of Owsley County during the same period. In Ashe County, slaveholders comprised 6.6 percent of the farmers in the county yet they accounted for 49.8 percent of the county's wealth. They also occupied virtually all of the county's political leadership posts. They were able to dominate politically because they were appointed by the governor and thus did not have to stand for popular election. As shown by Crawford, much of the general populace joined these elites in supporting the Confederacy. This was due to their shared racial prejudices and mistrust of the federal government. One portion of the county sympathized with the Union. Crawford argues that this allegiance reflected the attitudes of the elites living in that portion of the county. These elites, if not openly Unionist, discreetly supported the Union cause. This support was possibly due to their kinship and economic ties to Unionists residing in East Tennessee. Crawford ultimately suggested that the economic and social ties of the elites in Ashe County during the Civil War era shaped how the various portions of the counties allied themselves in the conflict.[32]

Paul Salstrom, in *Appalachia's Path to Dependency*, extended the roots of Appalachian poverty into the early rather than the latter portion of the nineteenth century. He argued that portions of Appalachia had been in economic decline prior to the Civil War. Through records documenting factors such as agricultural productivity and farm size, Salstrom was able to document stages of decline. As early as the 1840s, Salstrom found obvious evidence that the growth of the population combined with soil exhaustion was severely affecting farm productivity. While his study examined Appalachia as a whole, his conclusions warned against making region-wide assumptions. He argued that the settlement patterns in the different subregions of Appalachia caused them to develop in different fashions.[33]

Using a method foreshadowed by Walls, Wilma A. Dunaway applied Wallerstein's world-systems theory to the history of Southern Appalachia in constructing her massive dissertation entitled *The Incorporation of Southern Appalachia into the Capitalist World-Economy, 1700–1860*. It was a work in which she integrated the experiences of Native Americans, women, Africans, and African Americans with those of white males. The tome subsequently spawned a number of monographs.

In *The First American Frontier: Transition to Capitalism in Southern Appalachia, 1700–1860*, Dunaway correctly argued that Southern Appalachia was part of the world economy before any white settlers ever entered the region. The native inhabitants of the region were trading natural resources, namely animal furs, with white traders. These natives became the first exploited Appalachians as white traders gradually displaced the Cherokee Indians from their homelands. The next group of exploiters were absentee land speculators in the eighteenth century who bought up most of the land in the region. What little land was available to yeoman farmers was quickly seized. Those without land were forced into tenant farming. The consequences of the land shortage became obvious by the middle portion of the nineteenth century when, as argued by Dunaway, most whites were part of a "landless semiproletariat." She supported this contention through a database she constructed of more than 22,000 households.[34]

Dunaway unintentionally supported Salstrom's contention that one could not make region-wide assumptions about Appalachia by creatively defining the region. She adopted a broad definition of Appalachia that included the Shenandoah Valley of northern Virginia, the panhandle of West Virginia, and Madison County, Kentucky. These wealthy counties, comprised of prosperous farms and industrial entities, certainly skewed her statistics because they had little in common with the other counties in her sample.

Like Inscoe, Dunaway found that slaveholders in Appalachia were economically tied to their plantation counterparts in the South. In *Slavery in the American Mountain South*, Dunaway utilized a database of approximately 26,000 households to study slavery in the mountains. She identified 40,743 slaveholders in the "mountains." Also found within her sample were more than 300,000 Africans or African Americans within the region, most of whom were enslaved. Dunaway concluded that Appalachian slaveholders on small farms were using slaves as an export commodity to their counterparts living in plantations in the South. While her numbers were staggering, once again one had to look at her definition of Appalachia. Though ostensibly studying small-scale slaveholding on farms in Appalachia, she allowed her sample to include large-scale plantation slavery in areas such as Virginia's Shenandoah Valley.[35]

Dunaway once again unintentionally affirmed the dangers of applying broad conclusions to Appalachia as a whole. In 1850, Owsley County, Kentucky, contained 136 slaves, who were owned by members of a handful of families. The number of slaves in 1860 did not represent a significant change from the decade before.[36] The slave trade that Dunaway attributed to Appalachia in her monograph was not representative of slavery in Owsley County. This is an important distinction because Owsley County, Kentucky, was included in her sample.

A criticism critics leveled at Dunaway was that her attention to specific details was somewhat lacking. One example of this was evident in *Slavery in the American Mountain South*. She wrote about an Owsley County land agent in 1822 who was managing the properties owned by an absentee speculator named Robert Wickliffe. This was factually wrong since Owsley County was not founded until 1843.[37]

With the notable exception of Dunaway's global regional analyses, recent work on the Appalachian region has tended to focus on county-level studies. What the initial results suggest is that individual counties within the subregions of Appalachia developed economically, politically, and socially different from the neighbors. Two works focusing on Eastern Kentucky counties illustrate this trend.

Dwight B. Billings and Kathleen Blee's *The Road to Poverty: The Making of Wealth and Hardship in Appalachia* focused on the history of Clay County during the nineteenth century. The authors utilized a world-systems approach to examine the county's economic, cultural, and political development. According to the authors, what differentiated the county from its neighbors in Eastern Kentucky was that it was the last county to obtain a railroad line. Correspondingly, Clay County also avoided exploitation by coal magnates longer than other counties in its vicinity.[38]

Among the many myths addressed by Billings and Blee with this work was that Appalachia was completely isolated from the market economy of the United States during the nineteenth century. On the contrary, Billings and Blee demonstrated that early in the nineteenth century, Clay County, Kentucky, was among the foremost producers of salt in the western portion of the United States. Unfortunately, this brief moment of prosperity benefited only a few, namely the salt manufacturers who were headquartered on Goose Creek.

Salt manufacturing depended on slave labor. Ironically, it was this dependence on cheap labor that served to eventually doom the salt manufacturing industry within Clay County. Rather than upgrading their technology, which would have helped the Clay County entrepreneurs to compete with their counterparts in the Kanawha Valley of West Virginia, they continued to depend on a barbaric form of exploitation. In microcosm, this illuminated one of the key reasons that the North had such an overwhelming technological and manufacturing advantage over the South during the Civil War. The North's wage labor system, although exploitive in other ways, provided incentives for technological improvements in the manufacturing sector that never took place in the South.

Billings and Blee, like Waller, examined the role of feuding within the county. They demonstrated that feuding was one of the consequences of local elites fighting for economic and political control of the county. Through their analysis of local elites, Billings and Blee suggested that scholars examining the history of individual Appalachians counties should pay close attention to local politics. They vividly made the case that local politics is an important dynamic within counties, one that has traditionally been understudied due to the lasting influence of the colonial model.

Another recent study, Robert S. Weise's *Grasping at Independence: Debt, Male Authority, and Mineral Rights in Appalachian Kentucky, 1850–1915* examined Floyd County. According to Weise, the source of its poverty was its rich coal reserves. At the beginning of the time period examined in the monograph, Weise documents the existence of a vibrant "household economy" active within Floyd. This economy depended on both subsistence agriculture and market production. Weise suggested that one's standing within the patriarchal household economy depended on such factors as the level of debt or surplus. As shown within the court records examined by Weise, indebtedness was a constant for most of the inhabitants of the county. To alleviate their debt loads, which was creating conflicts within their respective households, male patriarchs began selling the mineral rights to their property. This willingness to sell their mineral rights in order to solve household problems made the inhabitants of Floyd County complicit with outside capitalists in the industrialization of the county.[39]

What seemed to be a painless way of gaining much needed capital proved the undoing of Floyd Countians. They lost control of the land on which they lived. Coal companies and the accompanying railroads destroyed some of the finest farmland in the county in order to easily extract coal. What land was not freely sold was often acquired through intimidation. The subsequent loss of one's livelihood and independence created rifts within households, as gender conflicts left patriarchs with a diminished social status. Without the ability to utilize subsistence farming for survival, the families in Floyd County became economically dependent on the coal companies.

This scholarly study of Owsley County naturally complements the monographs written by Weise and by Billings and Blee because it examines a Kentucky county that is perceived as being devoid of natural resources such as coal. It is also a county that never received significant transportation improvements, such as a railroad line. Lacking natural resources and transportation networks does not make Owsley County unique. The county is actually representative of a significant number of other Appalachian counties that have gone largely unnoticed in the scholarly literature because they were supposedly bypassed during the latter portion of the nineteenth century when Appalachia was violently incorporated into the economy of the United States at large. By these counties purportedly being ignored by capitalists, it has been extrapolated that they were left in a "Rip Van Winkle" state while natural resource rich counties became infamous for both their feudists and their organized labor troubles. By studying how a resource and transportation poor county developed, this study promises to open a window into Appalachian poverty that has previously been left closed.

A commonality between my study and those produced by Drs. Weise, Billings, and Blee is the influence of Robert M. Ireland's *Little Kingdoms: The Counties of Kentucky, 1850–1891*. Ireland detailed how the Commonwealth of Kentucky irresponsibly allowed the establishment of 120 counties, which he termed "little kingdoms" where centralized political and economic power came to be dominated by entrenched elites. Not surprisingly, these private fiefdoms became rife with corruption and fiscal irresponsibility.[40]

Ireland's "little kingdoms" thesis has gained so much acceptance that it has crossed over from scholarly circles to the popular media. The influence of Robert Ireland was obvious in a nine-part exposé published by the *Lexington Herald-Leader* newspaper, entitled "Little Kingdoms: Local Government at Your Expense." Although the monograph *Little Kingdoms* was written about Kentucky in the latter half of the nineteenth century, the *Lexington Herald-Leader*'s writers applied its terminology to describe continuing instances of misgovernance at the county level within the Commonwealth of Kentucky in the twentieth century.[41]

During my research of Owsley County, it became apparent to me that Ireland's "little kingdoms" theory had limited applicability to the complexity of Owsley County's economic and political development. Curiously, Billing and Blee's focus on local county courthouse politics also proved problematic in describing what was occurring in Owsley County, because Owsley's elites did not appear to wield much political or economic power over extended periods of time, although it was apparent that they were engaging in rent-seeking behavior. Surprisingly, the courthouse politics of neighboring counties proved to be one of the most important factors in Owsley County's retarded economic development.

While pondering the ramifications of the activities of outside elites in Owsley County, Ronald D Eller's *Kentucky's Distressed Communities: A Report on Poverty in Appalachian Kentucky* came to my attention. Using 1990 census data at the subcounty level, Eller identified "clusters of dis-

tressed communities" which transcended county borders. Not coincidentally, these were rural areas where the most persistent poverty in Appalachia
could be found. One of the four clusters of communities in Kentucky having poverty rates ranging from 46 to 63 percent encompassed contiguous
portions of Owsley, Clay, and Breathitt Counties. As observed by Eller,
these communities existed at the periphery of their counties, far from the
centers of the political and economic life within their respective counties.[42] Eller's observation confirmed that Owsley County was not just a
"little kingdom," as its obvious poverty extended beyond its borders.

Through the prism of Owsley County, this study will argue that
Owsley County is the product of a nondemocratic geopolitical structure
centered on the Three Forks of the Kentucky River. Power within this
structure was based on connections established by local elites to their counterparts in the central Kentucky cities of Lexington or Frankfort, or to governmental officials in Washington, DC. These connections tended to be
short lived, resulting in moments of development within the Three Forks
of the Kentucky River region.

1. The Creation of Owsley and Lee Counties

Native Americans were the first inhabitants of the land that would eventually comprise Owsley County. Native peoples intermittently occupied the region for at least 3,200 years, preferring to reside beside the main course of the Kentucky River and its tributaries.[1] There were no native populations residing in the region when the first land speculators of European descent began to arrive in the 1760s. These newly arrived individuals were attracted to the area by the lure of unsettled lands. In the watershed of the South Fork of the Kentucky River, these explorers encountered heavily forested land teeming with wildlife. To the naked eye, the South Fork of the Kentucky River appeared to be prime real estate. Among the land speculators to become enamored with the land in the region was Daniel Boone. He first hunted in the area between 1769 and 1771. It was not just the land that caught Boone's fancy. Like other land speculators of the era, he knew that the South Fork of the Kentucky River was part of a vast river network that included both the Ohio and Mississippi rivers. Desiring to lay claim to the perceived economic potential of the South Fork, Boone subsequently surveyed the region and utilized the data he obtained to secure land grants for himself. Unfortunately for Boone, his dubious abilities as a surveyor resulted in his filing of land deeds that infringed on the deeds that had been filed by other land speculators. After a significant amount of litigation, Daniel Boone lost his claim to all of the land that he had surveyed.[2]

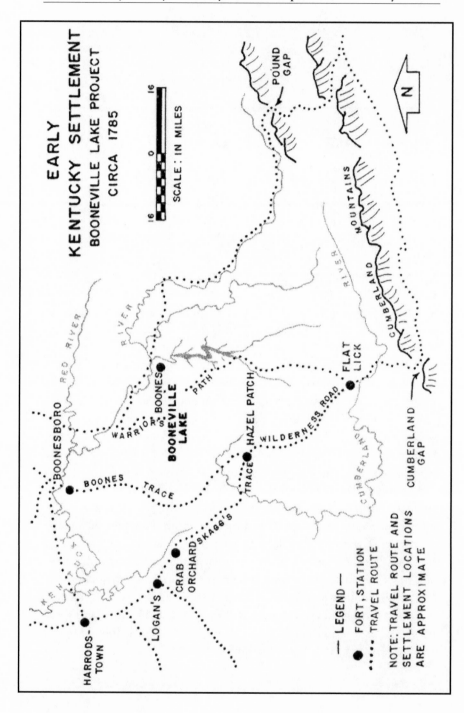

The migration of the first permanent settlers of European and African descent began in the 1790s. The family names of the early settlers included Gabart (which quickly evolved into Gabbard), Moore, Abner, and Bowman. According to a scion of the Gabbard family, "The greatest reason that they came here was to seek adventure. Allso [*sic*] to find a peaceful country to live in, and gain title to good Virginia lands."[3] Like the native peoples that preceded them, many of the first families to arrive settled along the South Fork of the Kentucky River and its major tributaries.[4]

The economic potential of the South Fork of the Kentucky River was first tapped in the nineteenth century by Clay County entrepreneurs residing at the headwaters of Goose Creek at Burning Springs. The Clay Countians operated fifteen saltworks that utilized the South Fork of the Kentucky River to get their salt to distant markets. Salt was a commodity of great value because it had a multitude of uses. Livestock required access to salt for their very survival. Salt was also a necessary ingredient for curing meat. Most importantly to the businessmen at Burning Springs, salt was in great demand in Central Kentucky by those involved in the salt-pork industry. The salt pork produced in the Bluegrass region was subsequently shipped to distant markets such as New Orleans, Louisiana.

Constructing an economic connection to the Central Kentucky town of Lexington proved quite a boon to the Clay County salt makers. Lexington was not only one of the largest towns in the western portion of the United States but was also a key cog in the national economy due to its hemp industry. Lexington's gentry, which included Henry Clay, had determined that their business interests represented the interests of the Commonwealth of Kentucky. From their perspective, it was thus a good use of public funds to construct roads and improve waterways that made it easier for Lexington entrepreneurs to get their goods to market. These individuals had determined that transportation infrastructure improvements required by their business interests should be the responsibility of the commonwealth, rather than of individual counties. The reason that they had come to this conclusion was that Kentucky counties had already proven that, regardless of how much money had been supposedly expended by

Opposite: On this map, "Boones" marks the location of the camp site that eventually became the town of Booneville in Owsley County. Note that Booneville Lake was a hypothetical geographical feature that was never constructed (U.S. Army Corps of Engineers, Louisville District).

county governments on improvements to transportation infrastructure, roads remained inferior and waterways were often impassible. Known as the "Bluegrass System," this proved to be an early model of the "American System" that was later espoused by Henry Clay and the Whig political party for application across the entire United States. While commercial interests across the commonwealth certainly welcomed this expansion of the market revolution into the political realm, many Kentuckians who depended on their farms for everything that they needed viewed the activities of the Lexington elites as an elaborate scheme to squander away the public's money.[5]

Since Lexington's salt-pork industry needed the salt being produced in Clay County, the Lexington elites and their like-minded associates throughout Central Kentucky ensured that the general assembly of the Commonwealth of Kentucky would provide needed transportation infrastructure improvements between Burning Springs and Lexington. In 1801, salt producers were granted the rights of eminent domain to secure the wood required to boil brine. They were also granted the right to transport their brine across property lines. Recognizing that improving transportation facilities was vital in extracting natural resources from the mountains, the General Assembly authorized a subsidy to connect the roads in the vicinity of the salt manufacturers to the Wilderness Road. This was followed a year later by legislation creating a lottery for improvements on the Kentucky River and its tributaries for Clay County's salt industry. These transportation improvements allowed salt from Clay County to be marketed not only in Kentucky but also in Tennessee and Virginia. Clay County's saltworks proved so prolific that they produced between 100,000 to 250,000 bushels of salt a year between 1835 and 1845.[6]

The Clay County salt manufacturers used the wealth they gained to expand into other industries, most notably coal mining and the timber industry. In order to ensure that their varied business interests were protected, the Clay County salt manufacturing families determined that they needed to control the decision-making offices of their local county government. Control of the local political system also had the potential of opening up new revenue streams, especially for those individuals who served as sheriff, tax assessor, and treasurer. Since the various salt manufacturers of Clay County were also business competitors, it is not surprising that conflict arose as different factions, led by the Garrard and White families respectively, competed with each other to seize political control of Clay County. Although the elite families feuded openly, they each seized control of key components of the local county government, thereby gaining the ability to protect their interests, as well as engage in rent-seeking behavior. In actuality, the political control of Clay County that was seized by both the Garrards and Whites proved to be much more profitable for a longer period of time than any other of the industries in which the families were engaged.[7]

These salt manufacturers provided a model to be emulated by other entrepreneurs residing in the Three Forks of the Kentucky River region. They had demonstrated how to make a local industry into an important component of Kentucky's overall economy, which subsequently led to the general assembly passing special legislation that privileged the economic needs of entrepreneurs over those of the general citizenry. The Clay County salt harvesters had also shown how to utilize their economic clout and political connections in Frankfort, the state capital, in order to seize political control of a county. Enterprising coal merchants residing in Estill County subsequently endeavored to emulate the example set by the Clay Countians.

Estill County in 1840 was the home of the McGuire, Beatty, and Congleton families. These families resided in the communities of Proctor and Beattyville, which are located on opposite sides of the banks on the Kentucky River near the confluence of the Three Forks. These families were connected to each other through their coal mining businesses. Coal mining in the Proctor-Beattyville area had dated back to at least 1790, when it was reported that twenty short tons of coal had been mined in the vicinity. Between 1790 and 1860, coal miners in the vicinity of Proctor and Beattyville produced 268,240 short tons of coal. For the sake of perspective, this small area accounted for the only significant production of coal in Eastern Kentucky between the years 1790 and 1823.[8]

Despite the wealth that these allied families had gleaned through coal mining, they had not been able to utilize their economic power to obtain significant political power within Estill County. They were obviously peripherally connected to the political elites controlling Estill County during the 1840s, since they were receiving spoils in the form of patronage, but they were not extended decision-making power.[9] It is not surprising that the Estill County elites, centered in Irvine, would have kept these McGuires, Beattys, and Congletons out of their immediate political sphere, because they did not share the same interests. Irvine elites focused on their economic infrastructure needs, which were centered in their hometown. They were not interested in using Estill County funds to improve the transportation infrastructure needs of a handful of coal mining families who lived in another portion of the county. The inability to obtain public monies proved a hindrance to their coal mining businesses of the McGuires and their business associates because they needed improved roads to efficiently get their coal from the mines to the Kentucky River. In order to obtain the required infrastructure to grow their businesses, the McGuires, Beattys, and Congletons needed to acquire control of a local county government. Since they were not able to overthrow those who wielded political power in Estill County, they were forced to seek another solution to their dilemma.

The McGuires, Beattys, and other coal mining families apparently turned to Estill's ruling elites for assistance in creating another county. On January 12, 1843, Representative Ansel Daniels of Estill County introduced a petition to the general assembly for the creation of a new county out of portions of Breathitt, Clay, and Estill counties. While the petition was ostensibly submitted on behalf of citizens from the three counties, there is no doubt that the impetus for forming the new county originated within Estill County. The general assembly, without any apparent debate over the issue, responded to the petition by calling for the creation of Owsley County on June 1, 1843.[10]

The namesake of the newly created county entity was William Owsley, a prominent politician and jurist who would soon thereafter become governor of the Commonwealth of Kentucky. Although the county was named after William Owsley, it was not a reflection of his popularity among the county's general populace. In his successful campaign for governor in 1844, William Owsley received only 151 votes in Owsley County. His opponent, William O. Butler, won the county with 216 votes.[11]

Owsley, the ninety-sixth Kentucky county in order of formation, was initially comprised of approximately 480 square miles. Like virtually all of Kentucky's counties at the time, Owsley County's borders were in constant flux during the early years of its existence. Its borders were redrawn on five different occasions before 1870. Only twice in those boundary changes did the county lose, or gain, more that ten miles of land. In both cases Owsley lost land to the creation of new counties, namely Jackson and Wolfe counties. The other boundary changes were made simply to satisfy the whims of local property owners, who probably preferred the tax rate in a neighboring county. The most extreme example of a frivolous change involved a property owner who successfully petitioned the general assembly of the Commonwealth of Kentucky to join Breathitt County. The property involved in the transaction amounted to less than a square mile of land.[12]

Owsley County's fluctuating borders were indicative of the priorities of the Kentucky General Assembly during this particular era. The legislature devoted much of its time to passing legislation affecting individuals, businesses, and municipalities without any consideration of the possible consequences. If an individual desired to create a county, all that was required was a legislator to introduce the bill to the general assembly. A delegate to the Constitutional Convention of 1890 characterized the process of creating a county as a system whereby "fifteen or thirty or forty people" created "outrageous legislation" to make laws that "were not for the benefit of the people at large, but only for the benefit of people who were to be enriched by them." The interested party, rather than the legislator who introduced the bill in question, often authored much of this special interest legislation. While no definitive evidence has been discovered that the McGuires or any of their associates authored much the legislation that impacted Owsley County until 1870, they certainly influenced the language contained therein. It was no coincidence that the names of members of these families were constantly appearing in legislation passed by the general assembly that impacted Owsley County. All of the pieces of special legislation passed by the general assembly would subsequently become law with little, if any, debate since the legislature as a whole tended to acquiesce to the desires of its individual members in regard to local matters.[13]

The legislation that created Owsley County mandated that the first meeting of the county's justices of the peace be held at the home of Archibald McGuire. Among the seven men selected by Governor R.P. Letcher to serve as justices of the peace was Hiram McGuire, who was Archibald's son. Archibald's nephew, James McGuire, Jr., was appointed by Governor Letcher to serve as the sheriff of Owsley County.[14] Serving as sheriff was a plum assignment that provided a substantial amount of power to one individual. In addition to law enforcement responsibilities, the sheriff also served as the primary tax collector for the county and was its chief elections officer.[15] As was evident from the very beginning of Owsley County's history, members of the McGuire family held key political positions.

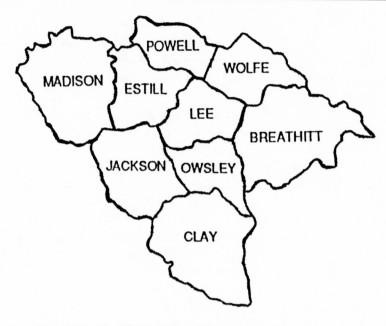

Counties in the Three Forks of the Kentucky River Region.

Securing the county seat on their property was the obvious next step in seizing control of Owsley County for the McGuires, Beattys, and allied families. The county seat traditionally served as the locale where a majority of the community's social, business, and legal transactions occurred. As a result of serving as the economic center of a community, the county seat inevitably also became the county's transportation hub. Having one's community declared a county seat meant an immediate financial windfall for landowners, as property values tended to immediately soar. Not surprisingly, competition among communities for the county seat designation was often fierce due to the aforementioned economic benefits. Archibald McGuire submitted a petition on behalf of the citizens of Proctor to the general assembly requesting that an election be held for the expressed purpose of permanently determining which of two communities vying to become the county seat would receive the designation. McGuire's wish was granted and the election was held in April 1844.[16]

One of the candidates was a small hamlet, known as Moore's Station, which bordered the South Fork of the Kentucky River. According to local legend, the community was established on a campsite that was utilized by Daniel Boone during one of his trips to the region between 1780 and 1781. The name of the locale honored James Moore, Sr., one of the first permanent settlers of European descent in the area. His son, Elias Moore, offered an acre of land to serve as the site of the county courthouse should the community be selected as the county seat. At the time of the election, seventy-five individuals populated Moore's Station. The community contained one school, a Methodist church, one tavern, and four stores. Moore's Station was particularly attractive to a many of Owsley's voting populace because it was centrally located and thus accessible to a majority of the county's residents. This was an important distinction, because one of the primary reasons cited in petitions calling for the creation of new counties in Kentucky during the second half of the nineteenth century was that the creation of new county seats made it easier for citizens to have access to places where most public business was conducted. This was also a local manifestation of the Jeffersonian view of democracy, because a centrally located county seat made maximum participation in government possible for the propertied white male masses.[17]

The second option before the voters was the town of Proctor, which was named after a locally renowned Indian fighter named Joseph Proctor. It was a community of twenty individuals whose homes were located primarily on real estate owned by Archibald McGuire. Since Proctor was located in the northern portion of Owsley County, it was not readily accessible to many Owsley Countians. Although the McGuires and their associates ran a vigorous campaign on behalf of their home community, they were foiled at the ballot box by Owsley Countians who opted to select Moore's Station as their county seat. Moore's Station was temporarily renamed Owsley Court House following the election. In 1846, the community was officially incorporated and renamed Booneville in honor of the famed explorer Daniel Boone.[18]

Following the election defeat, Archibald McGuire utilized his ability to secure special legislation from Frankfort to formally incorporate the town of Proctor. The act incorporating the community called for the town to be divided into lots, streets, and alleys. The titles to the newly designated properties were then made available to interested persons via a public sale. The legislation named Samuel Beatty, Nicholas McGuire, and Isaac Congleton to serve as trustees overseeing the sale of the property. Once the expenses of incorporating the town were recouped, all of the remaining revenue was given to Archibald McGuire.[19]

The election results concerning the county seat indicated a lack of deference on the part of Owsley County's citizenry towards those who were put into positions of authority over them by distant legislators in Frankfort, Kentucky. This is not surprising when one considers that the election was probably a local example of the conflict between market-oriented Whigs and Jeffersonian Democrats. Like the Clay County salt harvesters, the Owsley County coal mining entrepreneurs had made their local businesses important enough to the commonwealth's economy that the general assembly was passing special legislation on their behalf. The general assembly was actually empowering the McGuires and their associates to utilize Owsley County's public resources as they saw fit by putting them into positions of authority such as justice of the peace and sheriff. From a Whig perspective, what was good for the coal mining families in Proctor and Beattyville was good for the county as a whole; thus using county funds to improve the transportation infrastructure around their coal mining businesses was an appropriate use of Owsley County tax money. Most Owsley Countians, who tended to vote Democrat in elections, did not share the same view. They believed that transportation improvements that benefited the few were a colossal waste of their money.[20]

The average taxpayer in Owsley County had a net worth of $432 and depended on labor provided by family members to maintain a small farm on which enough food was grown to sustain the family through the year.[21] Farmers also relied on a variety of farm animals to provide staples such as meat and milk to diversify the family's diet. Animals, such as sheep and cows, provided the added benefit of supplying the raw materials that were utilized on the self-sufficient farms to make clothing. Due to Owsley County's geography, the farms were not very productive. Many of the farms were located on steep slopes that were prone to heavy erosion. The soils found in much of the county were comprised of thin layers poorly suited to agriculture. The limitations of the land for agricultural purposes were masked by the ability of those same soils to support woodlands. The plants that did grow in the soils of the county tended to suffer from stunted growth.[22]

Many of the small farms in the county were located among the trees. Farmers cleared the land they were going to use by either burning it or girdling all of the trees.[23] The portion of a farmer's land that remained woodland was considered to be unimproved property. Improved property was land that had been cleared. Despite the poor agricultural yield of their farms, most farmers in Owsley County engaged in commerce on a small scale locally. They were not producing enough surplus goods to be involved in shipping much produce to markets throughout Kentucky.

Henry Gabbard was typical of many subsistence farmers living in Owsley County. He was a farmer who supported a household that included another seven individuals. His farm in 1850 was comprised of thirty improved and 270 unimproved acres of land. The cash value of the farm was $300. His livestock, which included one horse, three milk cows, twenty-four sheep, and thirty swine, was worth $150. He grew 300 bushels of Indian corn and fifteen bushels of oats. By 1860, Gabbard's farm had shrunk to 120 acres, twenty of which were improved. He had dispensed with most of his livestock, with only one horse and the three cows remaining on the farm. There was also a change in the types of crops being grown, since Gabbard produced twenty bushels of wheat, 200 bushels of Indian corn, twenty bushels of beans, and twenty-five bushels of Irish potatoes that year.[24]

While Henry Gabbard's farm shrunk between 1850 and 1860, that was not indicative of a farming crisis throughout Owsley County. Other farmers, such as Levi Ross, thrived during this period. Ross's farm in 1850 consisted of 500 acres of land valued at $900. Of that acreage, only fifty was improved. His livestock consisted of two horses, four working oxen, two milk cows, twelve sheep, and thirty swine. His crop production was twenty bushels of wheat, 400 bushels of Indian corn, twenty bushels of oats, three bushels of beans, twenty bushels of Irish potatoes, and twenty bushels of sweet potatoes. The year 1860 found Levi Ross prospering. The farm had grown to 1,100 acres valued at $3,000. Of that acreage, 125 acres were improved. His livestock included three horses, one mule, two working oxen, and thirteen additional cattle. He also owned thirty-eight sheep and fifty hogs. The total value of his livestock was $500. His farm also produced 140 bushels of wheat, 900 bushels of Indian corn, and seventy-five bushels of oats. Levi Ross augmented his farm income by serving as an official "taster of mountain moonshine." Ross was the legal supplier of whiskey to establishments such as the tavern in Booneville and its counterpart in Proctor owned by Hiram McGuire.[25]

Unlike a majority of the farmers in Owsley County, Levi Ross was one of the 10,011 free people of color living in Kentucky in 1850. According to the national census undertaken that year, twenty-two free people of color resided in Owsley County. Isaac Butcher, a coal miner, was listed as a black head of household whose family was comprised of eight mulattos. By 1860, the free black population had declined slightly to eighteen within Owsley County. Apparently sometime between 1850 and 1860 Isaac Butcher and his family had migrated from the county, thus accounting for some of the drop in the local population. Among the newly listed free people of color found in the 1860 census of Owsley County was Berry Buford, a stonemason. Another was Arrena Goosey who, like her five children, was a mulatto. They lived in Beattyville as part of L.W. Blount's household. Arrena is listed in the census documentation as a "slave's wife." It is not clear who owned her husband, since L.W. Blount is not listed as a slaveholder in the Slave Schedule for the Federal Census of 1860.[26]

Whereas most farmers in Owsley County did not appear to be involved with markets in far-flung locales, the political elites in Proctor were actively engaged in commercial ventures beyond their immediate vicinities. As both coal merchants and large-scale agriculturalists, they were interested in getting their goods to market. They actively utilized contacts outside the region, especially with politicians in Frankfort, Kentucky, to seek improvements in the transportation infrastructure near their homes and businesses. The McGuires and Beattys in particular were seeking ways to improve their economic connections to the outside world.

Archibald McGuire was a member of one of the first white families to settle in present-day Kentucky. He was born at Fort Boonesborough in 1780. In 1844, he was the owner of 1,640 acres of land on the Kentucky River. Among his assets were nine slaves. By 1850, his farm consisted of one hundred improved and 1,641 unimproved acres of land valued at $5,000. He owned eight horses, twenty-eight cattle, twenty sheep, and forty swine. His farm produced 1,500 bushels of Indian corn, one hundred bushels of oats, and one hundred bushels of Irish potatoes. In addition to the farm, Archibald McGuire owned another $3,500 worth of real estate. Other assets included ten slaves, making him the owner of the second largest number of slaves in the county.[27]

Samuel Beatty was a close associate of the McGuires whose name occasionally appeared in conjunction with those of McGuires in legislation affecting Owsley County. Beatty moved to Estill County in 1841 from Missouri. He first appeared in the tax records of Owsley County in 1846. At that time he owned 315 acres of land on the Kentucky River and seven slaves. In 1850, his farm consisted of seventy-five improved and 338 unimproved acres valued at $8,000. His land, which was much more valuable per acre than that of any of the McGuires, was used primarily to grow Indian corn. The total value of all his real estate holdings in 1850 was $10,825.[28] Samuel Beatty had at least one son, and probably two, who were married to McGuires. James M. Beatty was married to Caroline McGuire. Decatur Beatty, Samuel's probable son, was married to Patsy Akers, whose father was James McGuire, Sr. Decatur Beatty's household in 1850 also included Robert Beatty Jimison, who eventually married Gilly Ann McGuire.[29]

The McGuires and Beattys held large amounts of land and between them owned thirty-four of the 136 slaves in the county. In addition to the intermarriage between the families, their business interests tied them together. The 1850 Census of Products of Industry showed the following capital investments in coal: $1,000 by Hiram McGuire; $2,000 by Samuel Beatty; $4,000 by Archibald McGuire; $400 by James McGuire; $600 by Decatur Beatty; $150 by William McGuire; and $2,000 by John G. McGuire. Other associates of the McGuire and Beatty families, namely J.C. Howerton and Isaac Congleton, were listed as coal merchants in the Census of Products of Industry a decade later. In 1860, coal mines owned by McGuires, Beattys, Howertons, and Congletons accounted for 232,000 of the 332,000 bushels of coal produced in Owsley County. The total value of the coal mined that year by the associated families was $25,250.[30]

The McGuires and their fellow political elites did not consider Booneville to be the permanent location of Owsley's county seat, despite the wishes of the voting populace. On November 26, 1851, the Kentucky house of representatives received a petition from Owsley County citizens asking that Booneville be stripped of its designation as the county seat of Owsley County. The act created in response to the petition became law on December 20, 1851. The language within the act specifically named Hiram McGuire and Isaac Congleton to serve as two of the four judges overseeing the election of a new county seat. Even though Isaac Congleton was a resident of Proctor, he was charged with oversight of the election in Booneville. Conflict over the act quickly erupted in Owsley County, with local Democrats upset that the Proctor forces had been allowed to oversee every aspect of the election in all locales. The Democrats got their local representative from Booneville to get the act amended on January 7, 1852. The amendment contained clear language stating that the only way that the county seat would be moved to Proctor was if a majority of Owsley's voters approved the move. The McGuires and their associates once again lost to the Democratic Party majority at the ballot box and Booneville remained the county seat of Owsley County.[31]

After two defeats, the McGuires and their associates abandoned their desire to move the county seat and instead concentrated on improving the roads in their portion of the county. At the time of this change in strategy, Proctor already had part of one of the finest roads in Owsley County passing through its boundaries. The Irvine-Pound Gap Road extended from Estill County to Virginia. It was a major thoroughfare through the mountains of Eastern Kentucky for traders taking their goods to market. While the Irvine-Pound Gap Road was a great asset, road improvements were required on the other roads in the vicinity of Proctor and Beattyville so that they could support the heavy wagons that were required in order to get the coal from the mines to the Kentucky River for shipment to markets outside of the region.[32]

Legislation was passed in Frankfort on February 18, 1861, to aid in the improvement of roads in the Beattyville and Proctor magisterial districts. The act called for an election to be held to determine whether the residents of the two magisterial districts would accept a $2.00 per year tax to improve local roads. The legislation also designated John G. McGuire of the Beattyville District and Isaac Congleton of the Proctor District to serve as the treasurer and commissioner of their respective districts should the voters pass the new tax. With these positions came the power to determine how to use the tax money, including the hiring of employees and the purchase of needed supplies. The voters of Proctor and Beattyville provided an election victory to the McGuires and their fellow elites and the tax went into effect.[33]

The McGuire family was quite wealthy at the dawn of the 1860s. Archibald McGuire's personal estate was valued at $9,000. His real estate was worth $4,600. James McGuire, Sr., owned $9,000 worth of real estate and had a personal estate valued at $5,000. John G. McGuire's personal estate was valued at $11,100. James McGuire, Jr., owned $4,000 in real estate. Unlike his relatives, Hiram McGuire no longer considered himself a farmer. He was a tavern keeper by trade, with real estate holdings valued at $2,500. Though some of the men appeared poorer than they had been a decade before, the reduction in their estates was probably due to property and money being passed to children as they reached adulthood. With even more McGuires related to the aforementioned individuals appearing on the census rolls with real estate holdings, it was obvious that the family wealth was extensive and spread among many more individuals than had been previously evident.[34]

During this period local matters were overtaken in importance by political developments nationally. The 1850s had radically altered the political landscape and the subsequent confusion was reflected in the votes cast by Kentuckians in presidential races that decade. In 1852, Kentucky voters favored Winfield Scott (Whig) over Franklin Pierce (Democrat) and John P. Hale (Free Soil). In 1856, Kentucky voters opted for James Buchanan (Democrat). In 1860, Kentucky voters threw their support to John Bell of the Constitutional Union Party. During this politically turbulent decade, the voters of Owsley County stayed remarkably consistent. They had tended to favor Democratic Party candidates since 1840 and continued that voting pattern to the election of 1860, when there were two Democratic Party candidates vying for the presidency. In that election they provided a majority of their votes to John C. Breckenridge (Southern Democrat).[35]

In the midst of this political turmoil was State Representative Abijah B. Gilbert. He was a member of the Democratic Party and represented Owsley County in the state legislature. Gilbert was also one of Owsley County's wealthier citizens. He owned a large farm consisting of 1,900 acres of bottomland on Sexton's Creek that had a cash value of $6,000 in 1860. On that farm he kept ten horses, four mules, six milk cows, six oxen, and thirty-five other cattle. In addition, he owned thirty-two sheep and ninety swine. His livestock was valued at $2,000. His farm was also producing a much wider variety of crops than that of most farmers in the county. His produce consisted of 200 bushels of wheat, fifty bushels of rye, 2,000 bushels of Indian corn, 200 bushels of oats, 40 bushels of peas or beans, 30 bushels of Irish potatoes, 20 bushels of sweet potatoes, and 3 bushels of flaxseed. Other products included 300 pounds of butter, 20 pounds of flax, and 50 pounds of maple syrup. Among those working on the farm were four slaves owned by Gilbert, two male and two female. Gilbert's political affiliation and property holdings suggested that he would be more sympathetic to the sentiments being expressed in the South as the United States of America was dividing than most of the people he represented in the state legislature. Although fellow Democrats in the state legislature expected that on the question of secession from the Union he would vote to secede, he instead voted for Kentucky remaining a part of the United States.[36]

The onset of hostilities between the United States of America and the Confederate States of America forced the people of Kentucky to choose sides. Although the Commonwealth of Kentucky officially opted for neutrality, a majority of Owsley Countians decided to cast their lot with the Union. Even though Abraham Lincoln (Republican) received only one vote in the county when running for the presidency in 1860, compared to five votes for Stephen A. Douglas (Northern Democrat), 370 for John Breckenridge (Southern Democrat), and 330 for John Bell (Constitutional Union), the people of Owsley County rallied to his cause a year later. In total, 13.64 percent of Owsley's white male population volunteered for service in the Union Army, which was the highest percentage of volunteers for any county in Kentucky. In comparison, the statewide average was 6.43 percent.[37]

Many of the men from Owsley County enlisted in the 7th Kentucky Infantry and served until October 5, 1864. One of these individuals was Captain Elisha B. Treadway. Treadway, who had served as a 2nd Lieutenant in Company F of the 3rd Regiment of Kentucky Volunteers during the Mexican War, helped organize Company A of the 7th Kentucky Infantry and served as its company commander. Among the volunteers in Treadway's company were a number of Archibald McGuire's relatives. On August 19, 1861, Thomas J. McGuire, Howard McGuire, Felix G. McGuire, Medley S. McGuire, Archibald McGuire, Huston McGuire, Jonathan McGuire, Warwick McGuire, and James G. McGuire all enlisted in the Union army at Camp Robinson. Unfortunately for the extended McGuire family, the war proved costly in human lives. Medley, Archibald, Jonathan, and James G. all perished during the conflict. While fighting for their country, the men of Owsley County saw action in a number of battles, including the Battle of Wild Cat in Kentucky and the Battle of Champions Hill, Mississippi, during the Vicksburg Campaign.[38]

The downside of so many men volunteering for the Union Army was that their families were vulnerable to the depredations that marked the conflict in the mountains of Appalachia.[39] Guerrilla bands ranged through the region and lawlessness was common. As described by an Owsley Countian, "...there has been more horse stealing and robbing than anywhere I know of at this time. Our country is in a deplorable situation"[40] It was these circumstances on the home front that led Major Elisha B. Treadway to leave the 7th Kentucky Infantry in order to form a Home Guard unit known as "The Three Forks Battalion" for the purpose of protecting his Unionist brethren. Treadway's successor in the 7th Kentucky Industry was Captain James M. Beatty, who assumed his duties on April 1, 1864.[41]

The only pitched battle within Owsley County during the Civil War occurred on April 15, 1864. The Battle of Booneville pitted Unionists from Owsley County against approximately eighty Confederate guerrillas who hailed from neighboring Breathitt County. While only one individual was killed during the fighting, resentment over the attack by Breathitt Countians festered, thereby straining relationships between the two counties throughout much of the twentieth century.[42]

The Civil War was a traumatic event that resulted in significant changes for the people of Owsley County. The most obvious change was that the community, like its counterparts across the country, had to adjust to the loss of men who were killed or maimed in the conflict. Owsley County also had to heal itself of the divisions within the community that became evident as guerrilla warfare raged throughout the countryside. A subtle, but no less significant, change occurred politically. A county that had favored the Democratic Party up to 1860 was in 1865 staunchly Republican. This identification with the Republican Party, which continues today, was a reflection of the service of so many of the men of Owsley County in the Union army. They had answered President Abraham Lincoln's call to service and had served under General Ulysses S. Grant during the Vicksburg Campaign. Unfortunately for Owsley County, the Commonwealth of Kentucky emerged from the conflict with a political hierarchy that would be dominated by the Democratic Party for more than a century.

Once the war was concluded and life in Owsley County returned to a semblance of normalcy, conflict once again arose within the county over the manner in which the McGuires and their associates had manipulated Owsley County to their benefit. The Beattyville and Proctor magisterial districts contained a number of improved roads that had been paid for through either the county's general fund or the revenues from the road tax passed in 1861. The McGuire faction controlled both sources of revenue due to the many pieces of special interest legislation that they had acquired over the early decades of Owsley's existence. In their zeal to develop their portion of the county, they had neglected the road needs of the rest of Owsley County. Resentment over the county revenue spent on the business needs of Proctor and Beattyville elites led to enough pressure being exerted by disgruntled Owsley Countians on legislators in the general assembly to repeal the 1861 road tax legislation.[43]

Asking for the repeal of the 1861 road tax was a punitive move on the part of the Owsley County interests that created the original petition, since only residents of Proctor and Beattyville were subject to the tax. Taxpayers in the vicinities of Proctor and Beattyville paid the tax willingly in order to improve the economic infrastructure of their local community. Unfortunately for Owsley Countians, the aggressive move against the interests of Proctor and Beattyville resulted in an even more aggressive retaliatory action by the political elites residing in those respective communities.

On January 14, 1870, Kentucky's general assembly was petitioned for the establishment of a new county made up of portions of Owsley, Estill, Wolfe, and Breathitt counties. The petition had been preceded by a remonstrance submitted on January 11 of the same year by Owsley County Representative Howell Brewer, who represented the county in the Commonwealth of Kentucky's house of representatives, on behalf of Owsley Countians opposed to the division of their county in order to create a new county entity. Unfortunately for Owsley County's residents, the petition for the new county proved successful, as the formation of Lee County was authorized on January 29, 1870, and made effective on March 1, 1870.[44]

The details in the legislation creating Lee County reflected the lessons learned by the McGuires and their business associates during their tenure in Owsley County. Having lost two elections in their efforts to get Proctor named the county seat, the McGuires took away the opportunity of the voting public to obstruct their plans by including language specifying that the county courthouse would be built in Proctor on a plot in the town square donated by Archibald McGuire. The act also named a number of McGuires and associates to serve as county officials. R.B. Jimison was named to serve as the county clerk. John G. McGuire was named to one of the two justice of the peace positions. James B. McGuire was awarded the position of constable.[45] As they did when they created Owsley County, the McGuires seized key political positions to aid them in manipulating the county to their benefit.

It appeared that Archibald McGuire had finally accomplished his dream of seeing Proctor become a county seat after more than a quarter-century of political machinations, but just as he was on the verge of reaching his goal, Archibald McGuire died. Ironically, the execution of his will was the first action by Lee County's court that did not involve an individual accepting a public office.[46] His death had a profoundly negative impact on the political machine that he had guided for decades. The cohesion and discipline previously evident between members of the McGuire family, Beattys, Congletons, Howertons, and Jimisons evaporated as individuals began acting in their own personal interests.

Conflict immediately arose in Lee County concerning the location of the county seat. Even though Proctor had been designated to serve as the county seat, questions began to be posed to Lee County's commissioners whether that designation was truly binding. Decatur Beatty and members of the McGuire family residing in Beattyville wanted their community to become the county seat of Lee County. J.C. Howerton and the McGuires living in Proctor were determined to ensure that their community remained the seat of the newly formed county. On March 10, 1870, Lee County's commissioners voted to keep Proctor as their county seat. The legitimacy of the vote was challenged because the meeting had been held at the home of J.C. Howerton. On September 1, 1870, Lee County's commissioners held another vote to determine the location of the county seat, which ended as a tie. The commissioners then decided that the solution to the quandary was to put the question to a vote by the general populace. Rather than waiting for the election to be held, J.C. Howerton and W.B. (William Barney) McGuire went to the Lee County court of claims and began filing the required paperwork to begin construction of the courthouse and jail on the land in Proctor that had been originally donated by Archibald McGuire for that expressed purpose. Infuriated by the affront, the commissioners decided not to hold the proposed election and instead voted as a group in November 1870 to make Beattyville the county seat. On the same day that the vote occurred, B.W. Luyman, a local attorney who included among his clients John G. McGuire, filed a motion to move Lee County's records from the location where they were housed in Proctor to Beattyville. Luyman's motion, which was supported by Decatur Beatty, carried the day, but the move of the records was challenged by an appeal that was filed in Lee circuit court by W.B. McGuire and J.C. Howerton. The courthouse battle then moved to the legal system. With Lee County in obvious political turmoil and McGuires on both sides of the issue, it was up to the state to settle the courthouse issue.[47]

The general assembly approved an act on January 28, 1871, that called for the determination of the county seat to be settled by an election. Three candidates were put forth: Proctor, Beattyville, and Canaan. None of the commissioners appointed by the Commonwealth of Kentucky to oversee the election hailed from Lee County. Curtis Jett and William Spencer were from Breathitt County, and John Farmer was a resident of Jackson County.

Not one McGuire, or any of their current or former associates, was included as an official in any capacity. Beattyville emerged victorious over Proctor by a margin of approximately three to one.[48]

The McGuires residing in Proctor refused to accept defeat. W.B. McGuire and Thomas McGuire filed a lawsuit to block the move of the county seat to Beattyville but were unsuccessful. In desperation, pro–Proctor forces even attempted to repeal the act that originally created Lee County.[49] Regardless of their protestations, the county seat issue had finally been settled for good.

For approximately thirty years, the McGuires and their associates diligently worked to empower themselves in order to construct the economic infrastructure required for their business endeavors to prosper at the expense of their neighbors in Owsley County. With the exception of Decatur Beatty and the handful of McGuires living in Beattyville, they ultimately failed to achieve their objective. Unfortunately, their thirty-year quest did leave a great deal of damage in its wake that would have lasting consequences. In the process of creating Owsley County, these elites took land, and the taxpayers residing therein, from Breathitt, Clay, and Estill Counties. In order to create Lee County, the McGuires and allied families took land from Breathitt, Estill, Owsley, and Wolfe counties. The constant loss of land resulted in all of these counties eventually becoming so small that each had, and would continue to have, an inadequate tax base to support even basic expenses such as county school districts and the salaries of county government officials. The shortage of tax revenue also meant that these counties could not adequately address their economic infrastructure needs, such as roads, because they could not afford the expenses.

The damage done to Owsley County was even more profound than just the loss of potential taxpayers. The land taken from Owsley to establish Lee County was the area where the Three Forks of the Kentucky River combined to form the main course of the Kentucky River. Owsley County was left with a portion of the South Fork of the Kentucky River that was so shallow that it was sometimes impassable by boat. The shallowness of the South Fork of the Kentucky River also meant that its economic benefits could only be maximized through the expenditure of revenue that Owsley County did not really have. The main course of the Kentucky River would soon become the centerpiece of Lee County's economy. Contrarily, Owsley County would have its economic development severely, and permanently, retarded by its inferior transportation infrastructure.[50]

Lee County, the 115th county created in Kentucky, contained approximately 200 square miles of land, 170 of which came from Owsley County. The total value of property in Lee County in 1871, which included the value of land, town lots, livestock, pleasure carriages, gold, silver or other metallic watches, gold and silver plate, and value under the Commonwealth of Kentucky's valuation law, was $468,151. In comparison, Owsley County's property valuation was $496,777. Thus at the time of Lee County's founding, Owsley County was perceived to be wealthier than its new neighbor. Despite differences in the factors used to determine total valuation, Owsley County remained wealthier in 1880, with a total valuation of $453,070, while Lee County's was $410,440.[51]

Lee County's economic fortunes began to change in the 1880s, when it was determined by politicians in Frankfort, Kentucky, and Washington, DC, that slackwater navigation of the Kentucky River was to begin at Beattyville. It was widely believed that slackwater navigation, which relied on a series of locks and dams, would enable the Kentucky River to be utilized year round to ship coal from the mountains of Eastern Kentucky, to markets in Louisville, Kentucky, and farther south, thereby displacing in the marketplace the coal that originated in Pittsburgh, Pennsylvania.[52]

The need for slackwater navigation had been evident to the coal industry of Eastern Kentucky for years. The industry's method of shipping coal was to load flatboats located on the many exposed gravel bars that could be found along the Kentucky River and its tributaries. Once their flatboats were loaded, the coal operators had to wait for a tide high enough to carry their goods to markets downriver. These loaded flatboats often fell prey to flash floods that broke them apart. In order to stem this constant loss, United States congressman John D. White secured $75,000 in the 1882 River and Harbor Act to construct a lock and movable dam in Beattyville. Three dam building experts from the U.S. Corps of Engineers were dispatched to Beattyville in 1883 to begin the planning process that would eventually lead to actual construction. A public meeting was held to allow Beattyville's residents to educate the engineers on the importance of the Kentucky River to the local economy. In Beattyville that year, there were approximately 650,000 bushels of coal, six million board feet of sawlogs, and 5,000 railroad ties shipped downriver. The combined value of all these commodities was $158,750.[53] Despite the near certainty of significant losses due to flash flooding, the Kentucky River provided the best means of getting the commodities to distant markets because most of the local roads could not support heavy wagons. Improvements on the Kentucky River thus held great promise in both reducing the losses incurred by entrepreneurs from the mountains and incorporating their local businesses into the market economy of the United States of America.

The Corps of Engineers began construction in 1885 on a sophisticated stone-filled timber dam, popularly known as a beartrap. Approximately 200 workers were initially employed to construct the dam. Housing for these workers was required, which created even more employment opportunities for individuals desiring a job. The sudden availability of employment in Beattyville resulted in such a large influx of laborers into Beattyville that there was not enough lodging for everyone.[54]

The onset of construction on the dam also attracted a number of outside capitalists to Lee County, such as the men who comprised the Three Forks Investment Company. The president of the Three Forks Investment Company was William Cornwall, Jr., who was also affiliated with the Louisville, Kentucky, based manufacturing company Cornwall & Bro. John H. Leathers, who served as secretary and treasurer, was the cashier of the Louisville Banking Company. Among the other officers and directors of the Three Forks Investment Company were J.W. Stine, president of the Richmond, Nicholasville, Irvine & Beattyville Railroad Company, Bennett H. Young of the Louisville Southern Railroad, C.D. Chenault, cashier for the Madison National Bank in Richmond, Kentucky, and United States congressman James B. McCreary, who was also a former governor of the Commonwealth of Kentucky. The Three Forks Investment Company initially secured one thousand acres of land within a half-mile of Beattyville that included both coal mines and substantial stands of timber. The company also secured a mile of riverfront property located above the site of the dam, which was ideal for constructing steam sawmills. The company's investors had no real plans to develop the real estate they owned, but instead preferred to sell the land to those entities that actually planned on developing the properties. Ultimately, those who invested in the Three Forks Investment Company made little, if any, profits from the business venture. They did succeed in making infrastructure improvements that benefited Beattyville and its residents. One of the contributions was the establishment of a bank. They also constructed a brickyard, which manufactured the bricks used to construct houses, railroad buildings, and a hotel. In addition, the company also graded and paved a number of roads that were needed as Beattyville expanded.[55]

The dam project itself was plagued by problems inherent in large-scale construction projects within Eastern Kentucky. The first problem faced by the engineers was getting needed supplies and materials to the construction site. Railroads could get materials and supplies to a location within forty-five miles of Beattyville, but from there the poor roads between the railroad hub and Beattyville severely hampered delivery. The Corps of Engineers did utilize, to a certain extent, the Kentucky River as a means of transporting needed materiel, but shipping goods upriver was a challenging endeavor in its own right. Complicating matters even further were the flash floods that materialized on a regular basis from the Three Forks of the Kentucky River. Despite myriad problems, the dam opened on October 30, 1886. Unfortunately for the advocates of slackwater navigation on the Kentucky River, the beartrap dam never did work efficiently. The artificial tide created by the beartrap moved much too swiftly, thereby endangering raftsmen and their valuable cargo. Within its first month of operation, it became painfully obvious that the dam was a colossal failure. The Kentucky River's swift currents had unexpectedly lifted up the wooden pilings that comprised the dam's outer structure. This resulted in the stone underlying the pilings being washed out. The failure of the beartrap dam meant that all future locks and dams constructed on the Kentucky River by the Corps of Engineers would be constructed of stone masonry.[56]

The people of Owsley County certainly envied the attention lavished on Lee County by outside capitalists, the Commonwealth of Kentucky, and the United States Congress during the 1880s. This sentiment is evident in letters published by *The Three Forks Enterprise* that also reflected the New South hype and boosterism of the day:

> Nature has been lavish of her rich and bountiful gifts, to this our section of the county. Here we have hidden and buried beneath our mountain peaks inexhaustible fields of the finest bituminous coal, and the richest and most yielding beds of iron ore; while peering, as if their tops would reach the skies, from our mountain tops, hillsides and valleys are to be seen, broad areas of the finest timber, which one could behold, from the tall and majestic oak, the giant of our forests, to any other conceivable kind and quality. Our beautiful and placid river whose waters furnish our only means of transportation, is another of nature's best gifts. But from lack of a sufficient enterprise and want of capital, we are unable to utilize these in such a way as to be pecuniarily valuable, in truth, they are of comparatively little value

to any of us, or to the outside world with our present illy-provided means of transportation. Our only means of egress or ingress to or from our place are our dirt roads, the dirt of which is good enough, but the roads are in a woeful condition; and at this present season of the year, travel over them is considered dangerous, that any one who regards his or her personal safety, would not dare undertake such a hazardous experiment. But with a buoyant expectancy and a willingness to wait, we console ourselves, that it may not be always thus with us. Sometimes, however, we think, that if we were not of the most jovial nature, seldom subject to a spell of the blues, that we would have a real heard spell of ennui, indeed. Now don't some one go and get sorry for us and build the Thre [*sic*] Forks railroad or some other such lock and dam the river or build us a turnpike, lest our excess of joy at such a realization should be more than we could well endure.— Soldier's Friend.[57]

While the letter by Soldier's Friend reflected frustration by an individual Owsley Countian, it also served as an advertisement for Owsley County to all of the outside capitalists who were operating at the time in Beattyville. The appeal apparently fell on deaf ears, because two years later another Owsley Countian wrote a letter pleading, "We can not build railroads and lock and dam our rivers ourselves; but the course of human events must sooner of later bring us into contact with the outside world."[58]

Both letter writers painted a portrait of Owsley County being ignored by the outside world while other counties in Appalachia were being industrialized. It is this viewpoint that has been perpetuated as one of the primary reasons that Owsley County is so impoverished today. Since present-day Owsley County is perceived as having no exploitable natural resources that can be extracted profitably, it has been extrapolated that this perception was also true during the late nineteenth century into the early decades of the twentieth. This line of thought suggests that at no time in its history was Owsley County attractive to outside capitalists. Thus, while much of Appalachia was industrialized in the latter portion of the nineteenth century, Owsley County was bypassed and never incorporated into the market economy of the United States of America. Contrary to this perspective, Owsley County was not overlooked by outside capitalists during the late nineteenth century. Many companies bent on exploiting Owsley County's natural wealth invaded the county just a few years after the complaints by Owsley Countians, such as Soldier's Friend, had been aired in Beattyville's newspaper. Unfortunately for Owsley Countians, they discovered that the arrival of industrialists was not the panacea that cured all of Owsley's economic ills.

Capitalists were drawn to Owsley by overwrought characterizations of the county's natural resources. The county's soil was perceived as being very productive. Ten-foot thick seams of coal were believed to underlie the soil at a depth of forty feet. Iron ore supposedly abounded within the county's borders. The "very finest" timber was also obviously available. One of the few rumors about Owsley County natural resources circulating among outside capitalists that actually proved to be completely accurate was that land was available at extremely cheap prices.[59]

The New Era Land Company of Louisville, Kentucky, began purchasing land within Owsley County in 1889. The company bought more than 3,000 acres in its first three years of operation in Owsley County. The Louisville Company also conducted business with other companies active in Owsley County. For instance, the New Era Land Company sold 6,446 acres of land to the Forman, Earle Company of Detroit, Michigan, in 1909.[60]

The Forman, Early Company, formerly known as the Nantahala Land Company, was not the only business headquartered in Detroit, Michigan, to purchase Owsley County timberland. Frank P. Chesbrough purchased approximately 900 acres in 1911. The Thomas Foreman Company opened business in Owsley County in January 1914. In its first month of operation, the company purchased 7,631 acres of land from the Forman, Earle Company. The Thomas Foreman Company acquired another 1,247 acres from the Laurel Land Company of London, Kentucky, four months later. The company continued to expand its land holdings within Owsley by acquiring lands belonging to individual Owsley Countians.[61] The Detroit companies buying timbered land within Owsley County all had ties to the booming automobile industry in their home city. The Detroit timber companies all needed access to substantial amounts of wood for both the manufacture of automobile bodies and the construction of spokes for wheels.[62]

Owsley Countians had worked tirelessly since the early 1880s to attract businesses owned by capitalists from outside the region to their community in the hope that those moneyed interests would construct the economic infrastructure that Owsley County required. After all, the business needs of capitalists operating in nearby Beattyville had resulted in the construction of roads that had benefited the local community. Owsley's populace was chagrined to learn that the infrastructure created by the capitalists operating within their county's borders was solely for the use of their businesses. Timber companies built two railroad lines into Owsley County. One was a narrow gauge track known as the "K & P." It was a small extension of the Louisville & Nashville Railroad that was used from 1905 to 1909. The other line was a branch of the Kentucky, Rockcastle and Cumberland Railroad. Both railway lines were abandoned once the supply of timber was exhausted.[63]

Despite numerous disappointments, Owsley Countians continued to champion their community to investors from outside the region. William Bullock, a local Booneville attorney, spoke of a future for Owsley County that included infrastructure improvements such as a turnpike from Booneville to Beattyville and a railroad line passing through Booneville that would extend to Charleston, South Carolina. Bullock believed that connecting Booneville to Charleston's ports would result in a boom for Owsley's fledgling coal industry.[64]

Bullock was a realist when it came to identifying Owsley County's economic weaknesses. He observed that all of the county's roads were made of dirt. These roads became difficult to navigate during the winter months because they were often muddy. Bullock identified timber as Owsley's primary economic commodity, since it covered two-thirds of the county's land. Unfortunately, the wealth being generated by the county's timber was not enriching many Owsley Countians, as timber harvesters were poorly paid. In Bullock's opinion, the only way to make the timber industry cost effective for Owsley Countians was to improve the waterway between Beattyville and Booneville or get a railroad line constructed to outside markets.[65]

While Owsley Countians were dreaming about a railroad, their counterparts in Lee were celebrating the arrival of the real thing. The Louisville & Atlantic Railroad decided in 1902 to extend a rail line to Beattyville that had previously terminated in the Estill County town of Irvine. The new railroad helped cement Beattyville's growing reputation as the "Queen City of the Mountains."[66] The arrival of the Louisville & Atlantic Railroad proved beneficial to the coal mining companies headquartered in Lee County, including those owned by members of the McGuire family. Beattyville's second railway arrived in 1909, when the Louisville & Nashville Railroad constructed a line that originated in Winchester, Kentucky.[67]

It would have been reasonable to assume that the arrival of railroad lines in Beattyville would have negated the need for improvements on the

Kentucky River. Coal and timber magnates could send their goods via rail to distant markets without the losses they had previously incurred while shipping their commodities down the Kentucky River. Instead, the arrival of railroads reinvigorated the interest of Lee Countians in having slackwater navigation of the Kentucky River extended to Beattyville. The beartrap dam project of the 1880s had been plagued by difficulties related to getting needed building supplies to Beattyville, since the nearest railroad hub had been more than forty miles away. The supply problem became a nonissue since the new rail lines could be utilized to ship building materiel directly to Beattyville.

Local leaders thus began clamoring for the construction of another dam in Lee County. The U.S. Corps of Engineers was opposed to the idea because they saw the extension of slackwater navigation to the Three Forks region as a waste of money. The Corps of Engineers had estimated in 1896 that extending slackwater navigation to Beattyville would have required the construction of seven locks and dams on the Kentucky River at a total cost of two million dollars. An additional $100,000 a year would have been required to operate and maintain the structures. This was a substantial sum of money for improvements on the upper portion of the Kentucky River that stood to benefit less than two thousand people.[68] As observed by Lieutenant William W. Hart of the U.S. Corps of Engineers, "The United States would have an extensive slackwater system on its hands, expensive to maintain, with little or no commerce to justify the expenditure."[69] The professional opinion of the Corps of Engineers mattered not at all, because Lee County's elites had the support of influential U.S. congressmen.

The Corps of Engineers determined that two locks and dams needed to be constructed within Lee County to extend slackwater navigation to Beattyville. Construction work on Lock and Dam 13 began in 1909. Serious problems soon arose because the company responsible for constructing the lock could not work in concert with the company assigned to build the dam. Lock and Dam 13 finally went operational in November 1914, more than two years behind schedule.[70]

The planned construction of Lock and Dam 14 was nearly scuttled the same year that work began on Lock 13. Theodore E. Burton, chairman of the U.S. House of Representatives' Committee on Rivers and Harbors, decided that the proposed Lock and Dam 14 should be omitted from future appropriations legislation because Lock and Dam 13 brought slackwater navigation of the Kentucky River close enough to Beattyville to serve the needs of the community. Kentucky's congressmen did not concur with the chairman's opinion. The Kentucky delegation made it a priority to attend all subsequent meetings of the Committee on Rivers and Harbors in order to ensure that Lock and Dam 14 survived the legislative process. Construction on the fourteenth, and final, lock and dam on the main course of the Kentucky River began in 1911 but was not completed until 1917.[71]

Beattyville became the economic hub of Eastern Kentucky during the early decades of the twentieth century due to its transportation infrastructure. The community's economic prosperity attracted migrants seeking employment. In 1900, the population of Lee County was 7,988. The population reached 9,531 just ten years later. Lee's population stood at 11,918 in 1920. Lee's surge in population was reflective of the strength of its economy. In contrast, Owsley County's population was 7,979 in 1910. By 1920, Owsley's population had declined to 7,820.[72] The population decline was partially attributable to Owsley Countians moving to Lee County in search of employment opportunities.

A sudden boom within the petroleum industry aided the diversification of Lee County's economy. Kentucky's oil industry had been in decline during the early years of the twentieth century due to the discovery of substantial oil fields in Wyoming, Kansas, and Oklahoma. Kentucky's downward trend was reversed in 1916 when Charles Dulin struck oil in Estill County. This sparked a "Klondike Rush" into Kentucky as individuals hailing from states such as Pennsylvania, Ohio, West Virginia, Indiana, Illinois, Kansas, and Oklahoma suddenly arrived to seek their fortunes. Estill's neighboring counties were particularly attractive to the speculators. The most productive source of oil found during this period, namely the Big Sinking Oil Pool, was first tapped in Lee County. Between 1919 and 1925, the Big Sinking Oil Pool produced 279,193 barrels of oil valued at $59,434,200.[73]

Petroleum interests were active in Owsley County by 1918. During that year, G.W. Garrett and Ike Wilder of Booneville began purchasing the rights to potential sources of gas and oil located underneath the property of individual Owsley Countians. Many people sold these mineral rights for a pittance. It cost Garrett $1 to buy the oil and gas rights to the 35 acres of land belonging to Joseph W. Bowman and his wife. The same price bought the oil and gas rights to Felix and Leah Smith's thirty acres.

Lee and Lucy Baker managed to obtain a much better deal with Garrett and Wilder than did many of their fellow Owsley Countians. They received $25 from the Booneville speculators for the rights to half of the oil and gas located underneath their 25 acre plot. By 1922, the price of oil and gas rights had apparently escalated significantly within Owsley County. It cost Garrett $100 that year to gain a half interest in the gas and oil located on a 5 acre parcel of land owned by Arch Judd and his wife, Lula.[74]

Garrett and Wilder were not the only Booneville residents to be purchasing the right to exploit the gas and oil reserves of their fellow Owsley Countians. In April 1919, Edward E. Rice began purchasing mineral rights from landowners residing along Upper Buffalo Creek and Island Creek. His business partner, R. Harry Smith of Louisville, Kentucky, financed Rice's purchases.[75]

The Petroleum Exploration Company established itself Owsley County in 1923. The company was incorporated in Maine but had its regional headquarters in Sistersville, West Virginia. Like other petroleum interests active in Owsley County, the Petroleum Exploration Company was purchasing the rights to oil and gas from landowners. Unlike their competitors, the company was also buying the right of way for pipelines, telegraph lines, and phone lines. The Owsley County court even gave the company the right to lay pipelines underneath county roads. The Petroleum Exploration Company utilized all of its rights to construct an extensive oil pipeline that connected a number of drilling operations within Owsley County to Lee County's transportation facilities. The pipeline network was extended in 1930 with the acquisition of lines running through Laurel, Clay, Perry, Owsley, and Breathitt counties from the Cumberland Pipe Line Company.[76]

The successes of petroleum companies operating in Owsley County came to the fore in 1927 with the publication of several articles in *The Courier-Journal.* In its July 1 issue, the newspaper celebrated the success of the Harry Lauder Syndicate of London, England, in drilling a well at Island Creek that was supposedly going to produce 30 barrels of oil a day. Just two days later, another oil strike at Island Creek overshadowed the British company's achievement. The Big Injun Oil Company drilled a well that purportedly produced 300 barrels of oil a day. It appeared, at least initially, that the Big Injun Well was going to provide a handsome profit to the owners of the Big Injun Oil Company. The ownership group, whose members hailed from Louisville or Beattyville, included in its ranks Monroe McGuire and V.S. Beatty. McGuire and Beatty were also part owners of the Monroe Oil Company, which was also drilling wells in the vicinity of Island Creek.[77]

The many petroleum companies operating in Estill, Lee, and Owsley counties did not remain in the respective counties for an extended period of time. The oil speculators quickly discovered that the petroleum fields found throughout Eastern Kentucky were quite shallow and thus emptied quickly. Even companies that managed to strike oil found it difficult to make a profit since drilling wells was an expensive undertaking.[78]

Obviously, *The Courier-Journal* had taken an interest in Owsley County's economic development during the mid–1920s. In 1926, an editorial writer from *The Courier-Journal* suggested to Owsley Countians that they should emulate the example of "their good neighbors in Lee" because Lee's residents had transformed their county into a "prizewinner in community betterment." In 1927, writers from the same newspaper lauded the successes of the many petroleum companies that were siphoning off Owsley County's natural wealth. The owners of the various petroleum companies striking oil were residents of Beattyville, Louisville, or London, England. *The Courier-Journal* was using the business success of these outsiders to insidiously push an agenda designed to characterize Owsley Countians as opponents of progress. This petty form of retribution was the direct consequence of the fiasco over the first incarnation of the Booneville Reservoir Project.[79]

In 1925, *The Courier-Journal* announced that a group of "progressive men" from the Louisville Hydro-Electric Company planned to construct a dam on the South Fork of the Kentucky River, near Booneville. The newspaper characterized the company's desire to locate their construction project in Owsley as a magnanimous gesture that marked a landmark moment in the county's economic history. The Louisville Hydro-Electric would become the first "foreign" investor within the county. The company's hydroelectric operation promised to create hundreds of jobs for Owsley Countians.[80] New jobs would inevitably be followed by an increase in the tax revenue realized by Owsley County. The county could then use the new funds to improve local roads and schools. What the Louisvillians at both *The Courier-Journal* and the Louisville Hydro-Electric Company failed to consider was the views of Owsley Countians, and other interested parties, who were going to be impacted by their grandiose development plans.

At a public hearing convened on March 18, 1925, by Captain C.W. Hall of the Federal Power Commission, the Owsley County residents in attendance voiced their opposition to the dam project. They observed that the construction of the dam was going to result in the flooding of nearly 75 percent of the county. Owsley County would become "a lake with a rim around it." Equally distressing to those who voiced their concerns was the loss of access to the many family graveyards that would have been submerged. To a majority of the Owsley Countians at the meeting, the arrival of the Louisville Hydro-Electric did not represent a rebirth of the county's fortunes. To the contrary, it marked Owsley's nadir. The lake created by the dam would displace most of the county's population. The migration of the dispossessed would then be followed by the dissolution of Owsley County.[81]

Owsley Countians found powerful allies in their bid to squelch the dam project. A representative of the Cumberland and Manchester Railroad stated that his company was preparing to construct rail lines into Owsley in order to remove virgin timber and coal from the area. Coal companies operating in Owsley County, such as the Highland Forge Company, supported the claims of the Cumberland and Manchester Railroad. Other "foreign" companies also came to the fore in order to protect their substantial investments in timber. These interests included the Thomas Foreman Company of Detroit, which owned 12,000 acres of timbered land, and the Bollepont Lumber Company. H.H. Hensley, who represented the Bollepont Lumber Company at the public hearing, was particularly adamant about protecting the 125,000 acres of Owsley County land that was owned by Detroit automobile magnate Henry Ford.[82]

As a result of the public hearing, the Federal Power Commission decided not to issue the permits required by the Louisville Hydro-Electric Company to construct the dam on the South Fork of the Kentucky River.[83] *The Courier-Journal* pinned the blame for the Louisville Hydro-Electric Company's setback both on Owsley County's residents and Henry Ford. Like Owsley's citizens, Henry Ford was subsequently disparaged in the pages of *The Courier-Journal.*

In 1926, an editorial writer for the newspaper called for the expansion of the Louisville and Nashville Railroad into Owsley County. It was hoped that the presence of the Louisville and Nashville Railroad in the county would dissuade Henry Ford from extending his D, T & I Railroad into the region. In the eyes of *The Courier-Journal,* the extension of Ford's railroad would have allowed him to exploit the natural resources he owned in Owsley, Clay, and Leslie counties. Through Ford, the newspaper appeared to be taking the stance that it was not in the best interest of the Commonwealth of Kentucky to allow "foreign" interests to capitalize on its natural wealth. In actuality, the newspaper had taken a hypocritical stance in its 1926 attack on Ford. If *The Courier-Journal's* editors had truly taken a stance against capitalists from outside of Kentucky, the newspaper would not have celebrated the successful oil strike in Owsley County by the Harry Lauder Syndicate of London, England, in 1927.[84]

Unlike Lee County, Owsley never got any of the private business interests operating within its borders in the early decades of the twentieth century to improve its transportation infrastructure. Railroad companies made surveys but never constructed any permanent rail lines. Petroleum companies drilled a number of wells and laid down miles of pipe but did not construct roads. In fairness to the capitalists, it was not their responsibility to construct the economic infrastructure required by Owsley County's citizens. That responsibility fell to Owsley's political elites. It was determined that Owsley elites should first pursue the financing necessary to construct good roads. It was hoped by Owsley citizens that the road construction would be followed by both river improvements and the arrival of railroads. This course of action represented a conscious decision to emulate Lee County's path to prosperity.

2. The Raw Deal

Owsley County was one of many counties in Kentucky to be dubbed a "pauper county" during the final decade of the nineteenth century. The term was used to describe any county that expended more tax revenue than it generated. The inability of a number of Kentucky counties to produce the tax revenues required to meet their obligations was the direct result of the irresponsible creation of 120 counties by the general assembly of the Commonwealth of Kentucky during the 1800s.[1]

As the twentieth century dawned, the Commonwealth of Kentucky began to shift the responsibility of building and maintaining roads to its counties. This shift was not unique to Kentucky, but rather a local manifestation of a "Progressive" movement sweeping across the South to construct "good roads." In following a regional trend, Kentucky's legislators created an unrealistic mandate for most of its counties. For pauper counties, financing road construction was virtually impossible. If Kentucky's elected political leaders wanted to spur road construction within each of the respective counties, they would have to devise ways to allow the counties to secure the needed funds for the task.

In 1909, Kentucky voters adopted an amendment to the constitution of the Commonwealth of Kentucky that allowed individual counties in Kentucky to borrow revenue for the purpose of bridge and road construction. According to the legislation the amount of debt that could be incurred by a county was limited to only 5 percent of the assessed total valuation of the county. This was followed in 1914 by additional legislation that allowed counties to begin issuing revenue bonds in order to raise the funds required for bridge and road construction. That same year, Kentucky created a "state aid" program that matched dollar for dollar the revenue generated by individual counties for road and bridge construction. This incentive served to encourage the leaders of Kentucky counties to borrow even more money that most could not afford to repay, as reflected by the sheer number of pauper counties that already existed at the time. Dissatisfied with the number of roads and bridges that had been constructed, Kentucky's elected leaders decided to abolish the state aid program in 1920 and replace it with "three to one" agreements. The new program provided a three dollar match for every one dollar raised by the respective counties for bridge and road construction.[2]

Like their counterparts across the state, Owsley County's political leaders seized upon the opportunities presented by the general assembly of the Commonwealth of Kentucky to obtain road money. The promise of matching funds also proved an irresistible incentive to Owsley's voters to help local elites raise bridge and road construction revenue. In 1918, Owsley Countians voted themselves a 20-cent annual road tax that stayed in effect for ten years. Owsley County's leaders used some of the road revenue generated by the tax to purchase a horse powered road grader in 1919. County Judge S.H. Rice purchased a tractor powered road grader several years later. Surprisingly, the purchase of the two road graders did not result in the construction of roads because Owsley County's magistrates could not come to a consensus over who would be allowed to operate the new equipment. During the period of time that the issue was vociferously debated, both of the road graders sat idle and quickly deteriorated.[3]

Conflict among magistrates over roadwork was not unique to Owsley County. Many of the counties in Kentucky that utilized magisterial districts for the division of roadwork discovered that their magistrates were a serious impediment to the effort to construct good roads. Magistrates throughout the state were tasked with the responsibility to construct roads, but were not required to obtain any type of training to acquire the technical skills needed to accomplish the task. Another problem was that the magistrates were given control over their respective district's share of the county's revenue for road construction, but were not really fiscally accountable for how the funds were used. This state of affairs was due to the notoriously poor record keeping of many Kentucky counties. Thus the fact that magistrates were spending money for road construction did not necessarily mean that roads were actually being constructed. As observed by a member of the Efficiency Commission of Kentucky in 1923, the magistrate road system as a whole presented "a pathetic picture of inefficiency and often of dishonesty."[4]

Despite the presence of two road graders within its borders, Owsley County had managed to construct only 250 miles of dirt roads by 1923.[5] Owsley resident Luther M. Ambrose assessed the roads in the county during the 1920s as being "no better than they were twenty years ago."[6] As all of the roads within Owsley County during the 1920s were made of dirt, this meant that they were basically impassible during certain times of the year. There apparently had been no attempt made to utilize gravel, or any other hard surface, to improve road local conditions. In comparison, Clark County had 390 miles of hard surfaced roads. Bath, Boone, Caldwell, and Harrison counties all had at least 250 miles of hard surfaced roads. Within Appalachian Kentucky, Pulaski County had 110 miles of hard surfaced roads and 2,200 miles of dirt roads. Rockcastle County had seventeen miles of hard surfaced roads and 425 miles of dirt roads.[7]

Despite the failure of the magistrates to construct roads, Owsley County's voters remained committed to raising the capital required for the task. In truth, they had no other real option than to continue funding road construction, since it had become evident that the county's economic stagnation would continue as long as the county did not construct the necessary transportation infrastructure to attract outside capital to their community. Thus in 1928, Owsley County voters opted to extend their 20-cent a year road tax for an additional decade. This commitment was significant because, as observed by Luther M. Ambrose, the average Owsley County resident had very little cash:

> Owsley County is not self supporting. There is not enough cash income within the county to buy the necessary food and clothing and pay the taxes. A great many families get their entire cash income from working away from home, either in the mines or in the Ohio Mills. Their average salary for school teachers [sic] is below the state "minimum." The only cash income during the time the crops are growing is from chickens and eggs and these go to the store in *exchange* for sugar, coffee, salt, tobacco, and dry goods. Dr. W.S. Anderson of the University of Kentucky told me that he sat all day in the cross-roads store at Major (White Oak Tree) and saw only ten cents in cash cross the counter in payment for merchandise or produce. Chickens and eggs are the currency. The chickens are being sold at about one pound weight for twenty five [sic] cents when they should have been kept

until they were big enough to be of value. Some logs are still floated out on the "tides" but most of the timber is gone except from a few large tracts like Buffalo which are owned by outside capital. Money is scarce and hard to get. Fewer cattle, sheep, and hogs are raised now than formerly. The whole economic situation is desperate, shall I say hopeless?[8]

Unfortunately for the voters, the taxes they willingly paid for road construction were usually being used for other purposes. For example, in the mid–1930s, county judge T.J. Green moved $4,500 from Owsley's road and bridge fund to the county's general fund. It was claimed by Green that the transfer was required in order to pay the county's debts. In truth, the primary beneficiaries of the diverted road funds were Owsley County's corrupt elected officials. Green himself received a direct payment of $1,500. Other elected county officials received payments that ranged from $700 to $1,000.[9]

For twenty years, Owsley Countians voluntarily provided their county's political elites with extra tax revenue in order to build roads and bridges. Owsley's elites supplemented the county's supplemental tax revenues by borrowing an addition $32,815.38 for road construction during the 1920s. The Commonwealth of Kentucky augmented Owsley's road and bridge fund by matching all of the road money that was raised by the county. Tragically, the expenditure of all this revenue resulted in the construction of very few roads.[10]

Following the onset of the Great Depression in October 1929, Owsley County's elected leaders determined that the county could not afford to service all of the debts that had been incurred during the previous decades. Their solution to the quandary was to simply repudiate the debts. They believed that ignoring their financial obligations was a constitutionally protected right, since Section 157 of the constitution of the Commonwealth of the Kentucky limited the maximum tax rate for a county's general fund at fifty cents per $100. Even at the maximum tax rate, Owsley County barely generated the tax revenue that was required to pay expenses mandated by the Commonwealth of Kentucky, such as the salaries of county officials. As long as Owsley County's taxpayers were paying the maximum amount of taxes allowable by law, creditors were forced to be satisfied with whatever tax revenue remained after the county paid all of its required expenses. The county's leftover revenue proved to be so low that there was not enough money available to even keep pace with the interest that was being generated by the debt. The unpaid annual interest was subsequently capitalized by those that owned the debt, thus Owsley's debt load continued to grow.[11]

The Great Depression was particularly devastating to Owsley County because it compounded existent problems in the agricultural segment of its economy. Farms in Owsley County had rarely been as productive as the average farm in Kentucky due to several factors. The thin soils found within the county had never been suitable for agricultural purposes. The continual sowing of crops in the same fields had further diminished what little agricultural potential existed in the soils. Most of the soils found within the county's borders yielded good crops for only three years. Once land had been farmed, it took up to fifteen years for the soil to be replenished to the point that it could once again produce an adequate crop yield. Most Owsley County farmers did not have enough farmland to wait during the years that were required for their soil quality to improve. The consequences of these problems were already evident in the 1920s.[12] Luther Ambrose assessed that "five families were living on land which would support one in comfort." An unidentified individual disagreed with Ambrose's conclusion; "my father estimated thirteen families where one might make a good living."[13] The out-migration of Owsley Countians between 1910 and 1930 thus proved beneficial because it reduced the number of people that required agricultural products to subsist. However, with the onset of the Great Depression, many of the people who had left Owsley County suddenly found that their economic opportunities had disappeared and they returned home. This resulted in Owsley County's population increasing by 24 percent between 1930 and 1940. Owsley County's population boom was not unique. Throughout Appalachia, individuals that had outmigrated from the region returned to their home communities as their jobs in the coal mines and timber industry disappeared.[14]

The population increase was accompanied by a corresponding rise in the number of farms in the county. In 1929, there were 1,351 farms in Owsley County. The number had grown to 1,591 farms by 1934. By 1939, there were 1,713 farms. The increase in the number of farms was not a positive development considering that the amount of farmland available within the county between 1929 and 1939 declined by 6 percent. The average farm in 1929 within Owsley County was comprised of 80 acres. Ten years later, the average had fallen to 58 acres. The growth in the number of individuals farming was also a reflection on the lack of availability of other forms of employment within Owsley County and its immediate environs. With the coal and timber industries suffering through a downturn in the business cycle, farming was the only real available option for many Owsley Countians to earn a living.[15]

The nature of farming in Owsley County changed drastically between 1930 and 1935. Throughout the nineteenth century, Owsley had been renowned for the livestock produced within the county, especially sheep. Despite the renown of the local herds, livestock production declined rapidly after 1930. There were 1,716 sheep in the county in 1930. The herds had dwindled to 898 just five years later. The number of hogs went from 4,355 to 3,166 during the same period. There were also changes in the types of plants grown on Owsley's farms. Oats were being grown on 2,249 acres of farmland in 1930. By 1935, only 468 acres of land were devoted to the crop. The decline in oat production mirrored the rise of tobacco as a major cash crop within Owsley County. Owsley County farmers produced 282,016 pounds of tobacco in 1930. The poundage increased to 434,905 in 1935.[16]

Some of these changes were the result of the farms shrinking in size. Sheep production required pastureland. Farmers who owned 85-acre farms in 1930 had enough land to maintain a herd of sheep. As farms rapidly grew smaller, both the pastureland and the sheep disappeared. The loss of the pastureland brought about even more problems for Owsley County farmers. Pastureland designated for sheep production was never plowed, thus it was not prone to much erosion. The increase in small farms meant that plowed fields that did erode easily replaced the pastureland. Compounding the erosion problem was corn and tobacco production. Since both crops were planted in rows, natural channels for water were created that further aided the erosion process.

The changes in the output of Owsley County's farms can also be attributed in part to the Agricultural Adjustment Administration (AAA). The AAA was a New Deal federal relief agency created by the Agricultural Adjustment Act of 1933 to address problems in the agricultural sector of the nation's economy. On the national level, the AAA dedicated its energies to reducing the supply of agricultural commodities to the levels required for public consumption. It was believed that the elimination of surplus production would result in price increases for the respective commodities. In areas where subsistence farming dominated, such as Owsley County, the AAA had to change its tactics. As part of the effort to foster agricultural production in these areas, the AAA negotiated a number of purchasing contracts for specific commodities. The purchasing contracts served to raise the prices of those commodities in the marketplace, thereby, in theory, providing greater profits to farmers. Owsley County farmers directly benefited from these contracts. Between 1933 and 1937, Owsley County farmers received $9,152.55 in benefit payments for adhering to the quota requirements imposed on the production of corn and hogs. Much of the revenue was probably the result of farmers being paid to reduce the number of hogs in the county, as evidenced by the fact that the hog population within Owsley County declined significantly during this period. Farmers participating in the hog program were paid $5 per hog, which they were allowed to keep as their quota. Any hogs that the farmer had in excess of their quota were required to be either traded or given away. It should be acknowledged that agriculturalists that joined the AAA's program were required to participate in both the corn allotment and the subsistence hog allotment. It is doubtful that Owsley County farmers would have willingly participated in reducing the number of hogs that they owned as they needed the hogs for subsistence. The era in which hog production declined was a period that saw Owsley County's population expand significantly. The AAA's subsistence hog allotment thus served to ultimately hurt people in Appalachia by taking away a means to feed their families in order to drive hog prices higher throughout the United States.[17]

The remainder of Owsley County's AAA payments between 1933 and 1937 were for the production of tobacco. Owsley farmers received $15,277.74 in payments related to tobacco production. Many Owsley County farmers abandoned subsistence farming in favor of tobacco production during the 1930s. In 1935, farmers in Owsley County produced 392,000 pounds of burley tobacco. By 1940, a total of 776,000 pounds of tobacco were being produced by Owsley Countians. It should be noted that the rise of tobacco production in Owsley County was most likely the result of the AAA policies. Although participation in the AAA's tobacco program was ostensibly voluntary, many farmers were forced to participate in the program if they grew any tobacco at all. The Kerr-Smith Act of 1934 was the culprit because it levied a 24 percent marketing tax on each pound of tobacco that was produced outside of the AAA program. The purpose of the onerous tax was to ensure that farmers could not profit from growing tobacco outside of the AAA program. For Owsley County farmers, the AAA's tobacco program meant that they lost control of their farmland. The Agricultural Adjustment Administration had assumed the power to determine how Owsley County farmers used their real estate. If an official from the AAA determined that a farmer was not going to plant a tobacco crop in a particular year in order to avoid overproduction, the farmer did not regain the ability to use their land as they saw fit due of all of the restrictions imposed by the AAA in order to participate in its program. For instance, in 1936, tobacco was deemed to be a "soil depleting" crop. If a farmer was instructed not to plant tobacco, they could not plant other "soil depleting" crops on the unused land. Unfortunately for the farmers, corn, oats, and wheat were among the edible crops that had been classed as soil depleting. The AAA's restrictions were so thorough that they even limited how farm labor and equipment was utilized on the land that fell under their purview.[18]

The Agricultural Adjustment Act of 1933, which was declared unconstitutional by the United States Supreme Court in January 1936, proved to be a disaster for farmers in Owsley County. In retrospect, the outcome was not surprising since the act was designed to raise farm commodity prices, rather than alleviate poverty. The true beneficiaries of the Agricultural Adjustment Act of 1933 were large farming operations, such as those found in the Midwestern portion of the United States, because they suddenly had the federal government guaranteeing price supports and control of surplus production during times that the agricultural sector of the economy was suffering through a downturn. In essence, the federal programs associated with the Agricultural Adjustment Act served to protect the economic interests of large agricultural operations at the expense of those who owned small farms. Farmers had to have a significant amount of acreage to produce a respective crop in order to glean the benefits of the higher commodity prices. In Appalachia in general, and Owsley County in particular, most farmers did not have access to substantial amounts of land. The farms in Owsley County had developed to provide the materials that were required for a family's subsistence. What little surplus was produced on the family farm was primarily used to barter for needed goods or services. The forced move from subsistence farming during the 1930s by the AAA had the net result of taking away the ability of Owsley County farmers to provide for themselves and their families. The diversity of foods produced on the farm was replaced by a dependence on a crop, namely tobacco, which could not be eaten. Suddenly, Owsley Countians were at the mercy of markets that fluctuated constantly, and that also tended to disadvantage low level producers. Since Owsley County, like many of its Appalachian counterparts, depended on its agricultural sector as the primary component of the local economy, the loss of the farmer's ability to produce required goods on their homestead left the population dependent on governmental welfare programs.[19]

Owsley County did not fare well in the competition for federal dollars during the New Deal era. For example, between 1933 and 1936, the Civil Works Administration (CWA) expended $29,000 for Owsley County. During the same period, the CWA expended the following in other Kentucky counties: $163,832 in Bell; $170,288 in Boyd; $99,943 in Breathitt; $65,542 in Clay; $57,611 in Laurel; $180,916 in Pike; and $141,396 in Whitley. The same trend was evident in the Works Progress Administration (WPA) between 1935 and 1937. The WPA expended $137,783 for Owsley County's benefit. The WPA was much more generous to other Kentucky counties: Bell received $584,444; Breathitt received $671,353; Clay received $539,462; Lee received $234,211; and Whitley received $697,559. The counties receiving the majority of the money all had active coal or manufacturing industries. Not coincidentally, those were also the counties with the largest human populations in Eastern Kentucky. Counties such as Owsley, which were judged by U.S. government officials to have little economic potential due to their lack of exploitable natural resources, received the least amount of money from the federal New Deal programs.[20] This negative perception of Owsley's economic potential was compounded by the state of its poor transportation infrastructure.

Just as Owsley County was beginning to emerge from the economic damage of the Great Depression, the long-ignored and repudiated road debt of the 1920s suddenly became a serious problem. On February 11, 1947, the Court of Appeals of Kentucky issued an opinion concerning *Griffin et al. v. Clay County et al. Burchell v. Same.* Clay County had issued $75,000 of bonded debt in 1928 that had accrued interest at an annual rate of 5¾ percent. Clay County, like all other counties, had been required by Section 159 of the constitution of the Commonwealth of Kentucky to create a sinking fund to pay off those debts over a maximum of 40-year period from the time that the debt was incurred. Unfortunately, Clay County's political elites never created the sinking fund. Clay's political leaders, like Owsley's, believed that Section 157 of the state constitution would protect them from the consequences of ignoring their creditors. Clay County discovered that the majority of the judges on the Court of

Appeals disagreed with their interpretation of the constitution. Clay County was ordered to "provide for the collection of an annual tax sufficient to pay the interest on said indebtedness, and to create a sinking fund for the payment of the principal thereof, even though an amount in excess of the maximum specified in Section 157 must be levied."[21]

The ramifications of *Griffin et al. v. Clay County et al. Burchell v. Same* were apparent to Owsley County's creditors. The Farmers State Bank of Booneville, on behalf of Charles A. Hinsch & Company of Cincinnati, Ohio, sued the Owsley County Fiscal Court later the same year. The case was argued before the Court of Appeals of Kentucky in 1951. In *Farmers State Bank et al. v. Owsley County et al.*, Owsley County's lawyers desperately attempted to demonstrate that their county had not made the same missteps as Clay, thus the same penalties should not apply. The key difference, in the eyes of Owsley's lawyers, was that the original owners of its bonds had sued Clay County. Owsley County had never directly borrowed money from Charles A. Hinsch & Company. The reason that Charles A. Hinsch & Company owned so much of Owsley County's debt was that it had purchased it from Owsley's original creditors, who had come to believe that they were never going to be repaid by the Owsley County Fiscal Court. Owsley's lawyers thus argued that the only parties with the constitutional right to file suit against the Owsley County Fiscal Court were the original holders of the debt. This strained argument fell on mostly deaf ears. The Court of Appeals of Kentucky found that the issues evident within the *Farmers State Bank et al. v. Owsley County et al.* case were so similar to the Clay County litigation that the same penalties should apply. Even the dissenting judges agreed with their colleagues in the majority about the apparent similarities between the cases. Rather than writing a detailed opinion on the Owsley County case, the dissenting judges instead referred interested parties to their dissent in *Griffin et al. v. Clay County et al. Burchell v. Same.*[22]

The dissenting opinion in *Griffin et al. v. Clay County et al. Burchell v. Same*, and by extension *Farmers State Bank et al. v. Owsley County et al.*, warned about the potential consequences of ruling against Clay and Owsley counties. It pointed to "the old and homely adage that 'you cannot get blood from a turnip,'" and observed that the counties in question had "no blood."[23] The respective counties also had no legal options. Individuals who found themselves deeply in debt could always seek protection through bankruptcy. That recourse was not available to the respective counties.

Thusly, regardless of whether the creditor had a valid debt, the dissenters concluded that it served the public good to protect all Kentucky counties under Section 157 of the of the Commonwealth of the Kentucky.[24]

The majority opinion in *Farmers State Bank et al. v. Owsley County et al.* reflected a level of agreement with the dissenters in the Clay County case. The judges warned that in subsequent cases that "the public generally is now on notice that this court will henceforth adopt a sound and health construction of our Constitution, and credit extended to taxing districts in disregard of our Constitution and the comments herein ... will be at the creditor's risk."[25] While the court of appeals pledged to protect the many counties in Kentucky that had chosen to ignore Section 157 of the constitution of the Commonwealth of the Kentucky, they made an exception for Clay and Owsley counties. Both counties were financially devastated by the decision.

In Owsley's case, the county lost what little ability it had to create its own economic infrastructure. It became totally dependent on outside entities to foster economic development within its borders. This put Owsley County, which was staunchly Republican in its political leanings, at the mercy of a succession of Democratic Party administrations at the state level. Not surprisingly, Owsley County never got decent roads constructed. As late as 1999, only 20 percent of the roads in the county had been paved.[26]

Lee County was also in economic decline in the 1930s. Like Owsley, the roots of its economic problems could be found in the 1920s. While the completion of slackwater navigation in 1917 supposedly heralded the reinvigoration of Lee County's river trade, it actually marked the nadir of the Kentucky River as a significant part of Lee's economy. By the time Lock and Dam 14 were completed, the Kentucky River had been supplanted by railroads as the primary means of getting Eastern Kentucky's natural wealth to distant markets.

The nature of river traffic on the Kentucky River also changed in the years that it took slackwater navigation to be extended to Beattyville. The locks built in Lee County had been designed to support flatboats and steamboats. By 1917, towboats and barges were the primary means of shipping goods via the Kentucky River. These forms of watercraft required larger locks than the ones that had been constructed in Lee County.[27]

The outbreak of World War I once again made Beattyville useful as a shipping center. The need to support the war effort put immense pressure on railroad companies. Railroads that would have ordinarily been used to ship coal out of Eastern Kentucky were instead being used to support the needs of the United States military. This proved a temporary boon to Beattyville because it had a ready supply of coal and an alternate means of getting that commodity to distant markets.[28]

The sudden relevance of the Kentucky River as a means to ship coal downriver sparked a revival in 1920 to the idea of extending slackwater navigation from Beattyville to Booneville. It was argued that the extension would solve two problems. The first was to a perceived sociological problem: "It is generally believed by people acquainted with the Kentucky mountains that as soon as a railroad gets into the district, feuds disappear and moonshining diminishes. This would equally apply to river transportation."[29] The other justification was much more practical. This was the argument that coal originating in Owsley County, of which there was little, could be shipped cheaper from the South Fork of the Kentucky River than it could via railroads. Despite strong support within the Three Forks of the Kentucky River region for the project, the United States Corps of Engineers vehemently and successfully fought off the attempt to start a lock and dam construction project within the vicinity of Booneville.[30]

In fairness to the Corps of Engineers, the difficulties they had endured related to dam construction in Beattyville would have dampened their enthusiasm for extending slackwater navigation to Booneville. The engineers had faced significant supply problems while constructing the beartrap dam in 1886. Getting supplies upriver via the Kentucky River to Beattyville had proven to be a monumental challenge. The poor roads between the nearest railroad hub and Beattyville had also created logistical nightmares. The conditions present within Owsley County in 1920 were far worse that than those that had been found in Beattyville in 1886. The South Fork of the Kentucky River was much too shallow for heavy stone to be shipped to Booneville during certain times of the year. Owsley also had no hard surfaced roads. Due to the difficulties related to the beartrap dam, the U.S. Corps of Engineers had refused to build any other dams in Beattyville until a railroad line had arrived in the community. Booneville did not have the required railroad in 1920, nor were there any prospects for getting a railroad line constructed.[31]

Booneville would have probably left the lexicon of the U.S. Corps of Engineers at that point had it not been for the horrendous Flood of 1937. The flooding that year was precipitated by rainfall that averaged nearly 16 inches across the Commonwealth of Kentucky. The resulting flood on the Kentucky River inundated many communities, including Heidelberg in Lee County. In January 1937, Heidelberg received 11.92 inches of rain. To put that in perspective, the community had received a total of 12 inches of rain between April 1, 1936, and October 1, 1936.[32]

Frankfort, the state capital, also suffered significant damage from the severe flooding. During January 1937, Frankfort received measurable amounts of precipitation on 21 different days. Frankfort's flooding problems were exacerbated by the inability of the Kentucky River to drain effectively into the Ohio River, which was also swollen with floodwaters. The entire length of the Ohio River hit flood stage over the course of January. Since the Kentucky River could not drain into the Ohio River, its tributaries also became swollen with water. The Ohio River's flooding significantly impacted Louisville, Kentucky. Floodwaters in Louisville crested at 57.1 feet, which represented an increase of ten feet over the previous flooding record for the city that had been set in 1884. The floodwaters on the Ohio, Mississippi, and Kentucky rivers ultimately displaced more than 50,000 families across Kentucky for an extended period of time, since the floodwaters were slow to recede. According to the Weather Bureau, the Flood of 1937 resulted in 250 million dollars of damage in Kentucky alone.[33]

The damage done by the 1937 flood spurred the U.S. Congress to address the need for flood control on one of the primary tributaries of the Mississippi River. The Flood Control Act of 1938 proposed the construction of 45 reservoirs in the Ohio River Basin. The legislation authorized the expenditure of $75,000,000 for planning and construction purposes. The selection of specific projects to be constructed was left to the discretion of the chief of engineers of the U.S. Army Corps of Engineers.[34]

The Flood Control Act of 1938 specified that three of the reservoirs slated for the Ohio River Basin were to be constructed on the forks of the Kentucky River. It was believed that damming each of the forks would enable the engineers to control the floodwaters arising in the mountains of Eastern Kentucky, thereby preventing the flooding of downriver cities such as Frankfort. The U.S. Army Corps of Engineers determined during its initial survey of the Kentucky River and its tributaries that Beattyville also stood to gain a significant amount of flood protection as a result of reservoir construction. Unfortunately for Beattyville, it was determined that the damming of the Three Forks of the Kentucky River would have only a minimal effect on Frankfort's flood problem. The three dams stood to ease the potential flooding of the state capital by mere inches. In order to spur construction of the dams at that point in time, the flooding relief in Frankfort would have had to have been measured in feet.[35]

In order to address Frankfort's problem, the Corps of Engineers proposed the construction of a dam in Jessamine County. This development pushed the construction of reservoirs on the forks of the Kentucky River down a suddenly growing queue. The proposed Jessamine Creek Dam drew opposition on a number of fronts. The dam would have stopped shipping on the Kentucky River at Lock #7. This development would have rendered all of the upriver locks and dams that had already been constructed useless. More importantly to many Kentuckians, especially those who were members of the Pioneer National Monument Association, the resulting lake would have buried the site of Fort Boonesborough.[36]

The Pioneer National Monument Association was founded in 1926 for the express purpose of saving historical sites in Kentucky. Initially, the organization targeted Fort Boonesborough and the Battle of Blue Licks Battlefield to serve as parts of the Pioneer National Monument. Within a matter of years, Boone's Station and Bryan Station were also added to the list of potential components for the creation of a national monument. Despite congressional support for the project, the entire endeavor would have collapsed with the construction of the Jessamine Creek Dam.[37]

When the Pioneer National Monument Association decided to take a stand against the Jessamine Creek Dam, they enlisted some significant allies. Among the organizations that lent their support to protect Fort Boonesborough was the Kentucky Historical Society, the Daughters of the American Revolution, and the Commonwealth of Kentucky's Daniel Boone Bicentennial Commission. The Pioneer National Monument Association was also greatly aided by one of its members, Tom Wallace. Wallace was the editor of the *Louisville Times*, one of the largest newspapers in the state. He was also a well-respected journalist who had many well-connected political contacts throughout the United States. His editorials and letters proved very damaging to the efforts to construct the Jessamine Creek Dam.[38]

Although the proposed Jessamine Creek Dam supplanted the original flood control benefit of the dams on each of the forks of the Kentucky River, the projects officially stayed active. The concept of a dam to be constructed on the South Fork of the Kentucky River was reaffirmed on

December 22, 1944, with United States Public Law 534, which permitted its construction for the new purpose of producing hydroelectric power. The legislation stipulated that construction on the project could not commence without a recommendation to the United States secretary of war by both the chief of engineers and the Federal Power Commission. Neither of the required recommendations was ever given.[39]

The theoretical existence of the Jessamine Creek Dam served to stifle development of the Kentucky River and its tributaries in areas upriver of Lock #7. What little momentum existed for the construction of dams on each of the forks of the Kentucky River disappeared. The Corps of Engineers did not even attempt to adequately maintain existing structures, such as the locks and dams that were constructed in Beattyville and its environs. These developments were due to the Flood Control Act of 1944, which authorized the Corps of Engineers to abandon all Kentucky River navigation projects upriver of Lock #7 once the Jessamine Creek Dam was constructed. By the early 1950s, it was becoming evident that there was little chance that the Jessamine Creek Dam would ever reach the construction stage due to the opposition of groups such as the Pioneer National Monument Association and individual Kentuckians such as noted historians Thomas D. Clark and Hambleton Tapp. The decline of the Jessamine Creek Dam's prospects did not mean that the Corps of Engineers had once again become interested in working on projects upriver of Lock #7. The Corps of Engineers drafted a report in 1951 recommending that Locks and Dams 8–14 on the Kentucky River be abandoned due to the lack of river traffic.[40]

The recommendation by the engineers to abandon so many locks and dams on the Kentucky River spurred the creation of the Kentucky River Development Association (KRDA) in June 1951. The organization's expressed purpose was to develop the untapped economic potential of the entire course of the Kentucky River and its major tributaries. The KRDA had a broad agenda that reflected the diverse interests of its members. The leadership of the KRDA was a reflection of the organization's broad base. Serving as secretary was Beattyville resident Van H. Reneau. Carruther Coleman of Lexington served a term as president. Other officers hailed from the Kentucky communities of Frankfort, Jackson, Winchester, Irvine, Richmond, and Hazard.[41]

Individuals hailing from the central Kentucky communities of Lexington and Richmond were primarily interested in constructing dams on many

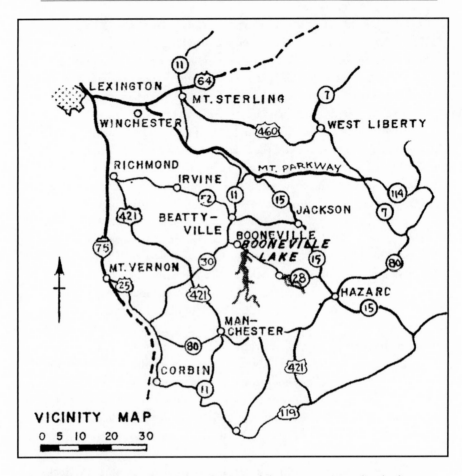

This map shows the locations of many of the communities that had representation in the Kentucky River Development Association (U.S. Army Corps of Engineers, Louisville District).

of the Kentucky River's tributaries in order to ensure an adequate supply of water for their rapidly growing populations.[42] As early as 1930, the inhabitants of both Richmond and Lexington had discovered that they could not always depend on the Kentucky River to supply the water that they needed. During the drought year of 1930, the water level of the Kentucky River was so low that little water was spilling over its dams. Downriver communities thus received little of the water that they had grown to depend on from the Kentucky River. The water shortage in Richmond proved so dire that water had to be delivered to the community via railroad cars.[43]

The leaders of upriver communities in counties such as Breathitt, Estill, and Lee were much more interested in flood control projects. The Three Forks of the Kentucky River region had historically been susceptible to flash flooding. One of the more devastating flash floods in the area would have been a terrifying memory to many individuals active in the KRDA. The Frozen Creek Flood of July 5, 1939, resulted in the deaths of fifty-two Breathitt Countians who were swept away by a 20-foot wave that had washed down a tributary of the North Fork of the Kentucky River.[44]

Many individuals in the Three Forks of the Kentucky River region had been anticipating the flood protection that would have resulted from the dam construction that had been authorized in the Flood Control Act of 1938. This anticipation had resulted in the phenomenon of "dam talk." Dam talk referred to informal conversations concerning reservoir construction that may or may not have had any basis in fact. The rumors were fueled by the periodic surveys of the Kentucky River and its tributaries that were being conducted by the United States Army Corps of Engineers. The presence of engineers in the area was misinterpreted by local residents as evidence that dam construction was imminent. When apparent work towards dam construction yielded nothing, the locals grew frustrated. Their disappointment was humorously captured by a local writer named Clennie Holon: "We believe that the best way to get that dam is to have another dam meeting of them Senators, Representatives and other big dignified men and then throw their big fat bodies right into the Kentucky River. Then after dumping a few bags of cement upon them, set back upon the bank and watch the river rise."[45] For individuals like Holon, the KRDA represented a new opportunity to push for the construction of dams on the forks of the Kentucky River.

In December 1953, the KRDA laid out an eleven-point agenda for the organization:

The recommendations follow:

1. The improvement of the navigation facilities on the lower portion of the stream (Kentucky River) as recommended in House Document 85 (73rd Congress) and that attention be given to the possibility of furnishing flood control to the lower portion of the valley incident to the navigational improvements.

2. That efforts be made to have suitable legislation enacted that will permit the Federal agencies involved to give proper economic

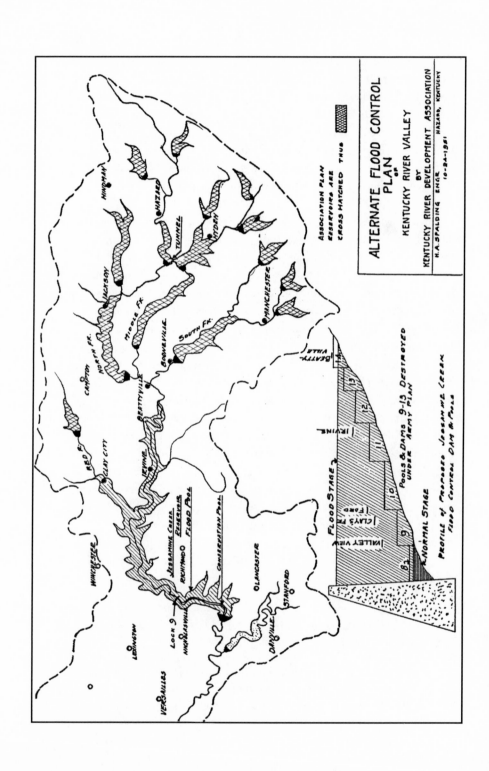

ALTERNATE FLOOD CONTROL
PLAN
OF
KENTUCKY RIVER VALLEY
BY
KENTUCKY RIVER DEVELOPMENT ASSOCIATION
H. A. SPALDING ENGR. HAZARD, KENTUCKY
10-24-1951

ASSOCIATION PLAN
RESERVOIRS ARE
CROSS HATCHED THUS

Pools & Dams 9-13 Destroyed
Under Army Plan

PROFILE of Proposed Jossamine Creek
Flood Control Dam & Pools

BEATTYVILLE
13
12
IRVINE
11
10
CLAY'S FERRY [FLOOD]
9
VALLEY VIEW
8
Normal Stage
Flood Stage

TUNNEL

HINDMAN
HAZARD
HYDEN
MANCHESTER
JACKSON
MIDDLE FK.
NORTH FK.
CAMPTON
BOONEVILLE
SOUTH FK.
BEATTYVILLE
RED R.
CLAY CITY
IRVINE
Jessamine Creek Reservoir
RICHMOND FLOOD POOL
CONSERVATION POOL
Lock 9
HIGH BRIDGE
OLIMPCHESTER
WINCHESTER
LEXINGTON
DANVILLE
STANFORD
VERSAILLES

weight to the value of water for industrial, irrigation, conservation and recreational purposes.

3. That where water power is present it should be developed rather than wasted, if stream improvement is undertaken.

4. That the extension of navigation above the Airdale Dam be disregarded, and that the dam be constructed as proposed.

5. That the immediate construction of a dam in the vicinity of Buckhorn is urged at a location to be compatible with the purposes of the association.

6. That consideration be given to the extension of navigable water to the vicinity of Booneville and that the Booneville dam and reservoir be constructed where and as now proposed.

7. That an immediate and thorough impoundment and flood control for the upper portions of the Kentucky River Valley and that the sites of those impoundments be those shown on the general plan of our Association with the possible additions on Maces Creek in Perry county and Bull Creek near Cornettsville in Letcher county.

8. That the Indian Creek dam on Red River be constructed where and as planned so as to furnish flood protection and water for irrigation to the Red River dam and reservoir be built where [*sic*] and River Valley.

9. That the possibilities of irrigation throughout the Kentucky River Valley be thoroughly studied.

10. That the prevention of pollution and construction and use of industrial waters be given primary consideration.

11. That the cut through the Panhandle to relieve flood conditions at Jackson on the North Fork, be given prior and immediate attention and completed at the earliest possible date.

A motion to approve the report was made by Mr. Spaulding and seconded by Mr. Reneau, and the motion carried without opposition.

Notable in the list of priorities was the "immediate" construction of a dam on the Middle Fork of the Kentucky River. The dam project on the South Fork appeared towards the middle of the listed priorities. Its mention seemed quite innocuous since it was surrounded by language suggesting a higher priority for "the extension of navigable water" to Booneville.[46]

The call for immediate construction of the dam on the Middle Fork

Opposite: **This map was widely distributed throughout Kentucky by the KRDA during the 1950s.**

of the Kentucky River was heeded. Congressmen Carl D. Perkins and James Golden and Senator Earle Clements pushed the project through the United States Congress's bureaucracy and had it fully funded before the end of 1954. Construction on the newly named Buckhorn Reservoir began in 1956 and was completed just four years later. One of the initial benefits of the Buckhorn Reservoir was that it ensured that the Corps of Engineers could not remove its services from the communities upriver of Lock #7 on the Kentucky River. Another benefit was that it did alleviate some, but not all, of Beattyville's flooding problems. Beattyville's political elites were encouraged by the obvious benefit of the Buckhorn Reservoir to their community.[47]

Beattyville's elites determined that construction of dams on the North and South forks of the Kentucky River would provide all of the remaining flood protection that their community required. The Beattyville elites knew that they did not have to concern themselves with the damming of the North Fork because that was the pet project of Congressman Carl Perkins, whose hometown of Hindman stood to benefit greatly from the project. Carl Perkins was a New Deal Democrat who had been elected to the United States House of Representatives in 1948 to represent Kentucky's 7th District. Once in Congress, he proved to be an astute politician. He quickly acquired the political clout that allowed him to personally ensure that construction of the Carr Creek Reservoir was underway by 1966. With the other two forks of the river either already dammed or having good prospects towards that end, it left only the South Fork of the Kentucky River to be addressed directly by Beattyville elites.[48]

Due to the proposals being made by the KRDA, the Corps of Engineers held two public hearings that concerned the development of the entire Kentucky River basin. One of the hearings was held in Hazard on May 22, 1954. The other hearing took place in Frankfort on June 2, 1954. Since the discussions were general in nature, a majority of the people who attended the hearings tended to favor large-scale construction projects along the Kentucky River. What little opposition was expressed was focused on specific projects. These public hearings left the U.S. Army Corps of Engineers with the strong impression that the KRDA had widespread support for all of its proposed projects along the entire expanse of the Kentucky River.[49]

Also in 1954, Congressman Perkins and Senators Earle Clements and John Sherman Cooper invited members of the KRDA to address a subcommittee of the U.S. House of Representatives holding hearings on public works projects. T.L. Arterberry and Russell Reynolds of Beattyville were among the KRDA's representatives. Both men testified about the harm caused by the frequent flooding of their home community. They proposed the construction of a dam on the South Fork of the Kentucky River in order to alleviate the threat of floodwaters to Beattyville. The chairman of the subcommittee suggested that there was no need to build an expensive dam since Lee Countians could solve their problems by simply moving to higher ground. Arterberry countered the recommendation by claiming that there was simply no place to go.[50] Arterberry's response reflected the myopic view of Beattyville's political elites in the 1950s. Leaving their home community for higher ground was a concept that they could not fathom. On the other hand, they had no problem with the residents of Owsley and Clay counties being forced to emigrate because their homes and farms were inundated by the creation of a lake that primarily served the business interests of political and social elites residing in Lee County.

The KRDA felt that the hearing before the subcommittee of the U.S. House of Representatives was a positive development for the organization since it created much needed momentum. It was the first time that Senator John Sherman Cooper had publicly assisted the organization. Cooper had been interested in the work of the KRDA from its inception, but had been careful not to embrace any of its specific initiatives. Cooper kept his distance because he did not want his participation in KRDA activities to be misconstrued as an indication of "immediate and beneficial actions." This was a legitimate concern in view of how quickly the Buckhorn Reservoir went from a KRDA priority to a finished project. In words that would prove prophetic, Cooper warned, "It is very disheartening to a community to receive assurances that studies are going to be made and thus draw the inference that construction will be authorized shortly, then to receive neither studies nor construction."[51]

Senator Cooper appeared to have the political wherewithal to champion the construction projects advocated by the KRDA. A strong advocate of the Tennessee Valley Authority, he believed that it was a legitimate use of federal power to supply services such as rural electrification and flood control to areas that could not be served by either individual states or private companies. These views, combined with a seat on the U.S. Senate Public Works Committee, made Senator Cooper a particularly

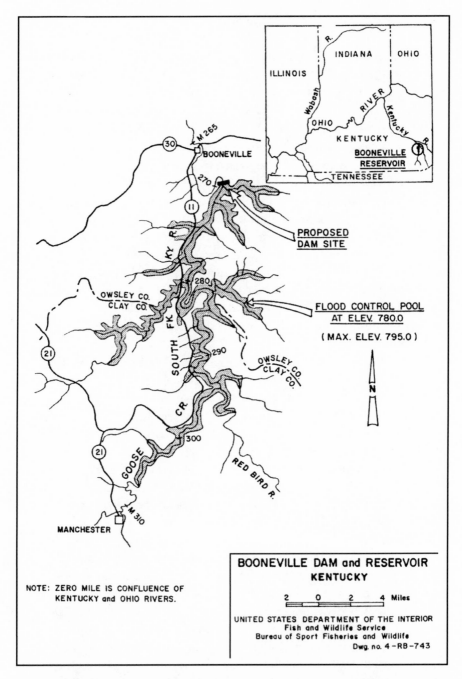

Created by the Fish and Wildlife Service, this map of the Booneville Dam and Reservoir often appeared in U.S. Army Corps of Engineers reports of the 1960s (U.S. Army Corps of Engineers, Louisville District).

valuable ally. Unfortunately for the KRDA, Cooper lost his reelection bid for his seat in the U.S. Senate to Alben Barkley in 1954. The setback proved temporary, as Barkley died in 1956. Cooper subsequently completed Barkley's term in office.[52]

Having reacquired his seat in the United States Senate, Cooper seized upon flood control projects as the means to endear himself to many of his constituents. This was important because, as shown in the previous election, he was vulnerable politically. He was a Republican senator in a state that strongly favored Democratic Party candidates. As a Republican, he was periodically out of step with the majority view in his own party on the national level because he was quite liberal on issues that affected rural America. For example, he defended the Tennessee Valley Authority in 1953 against efforts to cut its funding by President Dwight Eisenhower and many Republicans in Congress. In 1957, Senator Cooper publicly endorsed the KRDA's objectives, especially those related to flood control. Besides being politically expedient for his own long-term political future, another impetus for the move was a series of floods that struck Eastern Kentucky in January of that year. Pike, Bell, Clay, Johnson, Knox and Letcher counties were all declared to be disaster areas. The damages from the flooding episodes proved so severe that the American Red Cross provided approximately 4.5 million dollars in aid to the flood victims. What appalled Cooper was that none of the affected communities had any form of flood protection. Cooper endeavored to address Eastern Kentucky's needs by requesting that a number of flood control projects be undertaken on the Big Sandy, Cumberland, and Kentucky rivers. Cooper's sudden interest in flood protection caused him to develop close ties with the KRDA's Beattyville contingent.[53]

The KRDA also had the support of members of the Pioneer National Monument Association, most notably Cassius M. Clay of Paris, Kentucky. Clay pointed out that the lake that was supposed to be created by the Jessamine Creek Dam was not really intended to store water, but was instead designed to help regulate the amount of water flowing into the Ohio River. Since the dam was designed to catch flood waters rather than store water for central Kentucky, the size of its pool was going to fluctuate from between 150 acres to 37,000 acres. During the times that the reservoir was filled to capacity, farmland in Clark, Madison, Powell, and Estill counties was going to be submerged. Clay City in Powell County, and Ravenna in Estill, stood to be flooded when the Corps of Engineers had the reservoir filled to capacity. Rather than letting areas in Eastern Kentucky be flooded at times that the U.S. Corps of Engineers wanted to regulate the flow of water from the Kentucky River into the Ohio River, Clay suggested that the engineers should just adopt the water control plan that had been developed by the members of the KRDA. As observed by Clay, the KRDA's plan actually served the future water needs of Kentuckians.[54]

One might get the impression that the KRDA was universally celebrated by the coverage the organization was receiving in some of the newspapers published in the Three Forks of the Kentucky River region. Both the *Beattyville Enterprise* and *The Owsley County News* served to spread the KRDA's propaganda. They worked in concert, often reprinting each other's articles. The two newspapers failed to cover any story that might embarrass the KRDA in any fashion. They endeavored to create the impression that there was no opposition growing in Owsley County to the proposed construction of a dam on the South Fork of the Kentucky River. This stance was not surprising considering that both newspapers were owned by Beattyville elites.[55]

The people opposed to the construction of the dam on the South Fork of the Kentucky River did not have a newspaper to publicize their views. Instead, they generated petitions that were signed by a significant number of people who stood to lose their homes and farms. One such petition was submitted to the same subcommittee of the U.S. House of Representatives that heard from the KRDA's representatives.

> WHEREAS: (1) The building of the proposed reservoir would cover many thousands of acres of Owsley County and destroy the farming industry of the county; (2) It would destroy hundreds of homes, many of whom would not be able to settle elsewhere; (3) Hundreds of homes not covered by water would be isolated and worthless; (4) It would destroy highways, schools, and churches and reduce the area of taxable property of the county to the extent that it would be necessary to divide the county among the surrounding counties; (5) It would move many aged and ill people who would find it impossible to live elsewhere; (6) The cost of building such a reservoir would be greater to the Government than the property destroyed by floods and would not reduce the danger of floods since most of the damage done by floods is done by flash floods on the fork of some creek or river; (7) The building of such a reservoir would take from the people of that section their constitutional right to work and acquire property without fear of having it taken from them.[56]

Both the *Beattyville Enterprise* and *The Owsley County News* failed to mention the petition in their one-sided coverage of the hearings held in Washington, DC. Unfortunately for the KRDA, *The Courier-Journal* broadcast throughout the state that there was organized opposition to the proposed dam in Owsley County. The newspaper not only mentioned that the petition existed, but that copies had also been distributed to both Senator Cooper and the Louisville District of the U.S. Army Corps of Engineers. Despite the efforts of the KRDA and its allied newspapers, the existence of an opposition to the proposed South Fork reservoir could not be denied.[57]

The dam talk that galvanized opponents of the proposed dam was quite harmful to the KRDA. Despite the fact that no funding had ever been appropriated for the dam on the South Fork, its theoretical existence affected everyone whose land was potentially going to be underwater. Some individuals began constructing new homes but never finished them because they believed dam construction was imminent.[58] Other people, such as Mrs. Leonie Barger, were writing congressmen to gauge how they should react to the dam talk: "Congressman we want your advise [*sic*] what to do? Would you sell out? Or would you buy more land if you was I?"[59] Sadly, people made life-changing decisions on the basis of unsubstantiated rumors.

Major General William F. Cassidy, director of civil works for the Department of the Army's Office of the Chief of Engineers clearly indicated the interest of the Corps of Engineers in building the recently dubbed Booneville Reservoir in 1961. Although the United States Congress had given authorization for reservoir construction in both 1938 and 1944, no funding for the project had ever been appropriated. In 1960, there had been a comprehensive study of the Kentucky River and its tributaries that had put the construction of the Booneville Reservoir at the bottom of the prioritized queue of potential water projects in Kentucky. From Cassidy's perspective, building a dam near Booneville was not a project that he could "enthusiastically" support due to three factors. First, there was much greater need for the construction of three other reservoirs on the Kentucky River or its tributaries, namely the Red River Reservoir, Carr Creek Reservoir, and the Eagle Creek Reservoir. The second factor was the combination of the history of local opposition to the project and the related problems associated with resettling those displaced from their homes. Third, and most importantly, there did not seem to be an economic justification for building a reservoir on the South Fork. This was an important distinction because federal law required that reservoir projects pay for themselves within fifty years through such benefits as flood control, the production of electricity, and public recreation. The Corps of Engineers evidently was not convinced that a dam on the South Fork of the Kentucky River could even pay for itself within a half-century.[60] Cassidy concluded, " ... if concrete evidence were available that the substantial opposition to this project no longer exists, we would be pleased to subsequently consider the possibility of budgeting for an appropriation to start preconstruction planning of the project."[61]

Elvis J. Stahr, Jr., secretary of the army, voiced similar sentiments to Cassidy's in his report to the U.S. House of Representatives in 1962. Stahr repeatedly advocated not constructing the Booneville Reservoir because it was not required for flood control. As an alternative, Stahr and the U.S. Weather Bureau suggested improving flood forecasting along the entire course of the Kentucky River.[62] The fact that high-level officials connected to the U.S. Corps of Engineers would even suggest that improved flood warnings from the U.S. Weather Bureau could offer similar flood protection to a dam indicates how unnecessary they believed the construction of the Booneville Reservoir really was in solving flood problems in the Three Forks of the Kentucky River region. With such attitudes publicly expressed by U.S. Army officials, it is not surprising that in the twenty-three years since the reservoir project had been authorized the dam had not even progressed within the bureaucracy of the Corps of Engineers to the point that they would even consider requesting funding to begin the preplanning process.

King Justice, an Owsley County resident, responded to Major Cassidy's call for concrete evidence in January 1961. He presented copies of a petition to both the U.S. Army Corps of Engineers and Senator Cooper that purportedly contained the signatures of four thousand individuals who had previously opposed the Booneville Reservoir project. Most of the signatories were Owsley Countians. This was quite a feat, considering that only 5,369 people lived in Owsley County at the time. It was even more of an accomplishment when one considers that the signatures of children were legally unacceptable. Further reducing the pool of possible signatories was the portion of Owsley's population that had supported the Booneville Reservoir project from its inception. In drawing up the petition, Justice unintentionally admitted that a substantial percentage of

Owsley Countians opposed the dam project prior to 1961. Otherwise, he could not have found 4,000 individuals willing to switch sides. Justice's fantastic claim of 4,000 converts was also an indication of the petition's legitimacy. He was claiming that just about everybody in Owsley County had suddenly become supporters of the Booneville Reservoir project for no apparent reason.[63]

Many of Booneville's civic and political leaders supported Justice's position. The Booneville Lions Club "voted unanimously to go on the record as being in favor of the Booneville Dam and to make their actions known to all interested persons."[64] The resolution was drafted for the benefit of the U.S. Army Corps of Engineers and Kentucky's congressmen. The rural populace of Owsley County did not qualify as "interested persons." Most of Booneville's elites were careful not to let their rural neighbors know of their support for the dam project.

These men had good reason to avoid provoking their fellow Owsley Countians. To a majority of the populace, the dam represented a life and death issue. As expressed by Mr. and Mrs. L.L. Mainous of Booneville, the "big fellows that have been blessed with money" aimed to "drown us poor honest people that have worked to make our living on our farms."[65] Clay and Laura Thomas reflected the views of many when they wrote to John Sherman Cooper: "We love our home land and we dont want the graves of our loved ones covered with water."[66] Pleaz Turner saw opposition to the dam as a civic duty, observing that anyone opposed to the dam project who did not voice his or her opinion was "nothing less than a traitor."[67]

The opposition of his neighbors in Owsley County did not serve to temper King Justice's enthusiasm for the project because his economic interests lay in neighboring Lee County. He was the president of the Beattyville Concrete Block Company, which had the distinction of being the only concrete block manufacturing company in an eleven county area. Other prominent supporters of the Booneville Reservoir project were also from Beattyville, people such as C.M. Begley, secretary of the Lee County Republican Central Committee, G.D. Beach of C. Beach Insurance, and G.P. Congleton. Congleton was the president of Congleton Bros., Inc., which sold furniture, appliances, and hardware. Pacemaker Coal was also a component of Congleton Bros., Inc. One common theme raised in letters to Senator Cooper by these Beattyville elites was that they viewed tourism, in the form of lakes and parks, as the solution to all the economic ills of the surrounding region. The beneficiaries of the tourism would have been those communities located on the Kentucky River below the dam, such as Beattyville. In addition to economic opportunities presented by tourism, these men in particular stood to gain economically from the flood control benefits that a dam in Owsley County would provide.[68] As observed by unsympathetic Owsley County activist and Presbyterian minister Joe Powlas, these Beattyville elites had built their businesses in areas prone to annual flooding: "These merchants knowing that they will be flooded consistently build beneath the high water mark."[69] It stands to reason that a permanent solution to the flooding problem would have made the businesses owned by these Beattyville elites more profitable because they would not have been incurring constant flood losses.

By the early 1960s, the KRDA was obviously losing its effectiveness. The organization's leadership was not able to settle on specific projects due to its broad agenda. The KRDA was certainly not focusing on the issues that mattered to most of the people in Lee, Estill, and Breathitt counties. Beattyville's elites had worked within the KRDA to advance their cause but had grown frustrated by what they perceived to be the organization's inability to accomplish anything. Van Reneau's disappointment in the KRDA was evident in a letter he wrote to Congressman Perkins: "I have tried, cordially, and in a conciliatory manner, to either advance or retard the cause of the Kentucky River Valley from its stalled position of 'dead center' from which no development could materialize."[70] Despite his dissatisfaction with the KRDA, Reneau continued using the organization as a vehicle to push for the construction of the Booneville Reservoir. Other Beattyville elites gravitated to a new organization, namely the Middle Kentucky River Area Development Council (MKRADC).

The MKRADC, chaired by C.M. Begley of Beattyville, was much more aggressive than the KRDA in advocating for the construction of the Booneville Reservoir. The new organization made it a priority to gain the support of U.S. Representative Eugene Siler. The MKRADC coveted Siler's assistance because his congressional district included the areas in Owsley and Clay counties that were going to be flooded by the Booneville Reservoir. Siler had the potential to become a major obstacle if he joined his constituents in opposing the Booneville Reservoir project. Siler was known to have serious reservations about the proposed dam.[71] Congressman Siler usually gave "his full support to any proposed flood project in his district if it was endorsed by a majority of the people in the county in which the project would be located." Unfortunately for the MKRADC, Siler had received a large number of letters from Owsley Countians who were strongly opposed to the construction of the Booneville Reservoir.[72]

While the MKRADC was courting Congressman Siler, Senator Cooper was assisting Booneville elites interested in constructing the Booneville Reservoir. Cooper hosted a meeting on February 17, 1962, in Louisville between some Booneville residents and Colonel James Lewis, who served as the District Engineer of the Louisville District, Corps of Engineers. The purpose of the meeting was to allow the Booneville contingent to provide concrete evidence to the Corps of Engineers that the opposition to the Booneville Reservoir project no longer existed.[73]

The anti-dam faction in Owsley County was incensed when they discovered that the Louisville meeting with Cooper and the Corps of Engineers had occurred. Members of the group traveled to Louisville on March 12, 1962, to meet with Colonel Lewis in order to prove that the level of opposition within Owsley was as strong as it had ever been. Lewis was presented a petition signed by 2,300 Owsley Countians who were going to be directly, and negatively, impacted should the dam ever be built.[74]

Pleasant Amis, who made the trip to Louisville with those opposed to the construction of the Booneville Reservoir, did not hold a grudge against Senator Cooper for his role in helping the pro-dam group from Booneville meet with Colonel Lewis. Amis believed that Cooper had been misinformed about the views held by most Owsley Countians concerning the proposed reservoir project. Amis claimed that those in favor of dam construction amounted to less than 10 percent of Owsley's population. According to Amis, the Owsley Countians who favored building the Booneville Reservoir were "people that live away from here, and want to sell their land or people that owe more for their land than they can pay and therefore want to get rid of it." He also identified Beattyville businessmen as the primary advocates for the Booneville Reservoir: "They knew when they built their place of business near the river that it was too close to the water but they had a right to build it wherever they wanted to build." Amis suggested to Cooper that Beattyville's flood problems could be solved by simply moving businesses in Beattyville to higher ground.[75]

Pleaz Turner likewise believed that Cooper had been misled. He informed Cooper that many of the signatures that appeared on the pro-dam petition given to Colonel Lewis on March 12, 1962, were not authentic. As observed by Turner, the petition "contained the names of all the elective representatives of local government and the head of the local school system." Turner was in the position to know the views of many public officials in Owsley County because he was the superintendent of Owsley County schools. Turner was politically powerful in the community because he controlled access to a majority of the better paying jobs within Owsley County. It is extremely doubtful that any official connected to the Owsley County School System would have signed a petition espousing support of the dam knowing that Turner was so vehemently opposed to the project.[76]

Although the Beattyville elites who controlled the MKRADC believed that Senator Cooper was an ally in the effort to build the Booneville Reservoir, it was evident that his value to the cause was limited. Cooper had failed in 1962 to get an appropriation for the project included in the federal budget. King Justice was so upset by Cooper's inability to obtain funding that he warned, "When it comes time to start campaigning again up the Ky. River Valley I hope you have enough time to think up a good excuse or explanation why every water project in Ky. received an appropriation except the Booneville Dam."[77]

Since it was obvious to the MKRADC's leadership that Senator Cooper was going to need assistance in the U.S. Congress to get the Booneville Reservoir constructed, efforts were intensified to enlist Congressman Siler's support. C.M. Begley and representatives from Estill, Lee, Clay, and Owsley counties visited Siler at his home in Williamsburg in December 1962. Carl Reynolds, a Booneville resident, gave Siler a petition containing the names of 2,900 Owsley Countians who favored building the Booneville Reservoir. The petition also included the names of 298 residents of the county who were opposed to the project.[78]

The acknowledgement by the MKRADC that an anti-dam faction did exist represented a change in tactics for the organization. Rather than pretend that there was no opposition in Owsley County, they were instead going to argue that it represented a small fraction of Owsley's population. The anti-dam faction was characterized as a small group of people working insidiously against the desires of a majority of Owsley's residents. In order to demonstrate the harm being caused by those opposed to building the dam, C.M. Begley credited the group with getting a $100,000 appropriation for the Booneville Reservoir stricken from the federal budget.[79]

The MKRADC's representatives were chagrined to learn during the meeting that Siler remained skeptical about their claims. He was unconvinced that the anti-dam faction represented a minority view within Owsley County. As stated by Siler, he "had received numerous letters against the dam, but only four professing support." The meeting was not a total failure because Siler offered to schedule a public meeting with the Corps of Engineers so that all parties could debate the merits of the Booneville Reservoir project. Roy Royalty of Estill County offered to host the meeting in the Estill County community of Irvine. Siler courteously accepted Royalty's invitation.[80]

The U.S. Army Corps of Engineers balked at holding a public meeting in Irvine because "formal" meetings were reserved for projects in the investigation stage. The Booneville Reservoir project had not proceeded beyond the authorized stage since 1938. The key distinction between the two categories was that projects in the investigation stage were actually being considered for construction by the Corps of Engineers. Major David Carter, on behalf of Col. James L. Lewis, relented as long as the meeting in Irvine was not referred to as a "formal" public meeting. In a silly semantic exercise, a "public hearing" was officially scheduled for January 4, 1963.[81]

Public support for the MKRADC's position concerning the Booneville Reservoir began to emerge from a number of communities located in the Three Forks of the Kentucky River region. The Jackson Kiwanis Club of Breathitt County argued that the economic benefits resulting from the Booneville Reservoir would stem the "tremendous movement of citizens" from the region to more prosperous communities within the United States.[82] The mayor and the board of council of the City of Irvine passed a resolution maintaining that the Booneville Reservoir was going to provide multiple benefits to their community. The dam would solve the flooding problem that had made attracting industries to the community difficult. Irvine also stood to gain from the tourism industry that was going to be built around the new lake.[83]

Mart V. Mainous, an attorney in Irvine, was furious with the board of council for issuing the resolution. Mainous's reaction was understandable, considering his father resided on land in Owsley County that was going to be flooded by the dam. Mainous sent a letter of protest to Congressman Siler in which he stated, "2,500 Owsley Countians are violently opposed to the construction of the dam." Mainous reiterated the potential for violence several times. He also addressed the level of support for the Booneville Reservoir project in Estill County: "Few if any people of Estill County have an interest in the dam. It is seldom if ever discussed here. Of course some of the organizations have gone on record for it but this is mainly due to the constant prodding by the people in Lee County."[84]

With animosity building among all parties and the vitriol flying, the day of the public meeting finally arrived. Colonel James Lewis began the proceedings by giving a historical overview of the Booneville Reservoir's history from the perspective of the U.S. Corps of Engineers. Lewis laid the blame for the failure to construct the Booneville Reservoir on the United States Congress. Congress authorized the construction of a dam on the South Fork of the Kentucky River in 1938 but never provided any funding for the project. Lewis stated that the Corps of Engineers could "do nothing" on the Booneville Reservoir project until Congress made an appropriation in the federal budget.[85]

After blaming others for the lack of progress on the Booneville Reservoir project, Lewis then revealed a change in the institutional perspective of the Louisville District of the U.S. Army Corps of Engineers. The Corps of Engineers had justified the authorization of the Jessamine Creek Reservoir by claiming that damming each of the Three Forks of the Kentucky River would have only eased Frankfort's flood problems by a matter of inches. At the time that determination had been made, it had been patently clear that the Corps of Engineers did not want to be involved in any water projects in the Three Forks region. Conveniently, since they were suddenly committed to maintaining the Buckhorn Dam, they could suddenly justify the need for the Booneville Reservoir by utilizing data resulting from a flood that occurred in 1957. According to the Corps of Engineers, the Booneville Reservoir was going to relieve Irvine's flood problems by 7.1 feet. Heidelberg, in Lee County, was going to receive 7.8 feet of relief. Booneville and its environs were going to receive an extraordinary thirty feet of flood protection.[86] Lewis claimed that his data was based on "many years of detailed engineering and economic studies by our staff." That statement was contradictory. If years of work had in fact been done, then Lewis misled everyone about not being able to work on the Booneville Reservoir project without funding from Congress. If Lewis's assertion was not true, then where did the figures come from? When confronted with his inconsistent statements, Lewis admitted that the Corps of Engineers had little real data on which to base its conclusions.[87]

Senator John Sherman Cooper took the public meeting as an opportunity to stress his value to his political constituents. He pointed out that he personally was in position to shepherd the Booneville Reservoir project through the U.S. Senate. He was a member of the Senate Public Works Committee, which was the committee charged with authorizing dam construction. Once a dam was authorized, the next step in the process fell to the Appropriations Committee. Cooper happened to be the ranking Republican on that particular committee. These political appointments certainly gave the impression to pro-dam voters that Cooper would secure the funding required to get dam construction underway. Being a deft politician, Cooper recognized that the meeting was a political minefield because he had supporters on both sides of the dam issue. Although he had opted to publicly embrace the pro-dam faction, he made great efforts to avoid alienating his anti-dam constituents by demonstrating that he sympathized with their plight:

> Over in Pulaski County, where I live, Wolfe Creek Reservoir was built and it flooded the Cumberland River Valley. It flooded Fishing Creek, where my family had settled, where the graveyards were of my people, they were all covered up, and it wrenches sentiment certainly from those people who lived upon those lands.

Embedded in his story was the suggestion that opponents of the dam should reconsider their stance on the issue and make the same sacrifice for "progress" that his own family had been willing to make.[88]

Congressman Siler positioned himself at the public meeting as the champion of "the small fellows who have a little place in the hollows." This stance was understandable considering the boundaries of the 5th District, which he represented in the U.S. House of Representatives. His congressional district included Owsley and Clay counties. The inevitable depopulation of both counties by the construction of the Booneville Reservoir stood to cost Siler, a Republican, a significant number of dependable votes. Although Siler's district included all of the likely victims of the Booneville Reservoir, it included few of the potential beneficiaries. While Siler technically represented Estill County, he had no real relationship with his constituents there because he had been their congressional representative for three days. Lee and Breathitt counties were not part of Siler's district. It simply was not in Siler's political interest to support the MKRADC's position.[89]

Reverend Joe Powlas, at the invitation of Colonel Lewis, spoke on behalf of those who opposed the Booneville Reservoir. He began by reading a statement of opposition to the project by Arch Bell, a prominent Owsley County politician. This served to weaken the petition presented to the Corps of Engineers by Carl Reynolds that had supposedly been signed by all of Owsley's elected officials. Powlas himself suggested that Reynolds knew he was lying to the Corps of Engineers when he claimed that only 298 people in Owsley County opposed the Booneville Reservoir project.[90]

The U.S. Army Corps of Engineers were also within Powlas's sights. Powlas resented that the public meeting had been held in the first place. He was also concerned that so much of the presentation made by the Corps of Engineers had focused on land acquisition. Powlas correctly charged that the whole subject of how people's land was going to be valued was premature considering that no funding had ever been appropriated for the project. Powlas's argument reflected the harm that dam talk had done in the areas targeted for immersion. It was in the best interest of the people residing in areas to be flooded by the Booneville Reservoir to be given details on how to dispose of their land when there was actually funding to begin the process. At least then people would have a legitimate reason to make long-term decisions.[91]

Because economic development was at the heart of the justification for the Booneville Reservoir, Powlas attacked the concept on two fronts. Since the Buckhorn Reservoir had already been constructed, a model existed for Owsley Countians to test the theory that the resulting tourist industry would revitalize the region. He quoted a merchant with a store three miles from the Buckhorn Reservoir to illustrate the impact of the resulting lake on the local community:

> It is true that I receive most of the business of this area. In summer I do sell more pop and more gas, but this doesn't equal the volume of business I had prior to the dam. My business has been hurt by more than 25 percent. Before the dam, I had regular customers, families who traded with me year around. Now they are gone. When a fisherman comes, nine times out of ten he has everything he needs. This dam has certainly hurt my business.

Reverend Powlas also addressed the manner in which the economic benefit of the Booneville Reservoir had been determined. He charged that cost analysis always looked at the impact of the dam downriver. It never factored in the negative impact on upriver communities that would cease to exist.[92]

Powlas concluded by expressing sympathy for the residents of Estill and Lee counties who had suffered as a result of constant flooding. Nevertheless, their problems did not warrant eight hundred Owsley County families being uprooted from their homes. Since it was people in Lee County who wanted the dam constructed, Powlas suggested that a dam site be selected in Lee County. He ended his speech with a plea on behalf of Owsley County farmers: "We have heard of this dam now for many years. We are weary of it. They want to farm, they want to build, they want to plan ahead, and they want to live in peace. We ask that we be given the assurance that this dam will not be built in Owsley County."[93]

Pleaz Turner echoed similar sentiments, beginning with the point that he had been hearing about the dam since he had been a little boy. He likewise pointed out that the desire to construct the Booneville Reservoir originated outside of Owsley County: "Common sense ought to teach somebody that somebody down the line is responsible." Years of dam talk obviously weighed on Turner as he asked for a permanent resolution to the reservoir proposal: "People need to know something. They can't live from now on in jeopardy of their homes, their property and their future.... They need to know now how to plan for their future."[94]

It should be stated that the lake resulting from the Booneville Reservoir was also going to flood portions of neighboring Clay County. As in Owsley County, the perspective of the people in Clay County towards the Booneville Reservoir depended on their proximity to the water. If the water was going to flood one's home, then those individuals tended to comprise the opposition. Individuals who owned property above the water line usually opted to support the project. Ernest Trask, mayor of Manchester, fell into the latter category. He stated that the Booneville Reservoir represented the "salvation of economically depressed Eastern Kentucky." The dam would have provided an economic stimulus to Manchester, at the expense of those people residing in the rural parts of Clay County. Manchester would have occupied the opposite side of the lake from Booneville. Both of the respective county seats would have been the growth poles for the envisioned tourist industry.[95]

Carl D. Reynolds testified on behalf of Owsley Countians favoring the Booneville Reservoir project. He claimed that Owsley's anti-dam faction was comprised of the "higher income group of farmers." What characterized the higher income group was their ability to purchase cars and land. According to Reynolds, his constituents were tenant farmers who worked on the land owned by these "wealthy" farmers. Reynolds utilized the language of the African American civil rights movement to plead his case. He accused the landowners of enslaving poor farmers by giving them only a $3 or $4 daily wage. This enslaved group supposedly supported Reynolds' stance toward the dam because, after it was built, companies would move into the community that would pay a wage of $1.25 per hour. Reynolds' strained argument ultimately posited that it was one's civic duty to punish the wealthy farmers for enslaving the poor by having the tool of exploitation, namely their farms, buried underwater by the Booneville Reservoir.[96]

Clarence Begley, Chairman of the MKRADC, contradicted Reynolds' argument about wealthy farmers in Owsley County: "The records will show, I believe, that Owsley County has the lowest per capita income in the entire United States. Can we bring it down by putting in the Booneville dam?" Begley argued that it wasn't fair to either Eastern Kentucky or communities along the length of the Kentucky River to have their economic development impeded by poor Owsley Countians: "They will have to move some graves, but what could it do for Kentucky if we had control and we had a little industry and we had our recreational area?" Begley never defined which "we" he was referring to, but the description certainly applied to the political elites in his hometown of Beattyville.[97]

Although the public meeting was billed as a means to deliver information to the general public, it proved a major setback to groups favoring the construction of the Booneville Reservoir. The meeting had succeeded in providing concrete evidence to the Corps of Engineers and Congressman Siler that an organized opposition to the reservoir not only existed but dwarfed the pro-dam faction. Newspaper accounts compounded the disastrous impact of the meeting by publicizing across Kentucky the animosity held by many Owsley Countians towards those wanting to inundate their homes. One writer characterized Owsley Countians as having a "let us alone" attitude.[98] Other journalists observed that Owsley Countians were willing to fight to the death to protect their homes.[99] It was an immense task to undo the damage resulting from the meeting, but dam supporters certainly tried.

The Frankfort Chamber of Commerce quickly passed a resolution

supporting the construction of the Booneville Reservoir. The organization claimed it would have broadcast its views earlier had notification been
provided that a public meeting was going to be held in Irvine. The statement of support by the Frankfort Chamber of Commerce did not prove
to have much of an impact.[100]

George Long, a Booneville resident, contacted Siler directly in the
aftermath of the public meeting. Long acknowledged that nearly 100 percent of the Owsley Countians in attendance at the meeting opposed the
dam. His explanation for the phenomenon was "common sense will tell
you that those against the dam would turn out in full force, and those for
the dam would turn out in a token group."[101] Common sense actually
argued to the contrary. The reason that the meeting had been scheduled
in Estill County in the first place was to ensure that Owsley Countians
opposed to the dam would have a difficult time attending the meeting.
The fact that they showed up in such force represented how seriously they
took the threat of the Booneville Reservoir to their livelihoods. On the
other hand, "token" representation by the other faction helped support
Irvine attorney Mart V. Mainous' contention that Estill Countians were
indifferent towards the construction of the Booneville Dam and only acted
at the behest of people in Lee County who, not coincidentally, did attend
the public meeting.

Whatever momentum had been created towards the construction of
the Booneville Reservoir by the KRDA and the MKRADC had been
squelched at the public meeting in Irvine. Both the Corps of Engineers
and Congressman Siler had wanted evidence that there was no opposition
to the Booneville Reservoir. They instead found that the opposition to the
dam had been misrepresented to them by the MKRADC. The miscalcu-
lations by Clarence Begley and the Beattyville elites behind the MKRADC
meant that there was no impetus following the meeting on the part of Congressman Siler or the Corps of Engineers to request funding to begin the
preplanning process on the Booneville Reservoir.

Unbeknownst to the supporters of the dam project, Senator Cooper
had also determined that he had been misled. The MKRADC and its allies
had convinced him that the level of opposition to the Booneville Reservoir was minimal within Owsley County. As one of the first speakers at
the meeting, he had no reason to believe that he had been misinformed.
He changed his mind after hearing from the many Owsley Countians who
testified in opposition to building the Booneville Reservoir. Cooper talked

with Joe Powlas after the meeting and told him that he had chosen to support the dam project because he believed that was what most of the people wanted. The meeting had demonstrated to him that he had made a poor decision.[102] Being a deft politician, Cooper kept his change of allegiance secret from both factions. In future years, he publicly supported the Booneville Reservoir enough to convince pro-dam supporters that he was working on their behalf. In truth, if he had been a strong supporter of the dam project, he would have secured the funding required to construct the Booneville Reservoir.

The meeting in Irvine was not a total defeat for the pro-dam forces in Beattyville because the Corps of Engineers did not move to de-authorize the Booneville Reservoir. For Owsley County interests opposed to the dam, the project's authorized status meant that they had not gotten the closure that they had requested. The Booneville Reservoir project would thus continue to hang over the heads of Owsley Countians like the proverbial Sword of Damocles.

3. The War on the Poor

During the years that followed the conclusion of World War II, the United States of America enjoyed obvious economic prosperity. Unfortunately, the Appalachian region was not included in the postwar boom. Economic conditions actually began to sour in Appalachia during the late 1940s as lower coal prices and improved technology in the coalfields, such as the continuous miner, resulted in widespread unemployment. With few job prospects available within the region, many residents of Appalachia were forced to out-migrate from the mountains to other regions of the United States where economic opportunities abounded.[1]

Eastern Kentucky was especially hard hit by the economic malaise that was affecting the Appalachian region. As observed by B.F. Reed, "East Kentucky was just down in the dumps. Everything was lousy. Hazard was down and out. Harlan was down. All of East Kentucky was just [in] bad shape."[2] Although state government officials of the Commonwealth of Kentucky endeavored to address economic conditions in the eastern part of the state, the task proved daunting. The state government could scarcely afford to feed the local population, let alone provide to their rural communities the infrastructure improvements, such as new roads, that were going to be required to diversify Eastern Kentucky's economy. Despite the challenges, the state government in the mid–1950s began intensely studying the problems in Appalachian Kentucky in order to construct a plan of action to improve the quality of life for the residents of the area. While much of the planning focused on the need for the construction of economic infrastructure, private civic organizations, business leaders, and government officials formed partnerships, both locally and with other states, during the late 1950s to address problems found throughout the Appalachian region. This planning laid the foundation for many of the poverty programs that would arise the following decade.[3]

During the early years of the 1960s, national attention was once again drawn to Appalachian poverty through Senator John F. Kennedy's presidential primary campaign in West Virginia. Senator Kennedy's campaign was initially focused on using the West Virginia primary to test whether a Roman Catholic candidate for the presidency could win an election in a predominantly Protestant state. Instead of religious bigotry, Kennedy instead was confronted by an electorate wanting to know how he was going to address the deteriorating economic conditions that was negatively impacting many of the state's citizens. As he campaigned through West Virginia, Kennedy and his entourage were startled to see the poverty that was apparent in many of the communities that they visited. The reporters and photographers that were covering Kennedy's campaign publicized what they saw in publications that were read throughout the United States. For such poverty to exist at a time when most of the country was enjoying significant economic growth was appalling to many. On May 9, 1960, the day before voters cast their votes in the West Virginia presidential primary, Senator Kennedy pledged, "If I'm nominated and elected president, within 60 days of the start of my administration I will introduce a program to the Congress for aid to West Virginia." West Virginia voters in the Democratic Party primary gave Kennedy more than 60 percent of the votes cast, thus helping propel him to the presidency.[4]

Unfortunately for people in Appalachia, President Kennedy's sympathy toward their plight did not result in aggressive action on the part of his administration. Instead, targeted legislation emerged during Kennedy's presidency to alleviate specific problems. The Area Redevelopment Act of 1961 was emblematic of the Kennedy administration's efforts to keep the promise he made to the people of West Virginia. Passed as part of the president's "New Frontiers" agenda, the Area Redevelopment Act was designed to provide federal grants and loans to geographically designated areas in order to economically stimulate distressed urban and rural locales. In order to gain enough votes to ensure passages of the legislation, many more communities than had originally been intended by Kennedy's administration were granted eligibility for the funding, resulting in intense competition for limited dollars. With the monies spread broadly throughout the country, little consequential impact resulted from the Area Redevelopment Act.

To many people residing in Appalachia, President Kennedy's efforts to keep the promise he made to the people in West Virginia were underwhelming at best. This was probably an unfair opinion, since Kennedy's administration did a great deal of planning and organizing for efforts that would be launched by the next presidential administration. But, to the people in the region who expected him to ameliorate their economic conditions, there were few tangible initiatives that were directly affecting them. The frustration felt by the people of Appalachia could be seen in the aftermath of the flooding that struck Eastern Kentucky in 1963.

In March 1963, Eastern Kentucky was struck by two floods, caused by heavy rains, that struck within eight days of each other. The floodwaters wreaked havoc in approximately 50 counties, causing $80 million in damages. Roughly 25,000 people were forced to abandon their homes, some permanently. An editorialist from *The Courier-Journal* blamed the federal government for the catastrophe: "The floods that are tearing the economic life out of the mountains are the direct result of fifty years of federal neglect, and the situation they have created is so grave that only the Federal Government can correct it." The same writer also took the opportunity to lash out at the president, noting that he "has apparently lost all knowledge of and interest in the plight of the coal regions since his election." Despite the perceived inattention from the Kennedy administration towards Appalachia and its needs, the focus on the region's impoverished state remained in the national spotlight due to publications such as Michael Harrington's *The Other America*, Harry Caudill's *Night Comes to the Cumberlands: A Biography of a Depressed Area* and Jack Weller's *Yesterday's People: Life in Contemporary Appalachia*.[5]

President John F. Kennedy's untimely death in Dallas, Texas, in November 1963 led to the ascension of Lyndon Baines Johnson to the highest elected post in the United States. Unlike his predecessor, Johnson made poverty a centerpiece of his presidency. In his first State of the Union address, delivered on January 8, 1964, President Johnson declared "unconditional war" on poverty. He specifically pledged to "launch a special effort in the chronically distressed areas of Appalachia."[6]

In an effort to buttress President Johnson's rhetoric, the Council of Economic Advisors issued their *Economic Report of 1964*. The economists that made up the Council on Economic Advisors believed that poverty could be eradicated through government-stimulated economic growth, which would eventually result in full employment of the nation's workforce. This idea reflected the influence of the economic theories espoused by Maynard Keynes. Through the *Economic Report of 1964*, the Council of Economic Advisors espoused that eliminating poverty within the most prosperous country in the world should become a primary goal of the nation's economic policies:

> There will always be some Americans who are better off than others. But it need not follow that "the poor are always with us." In the United States today we can see on the horizon a society of abundance, free of much of the misery and degradation that have been the age-old fate of man. Steadily rising productivity, together with an improving network of private and social insurance and assistance, has been eroding mass poverty in America. But the process is far too slow. It is high time to redouble and to concentrate our efforts to eliminate poverty.
>
> Poverty is costly not only to the poor but to the whole society. Its ugly by-products include ignorance, disease, delinquency, crime, irresponsibility, immorality, indifference. None of these social evils will, of course, wholly disappear with the elimination of poverty. But their severity will be markedly reduced. Poverty is no purely private or local concern. It is a social and national problem....[7]

President Johnson signed the Economic Opportunity Act in August 1964. The landmark legislation created the Office of Economic Opportunity (OEO) to administer many War on Poverty programs, such as VISTA, the Job Corps, and the Community Action Program. Despite the high hopes for the War on Poverty effort, the OEO was provided an appropriation of only a little less than one billion dollars. This was a low funding level for an organization that was going to oversee the elimination of poverty across the entire country. Throughout the duration of the War on Poverty, the OEO was continually underfunded, which undermined the effectiveness of individual programs. This was not necessarily a reflection of the commitment of the Johnson administration to combat poverty, but an indicator of the financial constraints caused by the Vietnam War. As the Vietnam War escalated, the federal government prioritized spending on the conflict over domestic programs such as those associated with the War on Poverty.

A key component to the OEO's charge was the idea of "maximum feasible participation of the poor." The impoverished were to be given a voice, alongside those of political and community leaders, in how to address the problem of poverty within their own communities. In the eyes of the Johnson administration the poor had a unique perspective that was essential to decision-making at the local level. President Johnson, in particular, expected the poor to contribute to the War on Poverty effort in order to demonstrate that the programs created by his administration were a "hand up," rather than a "hand out."[8]

To Owsley Countians, the rhetoric emerging from President Johnson's administration signaled that their opportunity to shape their own destiny had finally arrived. They were going to be empowered by the federal government to throw off the yoke of poverty that had engulfed their community since the end of the Civil War. After all, Owsley County was among the most impoverished communities in Appalachia, which in turn was the most impoverished region in the United States.[9]

Economic circumstances in Owsley County at the beginning of the War on Poverty were certainly dire. Owsley's per capita income in 1960 was $450, which was one of the lowest per capita incomes registered by any county in the United States. Eighty-five percent of families within the county were deemed impoverished under federal guidelines. Twenty-five percent of the Owsley's inhabitants received welfare benefits. Sixty-five percent of the children registered in the county school district received free lunches. The county had a potential workforce that lacked a basic education since 70 percent of the students dropped out before graduating from high school. The quality of education was so poor for those who did complete their schooling that 76 percent of the county's youth taking preinduction examinations to join the military failed to pass the tests during an era when the military was desperate for soldiers to send to the Vietnam War. Medical services were available from one doctor. There was no dentist, pharmacist, psychiatrist, optometrist or marriage counselor working within Owsley County. The county also lacked railroads, water and sewage systems, libraries, public recreational facilities, agricultural extension services, and industrial facilities.[10]

In September 1965, Owsley County political and community leaders, including Pleaz Turner, Lucien Burch, Fred Gabbard, Carl Reynolds, and T.C. Sizemore, proposed the creation of the Owsley County Community Action Committee Inc. This organization was designed to serve Owsley County as an OEO community action program (CAP). It was hoped that it would eventually evolve into the conduit for all War on Poverty funds destined for Owsley County. It is curious that these Owsley elites waited until September to begin the process of establishing an OEO CAP for their community, considering that the OEO began disbursing grants to established CAPS during January 1965. The intent of the elites who organized the Owsley County Community Action Committee Inc. ran counter to the manner in which the OEO wanted to operate within the rural areas of Appalachia. The OEO envisioned CAPs as multicounty organizations, naively believing that a multicounty organizational structure would remove decision-making authority from local political machines. The members of the Owsley County Community Action Committee mistakenly believed, for no apparent reason, that their county was going to receive a special exemption to operate as a one county CAP from the OEO because it was purportedly the second poorest county in the United States.[11] After all, from their perspective, "on the basis of need" they "should stand at the top for help under the Appalachian program."[12]

The Owsley County Community Action Committee quickly discovered that efforts were afoot outside the county to add the responsibilities of serving as a multicounty OEO CAP to the MKRADC. The Owsley County Community Action Committee moved to block this effort by enlisting the aid of Congressman Carl D. Perkins. Perkins was selected to serve as Owsley's paladin because he was a politically powerful member of the U.S. House of Representatives. In selecting Perkins, Owsley Countians bypassed their elected representative to the same body, Tim Lee Carter. Carter had only recently succeeded Eugene Siler and was thus a newcomer to the United States Congress. The Owsley County Community Action Committee justified Perkins' inclusion in the process by pointing to Owsley's relationship to Lee County, which was part of Perkins' congressional district: "Owsley and Lee people are greatly interwoven. Most of the people here are kin or related to most of the people in Lee. While we realize this is not your congressional district ... the people are so close ... they are vitally interested in each other."[13]

While the Owsley County Community Action Committee was actively courting Congressman Perkins, Congressman Tim Lee Carter was actively working on behalf of his constituents in Owsley County. In November 1965, Carter toured Owsley County with OEO bureaucrats Ferd Nadherny, Tom Gee, and Ray Collins to show them firsthand the impoverished conditions in Owsley County. Carter hoped that the firsthand knowledge gained during the trip by the OEO officials would result in their steering poverty funding directly into the county's meager coffers. Carter's hopes reflected the naiveté of the new congressman, since it indicated a lack of understanding of how funding decisions were determined within the halls of power in Washington, DC. Unfortunately for Carter and the constituents living within his congressional district, the decisions made by OEO officials were not going to be made on the basis of a respective county's impoverished state, but rather by the desires of politically powerful congressmen. This unfortunate reality was probably the reason that the Owsley elites involved in the formation of the Owsley County Community Action Committee wanted Carl Perkins to champion their cause.[14]

Enlisting Perkins' aid, rather than that of Tim Lee Carter, was a naïve move on the part of Owsley's elites. The proposed MKRADC CAP was, with the exception of Owsley, made up of counties in Perkins' district, most notably, Breathitt County. For Perkins, there was no politically expedient reason to aid Owsley County, especially when his assistance would actually hurt the voters that kept him in office. The Owsley County Community Action Committee had unwittingly helped justify Owsley's inclusion into the group by claiming close ties to Lee County. T.C. Sizemore attempted to remedy the faux pas by arguing that Owsley County was never consulted in the creation of the multicounty program, thus their inclusion was "'taxation without representation,' wholly unfair and political discrimination."[15] Sizemore threatened Perkins that any effort to include Owsley County in the multicounty CAP would be fought editorially by his newspaper, *The Peoples Journal*. The effort went for naught, as Owsley County was included in the funding for the MKRADC by the OEO. The initial OEO grant of $83,856 was used to hire a professional staff for the MKRADC and determine its funding priorities.[16]

T.C. Sizemore's decision to threaten Congressman Perkins was not an isolated incident. Sizemore had a history of conflict. His father, a Clay County, Kentucky, sheriff's deputy for eighteen years, was killed during an election-day scuffle in 1932. Sizemore followed in his father's footsteps, serving as sheriff of Clay County from 1958 to 1961. He campaigned for the position as an outsider, promising to bring law and order to the corrupt county.[17] He bragged after taking office, "I beat the political machine in Clay County."[18] According to his own tally sheet, Sizemore arrested more than 1,000 people for liquor-law violations in his first 15 months on the job. As observed by a Clay Countian, "He's fanatical, the way he goes after some poor old fellow who has made himself a little whiskey; T.C. makes him appear to be Public Enemy No. 1."[19] Sizemore's actions resulted in violent reprisals against him and his deputies. Sizemore had his home and two cars blown up, all on separate occasions. Serving as one of Sizemore's deputies proved so hazardous that he could not replace the deputies that he lost. Sizemore blamed the violence on both bootleggers and his political enemies in Clay County. The violence served to feed Sizemore's ego. He utilized every action against him as an opportunity to promote himself.[20] As noted by Joe Creason of the *Courier-Journal*, "Sizemore isn't exactly a shrinking violet when it comes to having his picture in the newspaper or his exploits reported in full. He assumes no false modesty in detailing what he has done."[21]

The editors of both *The Beattyville Enterprise* and *The Jackson Times* criticized T.C. Sizemore's attempt to remove Owsley County from the MKRADC CAP. In an editorial published in both newspapers, the people of Owsley County were advised to ignore the "name-dropping editor" and his "childish remarks." Owsley Countians were thus put on notice that supporting Sizemore, rather than the MKRADC, would result "in nothing for Owsley County but disappointment."[22]

Owsley County's inclusion in the MKRADC CAP was a blow to the War on Poverty within its borders because of the manner in which the MKRADC operated. From the time it was established, the MKRADC had been nominally dominated by Beattyville elites. Both C.M. Begley and G.P. Congleton of Lee County had served terms as the titular leader of the organization. Although the Beattyville contingent had strongly influenced the direction of the MKRADC's efforts, the General Board included all of the representatives of the member counties to share in the decision-making. The MKRADC ceased to be a democratic organization as soon as it was reorganized to serve as a CAP. Prior to the War on Poverty, the MKRADC did not have access to a significant amount of revenue. The organization's primary purpose was to promote the entire region, thus the only way a county could benefit from its efforts was to cooperate with its neighbors. There simply was no tangible benefit to selfishly looking out for one's own interest. That scenario changed as soon as the federal government began sending significant sums of revenue to the organization. Courtesy of President Lyndon Baines Johnson, the MKRADC suddenly became an extremely valuable prize. Of course, the new nondemocratic structure was a closely kept secret that became apparent only after it was too late for the other counties to stop the effort. The General Board was kept intact in order to provide the impression that all member counties of the organization still shared in the decision making process. What was not made apparent was that the MKRADC had suddenly developed a two-tiered hierarchical structure, with the true decision makers predominantly representing the interests of only one county. The MKRADC's executive committee, almost completely comprised of Breathitt Countians, made virtually all of the financial decisions that impacted the member counties. The executive committee also directly controlled the roughly two million dollars a year in federal funds that were funneled through the MKRADC's coffers. It should be noted that not all of the federal monies sent to the organization originated from the OEO, as the MKRADC also served as a Concentrated Employment Program (CEP) for the United States Department of Labor.[23]

Cecil Kincaid, county judge of Lee County and a member of the MKRADC's General Board, was highly critical of the executive committee because he rightfully believed that he and his county had been disenfranchised. As described by Kincaid, he was a member of a General Board that had "little or no powers except voting on cut-and-dried issues."[24] According to Barbara Sue Deaton, who served as the secretary and bookkeeper for the MKRADC, the presence of General Board members was not even required for the General Board to hold a meeting. The MKRADC's director, Roland Sebastian, simply had the names of board members not in attendance added to the minutes of the meeting so that it appeared that a quorum had been achieved in order to make binding decisions. Kincaid recalled one such meeting that was held in Wolfe County. He had arrived at the site of the meeting, only to discover that only a few of the General Board members were present. Knowing that the General Board was not remotely close to having a quorum, he made the decision to return to Lee County. He later found out that the meeting had taken place, with the General Board hiring two Breathitt Countians to fill positions within the MKRADC. Although Kincaid did not believe that enough members of the general board had been in attendance to achieve a quorum, it ultimately did not matter because their participation in decision-making was not really required, or even desired.[25]

Breathitt County was positioned to take control of the MKRADC because it was a Democratic Party stronghold within Appalachian

Kentucky. As observed by former Kentucky governor Julian Carroll, "Breathitt was one of the last counties to be run by a political machine — where the support of one family meant winning the county."[26] The aforementioned family was the Turners, which first emerged as a significant political faction within Breathitt County in 1913 when a member of the family became the superintendent of Breathitt County schools. A member of the Turner family subsequently served as the superintendent of local schools through the 1960s. By 1938, the Turner family had also seized control of Breathitt County's courthouse. The Turner political dynasty managed to maintain its control of Breathitt County through its consistent ability to secure state and federal funding for their community, and by controlling access to most of the jobs available within their county's borders.[27]

During the War on Poverty era, the family matriarch, Marie Turner, was the superintendent of Breathitt County schools. Her husband, Ervine Turner, was a circuit judge whose district included Breathitt, Wolfe and Powell counties. Their son, John Raymond Turner, served Breathitt County as a state senator. A son-in-law, Jeff Davis Howell, was the head of the county Democratic Party organization and also had a financial interest in a local radio station. Howell was also an officer in the Citizens Bank of Jackson, which was under the direct control of the Turner family. Howell's wife, Treva, was employed within the school system as the assistant superintendent. Jerry Force, Treva Howell's brother-in-law, worked at the county newspaper.[28]

The political ties of the family extended across the state since Democrats seeking statewide office in the Commonwealth of Kentucky coveted their support. The Turner family could provide a large number of votes to statewide candidates due to the population of the county. In 1960, Breathitt County had a population of 15,490. In contrast, Owsley County's population was only 5,369.[29] The Turner family was so prominent within Democratic Party circles that they were accorded respect by politicians at the national level. It was not coincidental that "Lady Bird" Johnson, the president's wife, chose to use Breathitt County locales in May 1964 to illustrate Appalachian poverty to a national audience in the hope of prodding the U.S. Congress to pass the Economic Opportunity Act. The political power wielded by the Turner family, along with their privileged place within the Democratic Party hierarchy of the Commonwealth of Kentucky, served to empower Breathitt County officials to use the MKRADC as they saw fit. To this end, the Turners ensured that the MKRADC employed a nephew of Ervine and Marie to serve as "Executive Director of Poverty Programs." Another individual who was beholden to the Turner family, an employee of the Citizens Bank of Jackson, was tabbed to serve as the MKRADC's "Chairman of Poverty Programs."[30]

In December 1965, *Harper's* magazine published an article entitled "Mr. Shriver and the Politics of Poverty." The article was a wide-ranging account about the War on Poverty that included two extremely detailed paragraphs about an unnamed family that used OEO funds to strengthen their political base in an unidentified county in Appalachia. Without a doubt, the article was describing the activities of the Turner family and their Breathitt County associates. The writing style contained within the two paragraphs differed from the style evident in the rest of William F. Haddad's article. This was an indication that Haddad had reprinted, rather than paraphrased, the contribution to his story from a "local newspaper editor" in the vicinity of the Appalachian county.[31] T.C. Sizemore and his wife, Pat, used the article as the basis for a scathing attack on the Turner family and the MKRADC in *The Peoples Journal.* According to the Sizemores, a "national magazine" had publicly disgraced the Breathitt County faction. Not coincidentally, the Sizemores knew all of the details that had been alluded to by Haddad.[32] Whereas Haddad had not made any effort to identify the people he was writing about or where they lived, the Sizemore's had no such qualms. Pat and T.C. Sizemore had hoped that exposing the Turners' control of the MKRADC on a national stage would outrage the OEO and thus lead to Owsley County being extricated from the MKRADC's CAP. The ploy failed to generate any response whatsoever from the OEO, much to the dismay of the Sizemores.

While Breathitt County's political elites were consolidating their control of the federal funds being sent to the Three Forks of the Kentucky River region, Owsley Countians were fuming. All that Owsley County had received from the War on Poverty by February 1966 was some funding for the "Happy Pappies" program.[33] What was more notable was what Owsley County did not receive. Owsley had applied for a County Development Grant but had been denied. Owsley County officials had made an application for Neighborhood Youth Corps funding but that too never materialized. Efforts to obtain funds for Head Start and various Home and Community Sanitation projects also went for naught. For a county that had expected to receive special consideration from the OEO since it was supposedly the second poorest in the entire country, their lack of success in attracting federal funding was extremely disheartening.[34]

In another effort to extricate Owsley County from the MKRADC's CAP, the Sizemores alleged that Owsley's failure to get federal funding was proof that the MKRADC was misusing federal funds. In a desperate search for allies, the Sizemores sent letters to politicians at all levels of government, including Vice President Hubert H. Humphrey, Kentucky governor Edward (Ned) Breathitt, and Congressman Gerald Ford, who was the Minority Leader in the U.S. House of Representatives. The Sizemores made a compelling case in their letters that their county was being mistreated by the OEO by showing that neighboring counties were receiving significantly more federal funding despite not being as impoverished as Owsley. Jackson County had received $70,000 for a community information depot. Jackson County had also been successful in securing a County Development Grant, plus funding for both Head Start and the Neighborhood Youth Corps. Clay County had managed to secure more than one million dollars for various antipoverty programs. Most galling to the people of Owsley County was the reality that Breathitt County was widely acknowledged as one of the leading recipients of federal antipoverty monies in all of Appalachia.[35]

In response to one of T.C. Sizemore's missives, Senator John Sherman Cooper made arrangements for representatives of the OEO to explain to Sizemore that Owsley County had to be in a multicounty CAP in order to have a better chance of getting programs approved by the OEO. In examining the particulars of Owsley's situation, Cooper discovered that part of the problem was that Owsley County had not organized a specific community agency to work on its behalf within the MKRADC's bureaucracy. The Owsley County Community Action Committee should have been the agency to have represented Owsley's interests in this manner, but it really only existed on paper by 1966.[36]

A major reason that Owsley County never developed an effective local agency was that its community leaders were constantly at odds with one another. Pat Sizemore, in *The Peoples Journal*, addressed the negative impact of the constant political infighting among Owsley's elites:

> Here in Owsley, we are so badly divided, I wonder how we will ever get anything more. We stand to lose what we already have. Everybody else is jelous [sic] of everybody else. If John Doe is for a project, John Smith is automatically against it. One high county civic leader told a

country preacher in Owsley County: "If John Doe is for anything, I'm against it." The man gave the preacher no reason for his action.... Owsley County factions hold grudges.... They are too little to be big. As long as this attitude prevails ... Owsley will lose again, and again and again.[37]

Pat Sizemore's harangue against Owsley's elites was extremely hypocritical, considering that she and her husband were among the most active participants in the political infighting, due to their predilection to use their newspaper as a political cudgel.

T.C. Sizemore was a relative newcomer to Owsley County when he began publishing *The Peoples Journal* in December 1964. During the first year of publication, *The Peoples Journal* was very complimentary to many of the dominant elites in Owsley County, most notably Pleaz Turner, Lucien Burch, and Fred Gabbard. T.C. Sizemore's constant complimentary news coverage helped him and his wife to forge ties with Owsley's leading elites. This initial friendship resulted in T.C. Sizemore becoming involved in the formation of the Owsley County Community Action Committee. Sizemore's desire to ingratiate himself with Owsley County's political leaders was also a tacit acknowledgement that he had learned from the mistakes he had made by challenging Clay County's ruling elites during his term as sheriff.[38]

In early 1966, the relationship between the Sizemores and Owsley's dominant elites soured quickly. Owsley County officials stopped using *The Peoples Journal* to publish political ads or public documents, such as the financial statements of the Owsley County School System. This cost the Sizemores a significant, and dependable, source of revenue. This resulted in the venom that had previously been directed by the Sizemores towards the Turner family of Breathitt County suddenly being cast in the direction of Fred Gabbard, Lucien Burch, and Pleaz Turner.[39] Pat Sizemore raged, "I am sure every citizen of Owsley County is very, very familiar with the POLITICAL CLIQUE which has ruled our county for some 25 years now. Many of you, like ourselves, have been courted, used and finally thrown aside when no longer needed."[40] Although the personal attacks did not reflect well on the parties involved, the public bickering had no real tangible impact on Owsley County in general until the summer of 1966.

Illustrating the animosity that was growing between the former allies on the Owsley County Community Action Committee was the manner in which the respective parties viewed the Volunteers in Service to America (VISTA) program. The VISTA program was created by the Economic Opportunity Act, which was passed by the United States Congress in 1964. The program was modeled on the Peace Corps, but its volunteers served inside the borders of the United States. The first VISTA volunteers were trained in culture of poverty theory. They believed that it was the lack of opportunity that had created and perpetuated the fatalism and alienation that locked generations of poor people into a cycle of poverty. The young, idealistic college students who made up a majority of the program's volunteers believed that they could break the cycle of poverty through projects that empowered the poor. By 1966, the idealism that had been evident in 1964 had waned in the face of political reality. Within the Appalachian region, the VISTAs had seen many of their efforts to empower the poor blunted by either entrenched political elites that did not want their power and status threatened, or the absentee corporate interests that owned much of the land. The disillusionment felt by many of the VISTAs had led many of the volunteers to adopt a confrontational style towards those that held power within the region. As part of the effort to challenge entrenched elites, they actively mobilized the poor to demand that they be provided their "maximum feasible participation" in the decision-making bodies that impacted their local communities. Political elites throughout Appalachia responded to the efforts of the VISTA volunteers by openly questioning their motives, intentions, and morals. The elites also attempted to tar the young activists with the label of being "communists."

Despite the picture of the VISTA volunteers as an immoral disruptive force that was emerging within the region at the time, T.C. Sizemore decided to personally contacted Sargent Shriver with a request that 100 VISTAs be sent to Owsley County. The first ten workers arrived during the summer of 1966 with plans to provide educational services to children living in the rural communities of Indian Creek, Mistletoe, Lucky Fork, and Wolf Creek. They were immediately denied access to buildings within those communities that were owned by the Owsley County School System. According to Everett Byrd, chairman of the Owsley County Board of Education, "We do not even know what their program is. We asked them and they couldn't, or wouldn't tell us. We don't know if they are qualified for what they are trying to do." Byrd's excuse was not really the truth as to why Owsley County school officials were denying the use of educational buildings to the VISTA volunteers. Owsley County was merely following in the footsteps of Clay and other Eastern Kentucky counties who had also endeavored to keep VISTA workers out of their communities.[41]

The poor residents in the rural areas of Owsley County that were to be served by the VISTA volunteers had a different perspective on the local need for educational services than that held by the dominant elites in Booneville. Arch Gabbard of Indian Creek presented a petition to Owsley County school superintendent Pleaz Turner containing 135 names, although Gabbard claimed to be able to get up to 500 names if necessary, asking that the school system reconsider their decision not to allow the VISTA volunteers to use the buildings. Turner opted to decline the request. An angry Arch Gabbard observed, "If six or seven men in the county seat tell us everything we can do, then we are in bad shape. We are being denied our civil rights the same way as the people in Mississippi."[42]

The residents of the rural communities of Mistletoe, Island Creek, Wolf Creek, and Lucky Fork responded to the opportunity to have their children educated by individuals they viewed as future doctors, lawyers, and teachers by providing structures of their own to be used for school buildings. Members of these communities also offered to build permanent structures for future VISTA volunteers, including donations of land, in hopes that the VISTA volunteers would not abandon their county.[43]

The conflict between the Sizemores and the Turner, Burch, and Gabbard political organization proved very destructive to their community in the aftermath of one of the most tragic events in Owsley County's history. On January 5, 1967, the citizens of Booneville were forced to helplessly watch yet another Owsley County courthouse be consumed by fire. They were unable to douse the fire themselves because Owsley did not have a water system within the county. Fire trucks were dispatched from both Lee and Breathitt counties to fight the fire. The Breathitt County fire truck arrived at the scene of the fire with no water. The firemen from Breathitt had assumed that water would be available in Booneville. Lee County's fire truck did arrive with a supply of water, but appeared much too late to douse the flames that gutted the building.[44]

One of the most severe consequences of the fire that gutted Owsley's courthouse in 1929 was the loss of all of the county's records. Owsley County's records managed to survive the 1967 fire because they had been stored in fireproof vaults. Owsley did lose eight voting machines that had cost the county $22,500, $15,000 of which was still owed to the vendor.

E.L. Hughes, Owsley County's treasurer, estimated that it was going to cost between $250,000 and $300,000 to rebuild the courthouse. Unfortunately, Owsley County did not have the money required to replace the structure because its leaders had opted to woefully underinsure the courthouse and its contents. The company that insured the courthouse was obligated to compensate Owsley County only $36,000 for its loss. The funds were subsequently deposited in an account at the Farmers State Bank of Booneville.[45]

The Owsley County Fiscal Court proposed issuing revenue bonds totaling $150,000 in order to construct a new courthouse. The Fiscal Court then named a building committee, led by Fred Gabbard and Pleaz Turner, to oversee the courthouse construction project. Knowing that it was going to be difficult to get the voting populace of the impoverished county to vote for such a large amount of new taxes, Owsley's elites needed to scare people into supporting their position. Rumors began swirling throughout the county that Owsley was going to be divided, with the various pieces absorbed by neighboring counties, because it did not have a courthouse. The rumors subtly connected the courthouse issue to the fears that many already held towards the Booneville Reservoir project. The Sizemores responded to the rumors that were circulating throughout the county by sending a letter to Robert Matthews, attorney general of the Commonwealth of Kentucky, asking what were the legal requirements to dissolve a county. Assistant Attorney General Charles Runyon responded that the dissolution of an established county could only occur if the majority of the county's voters gave their consent. This served to assuage the fears of many of Owsley County's residents.[46]

The Sizemores advocated an alternative solution for replacing the ruined municipal building. They dispatched letters to U.S. Congressmen Thruston B. Morton, Carl D. Perkins, and Tim Lee Carter requesting that they use their political connections to appropriate the funds required to rebuild the courthouse. Senator Morton advised that there was little chance of obtaining federal funding to replace the building because courthouses were specifically exempted from funding by the Economic Development Administration (EDA). Both Perkins and Carter suggested to the Sizemores that they contact the Housing and Urban Development Administration for assistance. T.C. Sizemore did not make public the response he received from Edward H. Baxter of the Housing and Urban Development Administration, but it was obviously not the response that he desired. Sizemore complained that Owsley County was not receiving fair treatment from government officials because, according to him, federal monies accounted for 80 percent of the funds that were used to construct courthouses in the Kentucky communities of London, Richmond, Jackson, Hazard, and Barbourville. Through such rhetoric, the Sizemores convinced many Owsley Countians that they could get a new courthouse without accepting higher taxes or issuing municipal bonds. T.C. Sizemore even suggested that Owsley Countians should start fund-raising for the construction of a new courthouse through donations and fund-raising dinners while they waited for elected officials in Frankfort, Kentucky or Washington, DC, to act on their behalf.[47]

In 1967, the Owsley County Fiscal Court's proposal to issue $150,000 in revenue bonds for the construction of a courthouse went before the voters. Unfortunately for the elites, most Owsley County voters saw the courthouse bond issue as a tax that they probably could never afford to repay. The citizenry were obviously cognizant that their community had the lowest per capita income on average in the entire country. They also realized that their local population had been shrinking for decades, meaning that fewer people in future years would be responsible for paying the principle and interest on the bonds. If they were to prove unable to meet their obligations, it was widely believed that every taxpayer would lose everything because "every man's home in Owsley County is a surety or security for this bond indebtedness." Owsley's voters thus opted to protect themselves by voting down the bond proposal.[48]

In 1968, an identical bond issue once again appeared before the county's voters. Owsley County's political and business leaders, including Carl Reynolds, Charles Long, Fred Gabbard, and Lucien Burch, lobbied on behalf of the bond issue using the justification that Owsley Countians were delusional if they thought the federal government was just going to write a check in order to replace the courthouse. The only real option, according to the politicians, was for Owsley County to pursue federally backed low-interest loans in order to raise the money needed for the courthouse. In order to obtain the needed loans from the federal government, Owsley County was required to provide monies of its own to secure the debt. The only means available to gain the money that the county required was to pass the bond issue.[49]

The reasons posited by the politicians for supporting the bond issue in 1968 must have resonated with some voters, since the vote was closer than the year before. The margin of victory proved small enough that individuals politically connected to Fred Gabbard, Pleaz Turner, and Lucien Burch attempted to turn their narrow loss in the election into a victory by trying to disqualify enough voters to gain a majority at the polls. On November 28, 1968, Ed Combs and Jack Sebastian filed suit to have 117 people who voted against the bond issue expunged from the voter rolls. Their attempt to steal the election failed because the Owsley County court opted to dismiss their case.[50]

Owsley County was in a unique fiscal situation in 1969. It was the first time in at least 25 years that the county had a balanced budget. Former Owsley County judge A.M. Bell remarked that it could have been "the first time the county had any money to work with."[51] Ironically, just as the county was showing fledgling signs of financial stability, one of the ghosts of the past emerged in the midst of the courthouse battle. Charles A. Hinsch & Company of Cincinnati, Ohio, was selected by the Owsley County Fiscal Court to issue the $150,000 in revenue bonds should the voters ever give their approval to the proposed transaction. It is curious that nobody publicly made the connection that Charles A. Hinsch & Company was the same entity that had successfully sued Owsley County over the roadwork debts incurred by Owsley during the early decades of the twentieth century.[52]

On the eve of the election for the courthouse revenue bonds, it was revealed by *The Peoples Journal* that Fred Gabbard and Pleaz Turner were also going to have Charles A. Hinsch & Company issue revenue bonds totaling $600,000 for the construction of a new high school building in Booneville. The general populace had been unaware that efforts were afoot to fund a new school, because Gabbard and Turner did not require voter approval to fund the desperately needed construction project for the school district. The Sizemores and their political allies argued that voters should punish the Gabbard, Burch, and Turner political faction for incurring a debt that Owsley County would never be able to repay. Voter anger over the high school and courthouse funding issues resulted in candidates associated with Gabbard, Burch, and Turner being defeated at the polls.[53]

As a new decade dawned, Owsley County's voters appeared to have wrested control of their local government. Newly elected Owsley County judge Elijah Campbell, an ally of the Sizemores who had helped them defeat the efforts to issue revenue bonds in 1967 and 1968 for courthouse construction, began his term in office by firing everyone who had worked for the previous administration. The Sizemores in particular had great hopes that Campbell would provide the leadership that they believed the county so desperately needed. On his first day in office, Campbell filed papers with the Housing and Urban Development Administration to request federal funding for the construction of a new courthouse. He also named a new building committee for the courthouse. In short, he did everything that the Sizemores naively believed inaugurated a new era. What the Sizemores failed to take into account was that it was very easy to oppose a revenue issue when your political faction was not at the trough to collect political spoils. For Campbell and his cronies circumstances had definitely changed, as did their views towards funding for the courthouse. As Campbell himself stated, "A county is not a county without a courthouse."[54]

On June 1, 1970, the Owsley County Fiscal Court proposed another $150,000 bond issue for the construction of a courthouse. Not surprisingly, the Sizemores were incensed and turned the wrath of their newspaper on their former allies:

> This will be the 4th time the people of Owsley County have been called upon to vote for a Bond Issue of the SAME AMOUNT AND FOR THE SAME PURPOSE, WITH NO EXPLANATION OF WHO, WHY, WHEN, WHERE OR HOW THE PEOPLE ARE GOING TO BE ABLE TO PAY THIS HUGE DEBT AND WHY ANOTHER COURSE LESS EXPENSIVE HAS NOT BEEN TAKEN IN SECURING A NEW COURTHOUSE ... WHY ARCHITECTS HAVE NOT BEEN ASKED TO SUBMIT A PLAN FOR THE COURTHOUSE FOR PRESENTATION TO THE TAXPAYERS, VOTERS, AND PEOPLE OF OWSLEY COUNTY ... WHY BIDS HAVE NOT BEEN TAKEN FOR THE BUILDING OF A NEW COURTHOUSE TO DETERMINE THE LEAST AMOUNT AN ADEQUATE COURTHOUSE COULD BE BUILT FOR ... HOW LARGE THE COURTHOUSE WILL BE ... WHY MUST A COURTHOUSE BE BIG ENOUGH TO COST $150,000 OR A HALF MILLION DOLLARS BY THE TIME THE INTEREST IS PAID ON THE INITIAL AMOUNT OVER A PERIOD OF THIRTY YEARS....[55]

The Sizemores were even more indignant when they addressed the subject of Elijah Campbell. They noted that he personally helped them acquire and pay a lawyer whose legal services were required by the newspaper during one of the earlier episodes in the courthouse battle. The Sizemores urged local voters to ask the Campbell administration why, after years of opposition, the construction of a courthouse funded by revenue bonds suddenly had become a good idea for Owsley County.[56]

Under withering assault from the local newspaper, Judge Campbell played his trump card. Restating that a county was not a county without a courthouse, he connected construction of the building directly to the Booneville Reservoir project. He claimed that he had been told that the Booneville Reservoir was going to be built within five years and if the courthouse did not exist by then that the county would be dissolved.[57] With this act, Campbell attempted to shift the issue from the construction of a courthouse to the very existence of Owsley County itself. This clumsy political move fell on deaf ears due to Owsley Countians having heard variations of this nightmarish scenario in the dam talk that had been going on for decades. Voters turned out in large numbers and the bond issue was once again defeated at the polls.

After four defeats in as many years, the Owsley County Fiscal Court decided a change in strategy was necessary since it was apparent that the voters were not going to accept a $150,000 bond issue for the construction of a courthouse. Thus, in August 1971, the fiscal court decided to put a $200,000 bond issue on the ballot. Fortunately for Owsley Countians, the election proved a moot issue because the long desired assistance from Washington, DC, suddenly materialized courtesy of Senator John Sherman Cooper. The EDA approved a federal grant for the construction of a new courthouse totaling $302,000.[58]

The political infighting that engulfed Owsley County during the 1960s served to empower the MKRADC. According to Al Whitehouse, OEO chief of the Commonwealth of Kentucky, Owsley County's local community agency was charged with the responsibility of selecting a field worker for Owsley County. Since Owsley County never created a community agency, the MKRADC filled the post with an individual of their choosing. The MKRADC selected Carl Reynolds, the city clerk of Booneville, to fill the vacancy. This served to reward Reynolds with a $600 a month salary, plus reimbursement for expenses, for his services as the primary supporter of the Booneville Reservoir project within Owsley County. The appointment also ensured that Reynolds' political loyalty went to the Turners of Breathitt County, rather than to his fellow Owsley Countians.[59]

Congressman Tim Lee Carter grew frustrated from the reports he was getting from Owsley County concerning the War on Poverty. Carter had personally escorted members of the OEO in Washington, DC, through the county in 1965 and had nothing to show for his efforts. His irritation was evident when he wrote to Sargent Shriver, director of the Office of Economic Opportunity, "For godsake can't we do something to get these Youth Corps, Head Start, and Home and Community Sanitation projects going in this, the second poorest county in the nation? I am at a loss to explain why there are no funds for this county...."[60] Carter's complaint resulted in OEO officials sending a $20,000 appropriation for Head Start to Owsley County.[61]

Tim Lee Carter paid a political price for his staunch support of Owsley County during the War on Poverty years. He had personally brought unwanted scrutiny on the MKRADC from OEO officials in Washington, DC, and Kentucky. The Turners thus wanted him defeated in his reelection bid to the U.S. House of Representatives in 1966. Carl Reynolds was entrusted with the task of defeating Carter in Owsley County.[62]

Reynolds, an elected Republican Party official, had been a loyal supporter of Tim Lee Carter's prior to becoming an employee of the MKRADC. In Carter, Reynolds had a dependable ally in his unpopular quest to construct the Booneville Reservoir. Suddenly in 1966, Reynolds was surreptitiously trying to unseat Carter by falsely claiming that Tim Lee Carter had aligned himself politically with the Turners in Breathitt County and was thus the reason Owsley County was not receiving War on Poverty funds. T.C. Sizemore alerted Tim Lee Carter to Reynolds' activities. Although *The Peoples Journal* was supposedly nonpartisan, the Sizemores were using their newspaper to support Carter's campaign. The Sizemores genuinely admired Tim Lee Carter, so much so that they named a son after him. They were not going to stand idly by and watch Carter be defeated by Carl Reynolds. Reynolds nearly achieved his goal of defeating Carter in the county, failing by just 18 votes. Reynolds attempted to cover his tracks by calling Tim Lee Carter's campaign headquarters to inform them that he had personally delivered Joe Powlas's Cow Creek precinct to the Carter campaign. Reynolds' claim was an outright lie. Carter was extremely unpopular in the Cow Creek Precinct because of his support of the Booneville Reservoir project. There is no reason to believe that Reynolds would have even been welcome in the environs of Cow Creek since he too was a well-known proponent of the dam being built.

Despite pretending that he was still a staunch supporter of Tim Lee Carter, Reynolds had unwittingly revealed that his true loyalties were to those who paid his salary, namely the Turners of Breathitt County.[63]

The complaints made by the Sizemores in their letter-writing campaign also resulted in action by Congressman Gerald Ford, Republican leader of the United States House of Representatives. Ford requested that representatives of the OEO at both the regional and state level visit the region served by the MKRADC.[64] OEO officials from Washington, DC, and the Commonwealth of Kentucky visited the area in December 1966. Their report strongly criticized the MKRADC for its centralized bureaucracy that did not include input from the poor. It was recommended that MKRADC officials draft "clear, unambiguous objectives" on how to include the "maximum feasible significant participation of the poor in the policy making processes of the CAP."[65]

Despite public criticism toward its exclusion of the poor, the MKRADC did not change its heavy-handed ways. In March 1968, the OEO's Mid-Atlantic Regional Office threatened to stop funding the MKRADC's CAP in order to force the MKRADC to involve the poor in making decisions. The MKRADC responded to the threat by calling Congressmen Perkins and asking him to intervene on their behalf.[66] In addition to representing Breathitt County, Perkins also chaired the U.S. House of Representatives Committee on Education and Labor. This committee was responsible for oversight of the OEO. Perkins made one phone call to the OEO and said, "he was going to tell 'his people' in Kentucky that everything would be all right. OEO would be prudent not to make a liar out of him."[67] The OEO opted to follow Perkins' advice.[68]

Since OEO officials in the federal government were unwilling to act against the MKRADC, Kentucky governor Louie Nunn decided to address the problem. Late in 1968, officials from the Commonwealth of Kentucky removed Roland Sebastian as the MKRADC's director. The MKRADC was subsequently, but temporarily, under the stewardship of Mr. Lynn Frazer, OEO director for the Commonwealth of Kentucky. Frazer selected Billy Cradock to serve as the interim director of the MKRADC in order to oversee the daily operations of the organization. Having officials appointed by Nunn, a Republican, supervising MKRADC activities interfered with the activities of the Turners, so the family and their cohorts moved to reassert local control.[69]

On February 9, 1969, the MKRADC convened a meeting that

culminated with the election of Treva Howell as the new director of the MKRADC. Although the MKRADC wanted to pretend that Ms. Howell represented a new era for the organization, the ploy failed to deceive anyone because everyone knew that she was a member of the Turner family. The manner of her election reflected not a new beginning, but a reestablishment of the status quo. The meeting was held in Breathitt County and was presided over by Jerry Howell, who, in addition to serving on the MKRADC's executive committee, was Treva's brother-in-law. On the day of Ms. Howell's hiring, the MKRADC's executive committee filled seven vacancies to ensure that there were enough votes to elect Ms. Howell. Owsley Countians vociferously opposed Howell's appointment. For a Republican county like Owsley, whose resentments of Breathitt Countians dated back to the Civil War, it was the ultimate insult.[70]

Owsley Countians were not the only individuals upset with the election of Treva Howell. Dick Anderson, representing the Mid-Atlantic Region of the Office of Economic Opportunity, had warned the executive committee of the MKRADC the day before Howell's hiring that selecting her for the post would result in either the reduction or elimination of federal OEO funding. Lynn Frazer likewise believed that Howell was the wrong person for the job. Frazer walked out of the contentious meeting in which Howell was hired claiming that supporters of the Turner family were intimidating individuals opposing Howell.[71]

Such a blatant political move sparked a quick response from Governor Louie B. Nunn. He vetoed a $177,000 OEO grant to the MKRADC alleging that Democratic Party affiliation in general, and support of the Turners in particular, determined how money was distributed within the multicounty district. This particular reason helped explain why Owsley was getting little funding from the MKRADC. Nunn also charged that the presence of Howell's brother-in-law, Jerry Howell, on the MKRADC's board violated published federal regulations. This in turn meant that Treva Howell's selection to serve as the MKRADC's director was illegal. Governor Nunn also noted that OEO funds received by the MKRADC were deposited in accounts at the Turner-owned Citizens Bank of Jackson.[72]

Nunn's political action prompted Representative Carl Perkins to intercede on behalf of the MKRADC and Treva Howell. For Perkins, the whole situation was a political minefield. He had to support Treva Howell because the Turner political faction was a key constituency in his congressional district that had to be appeased if he wanted to be reelected. On the other hand, Perkins didn't want to offend Republicans at the national level since he was trying to secure a two-year extension of the OEO authorization act. He needed Republican support, including that of President Nixon and his OEO chief, Donald Rumsfeld, to keep OEO poverty funds flowing into Kentucky.[73]

Governor Nunn's veto prompted Rumsfeld to launch an investigation into whether there was justification to withhold OEO monies from the MKRADC. Mr. Richard (Dick) Cheney, special assistant to the director of the Office of Economic Opportunity in Washington, DC, and Dr. W. Astor Kirk, director of the Mid-Atlantic Region of the OEO, began the probe of the MKRADC in March 1969. Based on the findings of Cheney and Kirk, the OEO decided to restore the MKRADC's funding in September of the same year. The OEO investigators from Washington, DC, supposedly saw no evidence of any of the improprieties that had previously been documented by OEO officials at both the state level and the OEO's Mid-Atlantic Region headquarters.[74]

Not coincidentally, as soon as the OEO cleared the MKRADC, Congressman Perkins allowed the two-year extension of the OEO to emerge from the U.S. House of Representatives Committee on Education and Labor, which he chaired. The two-year extension, which had bipartisan support, had been held hostage throughout the investigation of the MKRADC. Had the investigation not yielded the findings he desired, Perkins had strongly signaled his intention to the Nixon administration to rewrite the legislation in a manner that would have made Democrats happy, but would have been unpalatable to Republican congressmen.[75]

Although Nunn was disappointed by the decision by Rumsfeld and the OEO staff in Washington, DC, to override his veto, he was not surprised that the investigation into the MKRADC had turned up no evidence of wrongdoing. Nunn alleged that the OEO investigators had never intended to find evidence of improprieties because they did not want to embarrass Congressman Perkins by having his close political allies implicated in the misuse of OEO funds. According to Nunn, one of the OEO investigators went so far as to publicly admit during the investigation that "everybody in Washington knows that Carl Perkins is the best friend that OEO has got and we are not going to kick our best friend in the teeth."[76] Despite the setback, Nunn publicly expressed his determination to make "the case of the taxpayers versus OEO."[77]

On November 6, 1969, Governor Nunn's opportunity arrived. He appeared before the U.S. House of Representative's Committee on Education and Labor and testified on the failure of antipoverty programs throughout the Commonwealth of Kentucky. Nunn was especially critical of "professional parasites, who siphon off under the guise of administrative costs a huge, unreasonable part of the funds that were intended for the needy."[78] Among those in the sights of the governor during the hearing were a number of CAPs headquartered in Eastern Kentucky, including the Kentucky River Foothills Development Council, Clay-Jackson Community Action Agency, and Knox County Economic Opportunity Council.[79]

Ostensibly, Governor Nunn's purpose was to speak generally about the failure of so many War on Poverty efforts in Eastern Kentucky. In actuality, a significant amount of Nunn's testimony focused specifically on the Turner family and their blatant use of the MKRADC to protect their political interests. This was not a surprising development since the hearing was a public forum where Nunn could make his charges against the organization and force the chair of the Committee on Education and Labor, Carl D. Perkins, to defend his political patrons in Breathitt County.

Governor Nunn entered numerous affidavits into the official records of the committee hearing that supported his contention that political support for the Turner family was a prerequisite for receiving poverty monies. He also charged that those who crossed the Turners risked not only their access to poverty funds, but also the access of their relatives. Nunn alleged that the Turners were able to demand complete loyalty from their followers for two reasons. First, the Turners controlled access to the jobs doled out by the MKRADC because they had direct control of the Executive Committee. Secondly, one of their associates routinely carried a gun on the job and did not hesitate to threaten people with it in order to keep them loyal.[80]

Turner family control of the MKRADC's funding cannot be understated because Ms. Howell used the money as she saw fit with no real oversight. According to Imogene Evanoff, an employee of the MKRADC, "Treva Howell shifted money from the appropriations of one county to another, or from travel funds or other budget accounts at will without consultation or approval of any Committee members."[81] Justin Rose of Wolfe County made a similar allegation, recalling that in April, 1969, Ms. Howell transferred $1,500 from Wolfe County's Emergency Food Stamp and

Medical Program using the justification that Breathitt Countians needed the funding more than the residents of Wolfe County.[82]

Congressman Perkins went to great lengths to express his outrage over the Turner family and their political supporters being depicted as gun-toting thugs in front of his committee by Governor Nunn. In contrast to Nunn, Perkins described the Breathitt Countians as "God-fearing people" who would not harm anyone. He then contradicted his initial statements by indicating that the people of Breathitt County would defend themselves against those who attempted to intimidate members of their community. The congressman then accused Nunn and his Republican administration of being the intimidators, noting that both highway officials and Lynn Frazer had been in the four-county area served by the MKRADC for months collecting affidavits to use in the governor's political vendetta against loyal Democrats in Breathitt County.[83]

Nunn's testimony about the Turner family was very detailed and, if true, was very damning of the conduct exhibited by his close political allies in Breathitt County. In order to stem any damage, Congressman Perkins decided to invite Ms. Treva Howell to defend herself against Governor Nunn's allegations. Treva Howell appeared before the Committee on Education and Labor on November 16, 1969. During her testimony, she revealed the extent of the MKRADC's efforts in the organization's four-county service unit during the War on Poverty era.

In terms of construction, the MKRADC had built a sorghum mill, a greenhouse, and a community store. All three of the structures were constructed within Breathitt County. While the potential benefits of a greenhouse were obvious, members of the committee questioned whether investing in a sorghum mill was a good use of federal money. According to Ms. Howell, the sorghum mill was a good investment because sorghum was going to overtake tobacco as a major cash crop in the Commonwealth of Kentucky within "a couple of years." The practical benefit of the mill, she also admitted, was that it saved local families the time consuming trouble of stripping sorghum by hand. Committee members also questioned the usefulness of the community store after Ms. Howell proudly described the building's dimensions as being 20 feet by 40 feet. To many of the representatives on the committee, the building appeared much too small to be of much use as a store. Ms. Howell argued to the contrary, claiming that, despite its size, the store promised to generate enough revenue to not only be self-supporting, but actually make a profit.[84]

When asked about the MKRADC's finances, Ms. Howell provided confusing answers that suggested at best poor accounting standards. Howell could not easily separate expenses that were paid using OEO funds from those paid from monies supplied by other governmental agencies. Treva Howell was asked how the MKRADC had expended the $176,000 that it was sent by the OEO in 1969. Howell claimed that $39,980 was spent on "conduct and administration." Another $114,005 went towards "community organization." When asked to specifically identify how the community organization money was used, Ms. Howell could not provide clear answers. The small amount of money that remained in 1969 was divided among the four counties for emergency food and medical programs.[85]

Ms. Howell also provided an interesting picture in how funds were allocated for each county by the MKRADC through the Headstart program. The MKRADC funded Headstart for only two-months during the summer of 1969, but received $196,483 for the program. Owsley County received $24,265 in Headstart funds while Lee County received $29,876. Wolfe County received a total of $51,500. The Breathitt County school system received $83,119 from Headstart. The independent school district in Jackson, Breathitt County's seat, received an appropriation of $7,712. Thus, between its two school districts, Breathitt County received more than 46 percent of the MKRADC's Headstart funding.[86]

The testimony provided by Ms. Howell ultimately proved detrimental to the MKRADC because it demonstrated there was little to show for all the money that had been funneled through the organization. The vast amount of money that had been sent by the federal government to the MKRADC had apparently gone into the pockets of the MKRADC's employees. Thus the only individuals whose poverty had been addressed were those Turner loyalists who had been fortunate enough to gain employment through the MKRADC. As observed by Congresswoman Edith Green of Oregon, "I can't find the poor people here that are being helped, if all of the funds have gone for administration."[87] While the MKRADC continued to exist after the hearings, it was greatly diminished and lost much of its access to federal funding.

In fairness to the Turners of Breathitt County, it should be acknowledged that their behavior was not unique. OEO CAPs all over Kentucky were engaged in questionable practices, as Governor Nunn himself admitted before Congressman Perkins' committee. Unfortunately for Owsley

County, the Turners of Breathitt County were extremely efficient in their rent-seeking behavior. Their ability to redirect OEO money intended for Owsley County to Breathitt County resulted in Owsley not being able to significantly improve its impoverished state during an era when the federal government was actively attempting to address poverty in Appalachia. President Johnson's War on Poverty, which had been initially viewed as a long-awaited opportunity for development in the second poorest county in the United States, would ultimately be bitterly remembered by an Owsley Countian as "the worst thing that ever happened to Appalachia."[88]

4. Lake Daniel Boone

The courthouse fire that ignited the battle over the construction of its replacement underscored the need for a water delivery system for Booneville in particular, and Owsley County in general. City of Booneville officials had actually begun the process of seeking funding for a water system prior to the fire. In February 1966, the city of Booneville submitted a grant proposal to the EDA to finance the construction of a water treatment plant, water distribution system, and a complete sewage system that included a sewage treatment plant. Booneville officials believed that the lack of these basic amenities was affecting the economic development of their community: "Owsley County, Kentucky, seems to be regressing rather than to be progressing in these times when anti-poverty programs are being conceived and geared to assist with the development of human and environmental resources in underdeveloped and deprived areas." Booneville officials supposedly had verbal assurances that fifteen different businesses, employing a total of forty-five people, would open in Booneville if they were to build a water and sewage system. These businesses included a coin-operated laundry, beauty shop, and car wash.[1]

While the creation of forty-five new jobs was a worthy goal, that really was not the purpose of the grant request. The water and sewage systems were desperately needed for the tourist industry that was supposedly about to exist in Booneville due to the pending construction of the Booneville Reservoir. According to the grant application to the EDA, construction on the Booneville Reservoir was going to commence no later than 1967.[2]

Carl D. Reynolds, Booneville city clerk and treasurer, pledged to build a new thirty-six–unit hotel in Booneville if the grant for the water and sewage systems was approved: "The plans for this motel are nearing completion and I own an excellent site within the city limits."[3] It is curious that he would have admitted a personal financial incentive in an application that he was widely credited with having written.

Augmenting the tourism justification utilized by Booneville officials to get the water and sewage systems built was a report prepared by Crawford & Crawford Engineers. The engineers noted that the Owsley County schools adjacent to Booneville were producing so much raw sewage that their septic tanks were unable to hold all the waste. Some of the excess waste being produced by the schools was being dumped directly into the South Fork of the Kentucky River. This was a problem that had to be addressed if the answer to Booneville's economic problems was a lake where people might be swimming. The remainder of the waste was showing up in some of the wells that people in the area were using for their drinking water.[4]

The EDA announced a $929,200 grant for the Booneville water and sewage system on June 24, 1966. Federal officials specifically cited the influence of the promised tourism industry in helping the community obtain the funding. Owsley subsequently utilized the money to build water and sewage treatment plants, along with related systems.[5]

As part of its normal operating procedures, the EDA moved on July 20, 1970, to close out the grants that funded construction of Owsley's water and sewage systems. Part of the process involved an audit of the projects completed with grant money. The audit found a shortfall of $28,000. Since Owsley County had taken out loans for a portion of those funds, the EDA only requested a refund of $4,270.[6] Officials from Booneville did not agree with the EDA's assessment that they owed the federal government. The Booneville politicians believed that they were in fact owed money by the federal government.

Charles E. Long, chairman of the board of trustees of the City of Booneville, complained that the EDA had refused two legitimate expenses that would have more than accounted for the financial shortfall. Both of the expenses in question involved Carl Reynolds. Reynolds had provided a plot of land for a sewage lift station site that he valued at $3,015. Reynolds also supposedly incurred $1,800 worth of administrative and engineering costs that he subsequently billed to the federal government. Long argued that it was unfair not to compensate Reynolds for these expenses because he was a nonpaid volunteer, even though he held a governmental post. Despite intervention on his behalf by Senator John Sherman Cooper, Reynolds did not receive the compensation that he felt was due to him. As pointed out by Thomas Dunne, special assistant to the assistant secretary for Economic Development, Reynolds was being treated in the same manner as any other municipal official in the United States. The grant guidelines specifically exempted municipal officials from receiving grant monies. Regardless of whether Reynolds was a paid employee or not, he was still the city clerk of Booneville.[7]

From the very start of the grant process, Reynolds had demonstrated that his voluntary service to Booneville had put him in position to benefit himself. Whether he wanted sewage and water pipes to a hotel he wanted to build or was trying to siphon money directly from the federal government to his pockets, he was obviously much more that just a nonpaid good Samaritan. The truth about Carl Reynolds actually became public at roughly the same time that the EDA grant for the water and sewage systems was being awarded to Booneville. He had been working for the MKRADC as the field worker for Owsley County, making $600 per month. His volunteer service as city clerk of Booneville had enabled Reynolds to appear as an independent representative voice of Owsley Countians when he was really working to push the agenda of his benefactors from outside of Owsley County.[8]

The relationship between Reynolds and the MKRADC cannot be emphasized enough because, according to the U.S. Army Corps of Engineers, it was the MKRADC and City of Booneville officials that reactivated efforts towards the construction of the Booneville Reservoir project in the mid–1960s. Reynolds was not the only Booneville official working towards the dam project. Charles Long was also involved. The MKRADC and Booneville officials were so successful working together that they managed to convince Kentucky's congressmen and the Corps of Engineers to petition for the funding required for the onset of preconstruction planning for the Booneville Reservoir. The congressmen secured a $100,000 appropriation in 1965. The initial appropriation was followed by another $150,000 in the 1966 federal budget.[9]

Among the acts of the MKRADC to build support for the construction of the dam was to change the name. Instead of referring to the dam as the Booneville Reservoir, the organization instead urged that everyone use the term "Lake Daniel Boone." The MKRADC's idea was subsequently endorsed by the general assembly of the Commonwealth of Kentucky. C.H. Bicknell introduced a resolution in January 1966 officially requesting that federal authorities begin calling the proposed reservoir "Lake Daniel Boone."[10] This proposition served two purposes. First, Lake Daniel Boone would become a point of civic pride because it connected Owsley County's future tourism industry to its historical past. It was hoped that celebrating the local historical identification to Daniel Boone would make individuals more amenable to having the dam constructed. Secondly, this provided "the legend and lore of Daniel Boone" theme for the tourist industry that was supposedly going to transform the whole region. Booneville officials claimed that a state park with Lake Daniel Boone as its centerpiece would initially attract 200,000 visitors annually, with tourists eventually numbering 800,000 per year. Hotels, restaurants, and stores would be required to service such a booming industry, which would in turn entice people who had left the county for employment opportunities to return home. The latter justification was based on a false premise, since the truth was that the Booneville Reservoir project was going to depopulate the county, as those rural people whose property was submerged by the lake would be forced to emigrate. The resolution yielded mixed results. Supporters of dam construction henceforth tended to refer to the project as Lake Daniel Boone. Not surprisingly, the name change did nothing to change the opinions of Owsley Countians who were already predisposed to opposing the project.[11]

On February 1966, Congressmen Tim Lee Carter and Carl D. Perkins joined U.S. Senators John Sherman Cooper and Thruston B. Morton in communicating to *The Peoples Journal* that they were disappointed that funding for the Booneville Reservoir project had not been included in the president's budget for fiscal year 1967.[12] Tim Lee Carter also felt it necessary to personally apologize to R.S. Bowman, an individual who wanted the Booneville Reservoir constructed. Carter was chagrined that people were blaming him and Senator Cooper personally with failing to secure funding for the dam. Carter swore to Bowman that the reservoir would not have been funded even if "ten angels" had testified on behalf of the project in front of the United States Congress due to the financial strain on the federal budget that was caused by the need to fund the war in Vietnam.[13] Despite the specter of the Vietnam War hovering over the budget for fiscal year 1967, all of Eastern Kentucky's congressmen pledged to dam supporters that "every effort would be made to secure funds" in the final budget for the 1967 fiscal year.[14]

Groups favoring construction of the Booneville Reservoir convened in Beattyville on February 16, 1966, to rally support for the dam. They wanted to make a public show of strength to Kentucky's congressmen to ensure that the politicians would redouble their effort to get funding for the dam project back into the federal budget. This was a critical point for dam supporters because they needed to maintain the momentum they had gained in the previous two years. They had received funding of their project while also managing to keep their opposition effectively muted. The delay of a year toward the construction of the Booneville Reservoir would potentially allow the anti-dam forces to reemerge. At the meeting, individuals from seven different counties pledged their support of the construction project to Major Morris L. Gardner of the Corps of Engineers, Louisville District. He was at the meeting to update everyone on some of the preplanning for the Booneville Reservoir that was underway. Among the men who had prominent roles at the meeting were members of the Booneville Dam Committee, which included long-time dam supporters Carl Reynolds, G.P. Congleton, Clarence M. Begley, King Justice, and Charles Beach.[15]

Senator Cooper invited the Booneville Dam Committee, also known as the Lake Daniel Boone Development Committee, to send representatives to testify before the Public Works Appropriations Subcommittee in Washington, DC, in order to help justify the insertion of the Booneville Reservoir project into the federal budget. In order to prepare their strategy for the meeting, the cognoscenti of the Lake Daniel Boone Committee and the MKRADC convened at Natural Bridge State Park on April 26, 1966. Letters of support for the Booneville Reservoir were solicited at the meeting from a number of organizations, including the Lexington-Fayette County Chamber of Commerce. What was plainly evident at the meeting was that the impetus for the creation of Lake Daniel Boone in the mid–1960s came from outside of Owsley County. Of the twenty-two individuals attending the meeting, only Fred Callahan and Carl Reynolds hailed from Owsley County.[16]

On May 4, 1966 representatives from Breathitt, Clark, Clay, Estill, Fayette, Franklin, Lee, Madison, and Owsley counties all testified before the Public Works Appropriations Subcommittee for the need to secure funding for the construction for the Booneville Reservoir project. Carl R.

Reynolds provided the supposed Owsley County perspective to the committee. The overwhelming message delivered was that the dam and resulting lake would create a booming tourist industry in a region largely devoid of jobs. According to Clarence Begley, an appropriation of only $1,069,000 was required to complete the preconstruction process by the Corps of Engineers, thereby bringing the desired tourism economy closer to existence.[17]

As in previous meetings, the supporters of the dam had to address the subject of local opposition to the project. According to the delegation, the opposition consisted of "one out-of-state preacher from a rural church" and individuals wanting to protect some graveyards.[18] Unfortunately for dam supporters, Senator Cooper had also invited the out-of-state preacher, Joe Powlas, to testify. Powlas came armed with petitions from Owsley County residents. Noting that some of the most valuable farmland in Owsley County would be inundated by the creation of Lake Daniel Boone, Powlas argued "we must remember that the rights of the man behind the plow are just as important and just as valid as the rights of the businessman."[19]

The most effective part of Powlas's presentation concerned the issue of flood protection. He argued that the Buckhorn Dam on the Middle Fork of the Kentucky River already extended adequate flood protection to the region. This particular point resonated with Senator Allen Ellender, who served as the Chair of the Senate Public Works Subcommittee. In a major blow to dam supporters, Ellender stated his intention to reexamine the plans for the Booneville Reservoir project in order to determine whether it was being built primarily for tourism rather than flood protection. Ellender pledged to oppose the Booneville Reservoir project if he determined that it was not required for flood control.[20]

Senator Cooper, on behalf of Kentucky's congressional delegation, demonstrated the true level of support for Lake Daniel Boone before a joint meeting in May 1966 of the Senate and House Appropriations Subcommittees. He requested $70,474,000 for twenty-two Corps of Engineers projects within Kentucky that were in some stage of planning or construction. These projects included $9,600,000 for the Fishtrap Reservoir, $9,000,000 for the Cannelton Locks & Dam, $8,700,000 for the Green No. 2 Reservoir, $7,558,000 for the Grayson Reservoir, $4,800,000 for the Carr Fork Reservoir, and $3,484,000 for the Barkley Locks & Dam. In addition, Cooper requested maintenance funds for an additional thirteen projects, including the Buckhorn Reservoir and Nolin Reservoir. Noting that the U.S. Army Corps of Engineers did need to reduce their budget due to the Vietnam War, Cooper pointed out that he did not include funds for construction starts for the Booneville Reservoir or the Eagle Creek Reservoir. The decision not to seek funding for the Booneville Reservoir project was a reflection of Cooper's secret opposition to its construction in Owsley County.[21]

The congressmen were doing more than just protecting their pet projects. They were also laying out their vision of the necessary water projects in Kentucky for the coming years. Among the projects they wanted included in the record for future funding requests were the Yatesville Reservoir, the Dayton-Bellevue Floodwall Project, and an unspecified water project for Beaver Creek near the town of Martin. In Cooper's discussion of future priorities, there was no mention of the Booneville Reservoir project.[22]

The renewed activity of 1965 and 1966 once again brought a flurry of letters from Owsley Countians to their congressmen wanting to know whether or not the Booneville Reservoir was going to be built. They wanted a definitive answer either way because their state of limbo was causing real harm.[23] Agnes Peters expressed the impact of the dam talk on the sale of property: "No one will buy such land, however much we may want to sell it."[24] D.L. Measel was concerned about an Owsley County resident whose house had burned down: "She is determined to rebuild, but inasmuch as the site will be covered by water if the proposed dam is built. Her children are trying to persuade her to delay or make other plans until they know more of the prospects of the dam."[25] The desire for a definitive answer transcended whether one was for or against the dam. As observed by a dam supporter, "All Owsley Countians would feel sorrow when the dam was constructed because everyone would have friends and neighbors who would be hurt as they were displaced by the lake."[26]

The congressional hearings in May 1966 proved to be the apex of the effort to construct the Booneville Reservoir. After the public testimony, there was a lull on all sides as they warily waited to see whether or not the congressmen would be able to get funds reinserted into the 1967 fiscal year budget. The wait turned into years as Kentucky's congressional delegation publicly, but unsuccessfully, pushed to gain funding for the Booneville Reservoir during each fiscal year to 1969. The congressmen communicated back to their constituents that the failure to secure the necessary monies was due to the Vietnam War. Desiring to plead their case in person, pro-dam constituents repeatedly requested the opportunity to speak once again before the Public Works Subcommittee in hopes of reigniting momentum for dam construction but they were continually rebuffed.[27]

In February 1970, the board of directors of the Peoples Exchange Bank of Beattyville, Kentucky, which included Gentry Congleton, Charles Beach, Jr., and G. Arco Begley, publicly expressed its desire to see the Booneville Reservoir constructed. These Beattyville elites hoped to encourage Kentucky's congressmen to redouble their efforts to get dam construction on the South Fork of the Kentucky River underway. The bank's board received an assurance from Senator Cooper in April of that year that a congressional hearing was going to be scheduled to discuss the prospects for constructing the dam.[28] The promised hearing never took place.

The troubles concerning the MKRADC, which had been under growing federal scrutiny since 1966 over its use of OEO money, had limited the ability of the MKRADC to effectively push for the construction of the Booneville Reservoir project during this critical period. The MKRADC addressed its credibility issues by joining with the Upper Kentucky River Development Council to create another organization. The Kentucky River Area Development District (KRADD) officially came into being on March 13, 1968. Its membership included the counties of Knott, Perry, Letcher, Leslie, Breathitt, Lee, Owsley, and Wolfe counties.[29]

KRADD supplanted the MKRADC as the primary organization clamoring in favor of the Booneville Reservoir project. The organization officially proclaimed its support of the project on December 9, 1968. Like the MKRADC before it, the new organization was provided a carrot by Kentucky's congressional delegation. The congressmen secured a $230,000 appropriation for fiscal year 1970 to complete the Booneville Reservoir's preconstruction planning.[30]

With the appropriation of money came the inevitable response from Joe Powlas. He charged that the only reason that the Booneville Reservoir still existed, even in theory, was due to the U.S. Army Corps of Engineers: "I was told by a leading Senator that the Corps of Engineers MUST have projects — that as a carpenter must go from one house to another, so must the Corps of Engineers go from one project to another." Dam construction thus served to keep the Corps of Engineers' 500-person workforce gainfully employed. As such, it was a "PITIFUL and SHAMEFUL excuse for the construction of projects which are not needed, which are not wanted, and which can only cause hardships for people, not to mention the wasteful spending of the taxpayers' money!"[31]

Although funding was secured to complete the preconstruction planning process, the success of the KRADD proved short-lived, as the Booneville Reservoir project failed to be included in the president's budget process for the 1971 fiscal year. Rather than depending solely on their congressmen to press their case, KRADD created a document for inclusion in the record of the Public Works Appropriations Subcommittee meeting held in May 1970 in hope of having funding reinserted into the 1971 fiscal year budget. One of the signatories of the document was none other than Clarence M. Begley. The document reflected lessons learned from the hearing before the subcommittee in 1966. Although tourism was included as a benefit, it was greatly downplayed in favor of flood control. The authors of the document certainly held grudges towards the U.S. Congress, as they closed with the statement, "We can forgive and forget the past 32 years that have elapsed since Congress first authorized this dam, if we can get construction funds now."[32] The arrogant plea failed to generate the desired result.

The money appropriated in 1970 to complete preconstruction planning was not enough, so another $245,000 was appropriated in 1972. The appropriation was not even worthy of an editorial response from either T.C. or Pat Sizemore of *The Peoples Journal*. They reprinted an article with a Washington, DC, byline that included some information about the money for the reservoir and put it on the fourth page of their paper.[33] The Sizemores, along with many other Owsley Countians, had regarded Lake Daniel Boone a nonissue for years. Like the Jessamine Creek Reservoir before it, everyone knew that it was never going to be built long before the Corps of Engineers placed it on the inactive list. This was due to the project's history of public opposition and the repercussions of the Red River Gorge controversy.

The Red River is a tributary of the Kentucky River that the Kentucky River Development Association proposed be dammed as part of its development plan for the Kentucky River basin during the 1950s. It was openly discussed during the public hearings held by the U.S. Army Corps of Engineers at Hazard on May 22, 1954, and at Frankfort on June 2 of the same year. What was notable about both meetings was that nobody had an objection to the concept of building a dam on the Red River. The Red River received congressional authorization to be dammed as part of the

Flood Control Act of 1962, which was passed on by the U.S. Congress on October 23, 1962. It was a reservoir project that was greatly desired by individuals residing in Powell County, where the dam was going to be built, and communities like Frankfort, Richmond, and Lexington that would be assured of a source of water when the need arose. Unfortunately for those wanting the Red River Reservoir constructed, some of the land targeted for flooding included the Red River Gorge, which was known for its scenic beauty, including sandstone cliffs and natural bridges.[34]

One of the key recommendations to construct a reservoir on the Red River came from General Elvis Stahr, who was the acting chief of engineers, Department of the Army, during October 1961. Through an investigation of the Red River, the U.S. Corps of Engineers determined that placing a dam about 1.5 miles below the confluence of Indian Creek and the Red River would result in the creation of lake that would be approximately 20 miles in length, and would bury portions of Powell, Menifee, and Wolfe counties under water. The area to be inundated was rugged territory that was sparsely populated.[35]

Unlike the individuals who were going to be impacted by the Booneville Reservoir, the people living in the vicinity of the proposed Red River dam favored construction of the dam. James Crowe, Powell County judge, expressed this community-wide sentiment to John Sherman Cooper when he wrote, "Speaking for myself and for, I feel, the majority of the people of this county, I wish to say that we are heartily in favor of this project and we are eager to see construction work begin as soon as possible." The reasons why everyone supported the dam proposal were the constant flash floods that raged down the Red River. Vendetta L. Derickson of Stanton, who was serving in the Kentucky senate, expressed to Senator Cooper her (and that of her late husband) concern over "seeing and suffering the tremendous losses from these yearly floods." A local farmer, R. Foster Adams, wrote to Cooper about the damage that floods caused to the local economy: "At least one crop is lost due to the floods each [sic] five years. This year for example, practically the entire corn crop has been lost during floods which occurred in June and July." The Kentucky house of representatives weighed in on the side of dam construction on March 1, 1962, passing a resolution introduced by Powell County representative Luther Patrick that urged the U.S Army Corps of Engineers to quicken the pace of preconstruction planning in order to protect the Red River's residents from constant flooding caused by heavy rains.[36]

The Corps of Engineers held a public meeting on March 15, 1963, in Stanton, Kentucky, to share with the public how their planning was progressing on the possible construction of a dam on the Red River. They were also interested in gauging the level of support the dam had within the community. According to the transcripts of the meeting, there were 95 people in attendance. In stark contrast to the meetings that had been held by the U.S. Army Corps of Engineers concerning the Booneville Reservoir, not one person spoke in opposition to the Red River dam. Encouraged by the evident local support, the engineers continued the brisk planning that was underway for eventual construction of the dam on the Red River.[37]

Unbeknownst to the people residing in the vicinity of the Red River Gorge, as well as Kentucky politicians, and the U.S. Army Corps of Engineers, the Sierra Club had taken an interest in the Red River Gorge. The organization was surreptitiously planning to make the Red River Gorge into one of their environmental battlegrounds, which already included locales across the country such as the Tocks Island Dam on the Delaware River.

Founded in 1892, the members of the Sierra Club were initially interested in organizing wilderness outings and protecting Yosemite National Park. John Muir, the first president of the Sierra Club, had been instrumental in getting Yosemite National Park established in 1890. Between 1908 and 1913, Muir and the Sierra Club unsuccessfully attempted to stop the California city of San Francisco from constructing a reservoir that dammed the Hetch Hetchy Valley in Yosemite. Bitterly disappointed in the loss of the Hetch Hetchy Valley, the organization became much more militant as it adopted as its mission saving other national parks and wilderness areas from the ravages of development.[38]

During the 1950s, the Bureau of Reclamation created the Colorado River Storage Project (CRSP). The CRSP contained proposals for a number of dams, including the Echo Park Dam and the Glen Canyon Dam. It also contained proposals for a number of irrigation projects designed to supply water from the Colorado River and its tributaries to farmers and ranchers in the states of Wyoming, Colorado, New Mexico, and Utah. One of the construction projects included in the CSRP was the Echo Park Dam on the Green River in Colorado. This project in particular drew the ire of conservationists, including the Sierra Club, because it was going to flood portions of Dinosaur National Monument. While the CRSP was being debated in Congress, the Sierra Club and other conservation organizations launched a successful nationwide campaign to stop the construction of the Echo Park Dam. It proved to be the conservation movement's most public battle since the unsuccessful attempt to save the Hetch Hetchy Valley. Unfortunately, while the Sierra Club, the Wilderness Society, and their other allies were desperately attempting to stop the dam proposed for the Dinosaur National Monument, Congress authorized construction of the Glen Canyon Dam.[39]

Located near the border of Arizona and Utah, Glen Canyon's natural beauty was not well known outside of its immediate environs. Once construction of the Glen Canyon Dam had commenced on October 15, 1956, members of environmental organizations such as the Sierra Club and Wilderness Society began to visit. What they saw were beautiful canyons that contained unique flora and prehistoric Native American archaeological sites with accompanying petroglyphs. Although several environmental groups, led by the Sierra Club and its executive director, David Brower, tried to launch an effort to save Glen Canyon, it was much too late. Glen Canyon was completely dammed by 1963, which resulted in Lake Powell's creation and the inundation of the Glen Canyon.[40] Glen Canyon subsequently became a powerful symbol to environmentalists as to what could be lost if they were not vigilant. With the militancy among environmental groups that was evident following the Glen Canyon debacle, it was almost inevitable that the Sierra Club would have taken a keen interest in the Red River Gorge, since its geological features were very reminiscent of those found in Glen Canyon.

The Kentucky section of the Sierra Club was organized in March 1967 at a Holiday Inn in Lexington. At the time of its founding, there were only 27 members of the Sierra Club in Kentucky. After the meeting, two of the club's organizers, Jim Kowalsky and Carroll Tichenor, held a brainstorming session to determine how best to attract national attention to the cause of saving the Red River Gorge. As fate would have it, Ms. Tichenor had recently seen a television broadcast of U.S. Supreme Court justice William O. Douglas hiking in Oregon to bring attention to an environmental site that he wanted to see protected from development. Douglas had been using his celebrity as a member of the U.S. Supreme Court since the 1950s to aid environmental causes that he supported. Douglas's love of the wilderness could be traced to his childhood, when he contracted polio. In order to strengthen his legs from the effects of the disease, Douglas would take long hikes in uninhabited areas in the vicinity of his home. As he grew older, he began to make long distance hikes in order to explore natural wonders across the United States and Canada. He kept meticulous diaries, which became the source materials for the numerous books that he authored extolling the virtues of the wilderness areas of North America. Not surprisingly, Douglas's willingness to support environmental causes had made him a close ally of the Sierra Club nationally. Douglas even ignored potential conflicts of interest to support the cause of the Sierra Club in his professional life. In the 1972 U.S. Supreme Court case *Sierra Club v. Morton*, Douglas wrote a dissenting opinion that argued that natural sites or organisms such as trees should be extended legal standing in the courts of the United States in the same manner as human beings. If Douglas had been successful in arguing his point, conservationists would have gained the ability to bring lawsuits on behalf of plants, fish, archaeological sites, etc. Knowing that already-established close ties to the Sierra Club at a national level would likely make Douglas a willing ally, Tichenor and Kowalsky decided to invite him to stage a hike in the Red River Gorge in November 1967 so that the national media could broadcast images of the threatened gorge to televisions throughout the country.[41]

Having settled on an event to draw publicity, the Sierra Club turned its attention to putting a Kentucky face on their national campaign. Towards that end, they held a dinner in Louisville in May 1967 with the hope of attracting Kentuckians to join their group since most of the members were people who had just recently moved into the state. As noted by a Sierra Club organizer named Johanna Henn, "The club badly needs local people to join, especially those that know their way around in Kentucky politics to lead and give advice. Evidently the court house politics the way it operates in Kentucky is bewildering to outsiders...." Among the attendees at the dinner were two of the newest members of the Kentucky chapter, Harry and Anne Caudill. Harry Caudill, a lawyer from Whitesburg and a nationally renowned author, proved to be a valuable asset. He personally knew governmental officials at both the state and national level. He corresponded with many of these officials as he sought to save the Red River Gorge. He also helped the Sierra Club enlist other well-known and influential Kentuckians to the cause such as Wendell Berry.[42]

As was required by their guidelines, the U.S. Army Corps of Engineers held a Public Real Estate Hearing in Stanton on August 16, 1967.

Prior to the meeting the engineers had widely distributed a pamphlet detailing the manner in which the federal government was going to be compensating those whose land would be flooded as a result of the construction of the Red River Reservoir. During the meeting, the previously unknown members of the Kentucky Chapter of the Sierra Club made their presence known by providing a list of reasons why the dam should not be constructed. The locals, who wanted the dam constructed, resented their presence and thus voiced their displeasure. As observed by one of the residents of the area, "Local people were tired of being flooded and did not need the advice from outsiders."[43]

Two weeks after the Public Real Estate Hearing in Stanton, the Kentucky Chapter of the Sierra Club received some valuable assistance in their effort to recruit native Kentuckians to their cause. The *Courier-Journal* published an extremely one-sided article entitled "Conservationists Begin Fight to Held [*sic*] Up Dam," announcing that the Sierra Club was going to launch a nationwide effort to rally "fighting conservationists" in order to stop the construction of the dam on the Red River. In the article, the newspaper published the contents of a recruiting letter that the Sierra Club was circulating throughout the United States. The article also reprinted all of the specific charges of the harm that the members of the Kentucky Chapter of the Sierra Club alleged, at the Stanton meeting, was going to result should the reservoir ever be constructed. There was apparently no effort made by the unnamed individual who wrote the article to ask the U.S. Army Corps of Engineers, government officials from the Commonwealth of Kentucky, or the people living in Powell, Menifee, or Wolfe counties, for their perspective on the dam issue.[44]

It was becoming obvious by October 1967 that the fledgling Kentucky Chapter of the Sierra Club was making headway in its campaign to stop construction of the dam on the Red River. Their complaints had attracted the attention of Stewart Udall, United States Secretary of the Interior. In response to what he was hearing, Udall opted to make a request of the Bureau of Outdoor Recreation to investigate whether there was any merit to the charges being leveled by the Kentucky Chapter of the Sierra Club.[45]

The Sierra Club was also making headway in putting a Kentucky face on their campaign. On November 1, 1967, the Sierra Club began distributing a letter authored by noted wildlife artist Ray Harm. In addition to bringing attention to the threat to the Red River Gorge, Harm's letter served to provide an explanation as to why there was sudden widespread opposition to the dam when none had been evident in all the years of planning that had been done on the project: "*The project has been little publicized.* I learned of the project *only four months ago. But we are aware of it now*, and are preparing ourselves with information about the project — our opposition is valid though admittedly late."[46]

In an effort to stem the Sierra Club's momentum, an editorial writer for the *Lexington Herald* charged that any delay in construction had the potential to "kill" the entire Red River dam project. The writer urged Lexingtonians to ignore the Sierra Club and its allies, who were printing sympathetic articles in Louisville newspapers such as the *Courier-Journal*, because they were unacquainted with the consequences for central Kentucky if the dam was not built. According to the editorial, the dam had to be constructed in order for Lexington to be assured of water during times of drought. The writer attempted to scare the people of Lexington into supporting dam construction by observing that Lexington's population was three times the size it had been in 1930, when the city suffered severely from the low flow of water from the Kentucky River resulting from the drought of that year.[47]

Although he was a strong supporter of the Red River Gorge project, Senator John Sherman Cooper began to feel pressure from his constituents on both sides of the Red River Gorge controversy. Cooper decided that his best course of action was to ask both the Department of the Interior and the Department of Agriculture to review the claims of the Sierra Club's members. The Department of Agriculture had to be included in the review because the Red River was located in the Daniel Boone National Forest. Cooper hoped that the reviews would conclude in the debunking of the Sierra Club's charges.[48]

The Sierra Club and its allies succeeded in getting national attention focused on the Red River Gorge on November 18, 1967, when U.S. Supreme Court justice William O. Douglas staged a three mile hike through the Red River Gorge. Accompanied by hundreds of supporters, Justice Douglas made many observations for the reporters covering the event. In particular, he lashed out at the United States Army Corps of Engineers: "I'm no engineer but I don't believe you need to flood a whole valley as unique as this for flood control." It should be noted that many supporters of dam construction were also on hand, protesting the influx of outsiders who they perceived were interfering in local issues.

Unfortunately for the local inhabitants who wanted the dam constructed, Justice Douglas's appearance attracted national media outlets such as *The New York Times*.[49]

By early 1968, the Sierra Club and other environmental organizations had begun to turn the tide of public opinion on the dam project. Many members of Kentucky's academic community had joined the Sierra Club and were providing their expertise to rebut any argument put forth by the U.S. Army Corps of Engineers. For example, Dr. Dudley Martin prepared a detailed study, entitled "Water Supply for Lexington, Kentucky, in Relation to the Kentucky River," that used data from the Lexington Water Company to refute the claims that Lexington was suffering from a water shortage. Carl M. Clark, an agricultural economist at the University of Kentucky, prepared a study entitled, "Kentucky's Red River Valley: A Brochure on Behalf of the Preservation of the North Gorge as a Wilderness," that convincingly demonstrated that the area to be dammed had more economic potential in its natural state than it had as a lake. Dr. Roger Barbour, assistant professor of zoology at the University of Kentucky, conducted a general scientific survey of the gorge that was endorsed by eighty-five of his colleagues across the state. These reports were circulated widely, including to members of the United States Congress who had the power to stop the funding required for constructing the dam.[50]

The Office of the Chief of Engineers released the *Red River Reservoir Kentucky Reconnaissance Study* in March 1968 that surveyed other potential sites along the Red River for a dam that would prove acceptable to the environmentalists. Although the study concluded that the original site remained the best location for the dam, it did indicate a willingness on the part of the Corps of Engineers to negotiate with the Sierra Club and its supporters for an alternate site if that would quell the opposition. The Sierra Club's response, which was included as Appendix "B" in the study, indicated that the Sierra Club was willing to consider an alternate site if that would save the Red River Gorge. It should be noted that the Sierra Club shrewdly gave the impression in their response of a willingness to cooperate without actually committing to any specific course of action.[51]

The *Red River Reservoir Kentucky Reconnaissance Study* also drew the attention of the United States Senate Subcommittee of the Committee on Appropriations at a hearing held on March 15, 1968. Senator Allen J. Ellender, who chaired the subcommittee, had been alarmed by the claims made by the Sierra Club. His concern was heightened by what he discovered while reviewing some of the reports made by government officials, such as Stewart Udall, United States secretary of the interior. Udall grudgingly gave approval to damming the Red River even though he personally had some reservations as to the wisdom of the effort:

> In retrospect, if we were starting with a clean slate in our considera-
> tion of the Red River under today's criteria which give heavier
> emphasis to protection of natural values than was true a decade ago,
> we might well decide: (1) that no dam should be built on this river
> and attempt to meet the needs in some other fashion: or (2) propose a
> dam at a lower site. In conclusion, therefore, while we prefer either
> no dam or a dam at the lower site, we realize that, in view of the cost
> differential, including the rebuilding of roads and the provision of
> necessary access sites, time delay, and the lack of substantial disparity
> between the effects on the natural values of the area, the Administra-
> tion and Congress may wish to proceed with the authorized project as
> recommended by the Corps of Engineers.[52]

Despite Senator John Sherman Cooper's assertions at the hearing that the claims made by the Sierra Club had no basis in fact, Ellender was deeply concerned about the effect that their protests were having on the project. The additional studies performed by the Department of the Interior, U.S. Forest Service, Department of Agriculture, and the U.S. Army Corps of Engineers in response to the Sierra Club's charges had resulted in the delay of construction by one year. This delay resulted in an estimated increase in the cost of the dam to the U.S. government of $600,000.[53]

Members of the Kentucky Chapter of the Sierra Club got their oppor-tunity to address members of the United States Congress in May 1968. Eight members of the organization addressed the U.S. Senate's Subcom-mittee of the Committee on Appropriations and five addressed a commit-tee of the House of Representatives. Notable among this group was Ray Harm, who was the only member of the Sierra Club to address both the Senators and the House of Representative's members. Also testifying on behalf of the Sierra Club was Dr. Mary Wharton, a botanist who was head of the biology department at Georgetown College, and Dr. Robert Kuehne, assistant professor of zoology at the University of Kentucky. These three experts were able to demonstrate to Senator Ellender that Senator Cooper was mistaken in his assertion that the Sierra Club did not have any scientific facts to support their positions concerning the Red River Gorge. It became evident during the hearings that the scientists representing the Kentucky Chapter of the Sierra Club actually knew much more about the local fauna and flora than did the specialists employed by the U.S. Army Corps of Engineers.[54]

During the hearings before Congress, the Kentucky Chapter of the Sierra Club, along with the Kentucky Academy of Science, the Audubon Society of Kentucky, the Nature Conservancy, Kentucky Ornithological Society, Izaak Walton League, American Association for the Advancement of Science, American Nature Study Society, and the Kentucky Federation of Women's Clubs, all endorsed constructing a dam on the Red River at a location farther downriver than the site preferred by the Corps of Engineers. According to the engineers, the lower site would have spared most of the scenic Red River Gorge area from being inundated. It should be noted that the conservationists were not really advocating constructing a dam on the Red River. They simply took this tact in order to delay any effort to construct a dam.[55]

In a desperate move to alleviate the damage done during the May 1968 hearings, Senator John Sherman Cooper decided to drop his request for $760,000 to commence construction on the Red River dam. Instead, he offered an amendment to House Bill 17093 that requested $300,000 be allocated for additional surveys along the Red River in order to identify alternate sites for a dam. Although Cooper's amendment was denied, members of Congress did require the U.S. Army Corps of Engineers to conduct another round of surveys on the Red River.[56]

While the U.S. Army Corps of Engineers was preparing studies, the Sierra Club and their fellow environmental organizations launched a brilliant public relations campaign to bring attention to their cause. Harry Caudill published an article, entitled "A Wild River That Knew Boone Awaits Its Fate," in *Audubon*, that tied the controversy to a well-known figure from Kentucky's past. *Time* took its cue from Caudill a year later when their article also focused on the Daniel Boone connection. Other articles were published in such diverse publications as *Smithsonian*, *National Parks and Conservation Magazine*, *The ASB Bulletin (The Official Quarterly Publication of the Association of Southeastern Biologists)*, *American Forests*, *Science*, *Sports Illustrated*, *AAAS Bulletin*, and *Sierra Club Bulletin*. The most eloquent defense was provided by Kentucky poet Wendell Berry's 1971 monograph entitled *The Unforeseen Wilderness: Kentucky's Red River Gorge*. Berry's moving text was accompanied by beautiful pictures of the gorge that clearly demonstrated that the locale was a true national treasure. It should also be noted that the Red River Gorge controversy spawned a number of scientific studies that were also being published, such as *Fishes of the Red River Drainage, Eastern Kentucky* by Branley A. Branson and Donald L. Batch, and "Solidago Albopilosa Braun, a Little Known Goldenrod from Kentucky," authored by Marilyn L. Andreasen and W. Hardy Eshbaugh. These scientific studies brought up more difficult issues that had to be addressed by the Corps of Engineers during their congressionally mandated studies of the Red River Gorge.[57]

The president of the National Audubon Society, Dr. Elvis J. Stahr, Jr., received a tour of the Red River Gorge from Colonel R.R. Wessels of the Louisville District of the Army Corps of Engineers in December 1968. After completing his daylong visit, Stahr concluded that "This remarkable area would make a great National Park." Ironically, it was General Elvis J. Stahr, Jr., secretary of the army, who supported construction of the Red River dam in his report to the U.S. House of Representatives in back in 1962. Despite his earlier position, Stahr proved to be a formidable protector of the gorge. He utilized the contacts made during his military career to speak on behalf of the conservationists who were trying to save the Red River Gorge to officials at the highest levels of government.[58]

The pressure brought forth by the Kentucky Chapter of the Sierra Club, Dr. Stahr and the National Audubon Society, the national media, constituents, and militant conservationists across the country proved to be more than Senator John Sherman Cooper could bear. In February 1969, Cooper formally requested from the Senate Appropriations Committee that no money should be appropriated for constructing the dam on the Red River at the site that would have inundated the Red River Gorge. Although this request meant that construction at an alternate site would be delayed an additional two years, it would allow the engineers and the environmentalists to find a site for the dam that would be acceptable to all parties. This proved to be a forlorn hope since no site would have been truly acceptable to the environmentalists by that time. On February 26, 1969, Kentucky governor Louis Nunn issued a statement that endorsed Senator Cooper's position, although Nunn did express his sympathy for those individuals residing in the vicinity of the Red River who were still suffering through the constant flooding. Not surprisingly, since both Cooper and Nunn were Republicans, President Richard Nixon acquiesced to Cooper's desires and instructed the director of the Bureau of the

Budget to ensure that no funding be included in the budget for the 1970 fiscal year for dam construction on the Red River.[59]

Supporters of the Red River Reservoir continued their efforts to get the dam constructed by calling for the dam to be constructed on one of the alternate sites on the Red River that would have specifically spared the Red River Gorge area. This solution was unacceptable to conservationists who felt empowered by their previous successes to protect the entire expanse of the Red River. Officials in downriver communities such as Lexington began to abandon the Red River Reservoir project due to the controversy. Although they gave up on the construction of a reservoir on the Red River, that did not mean their communities still did not require a dependable source of water. The alternative to the Red River Reservoir briefly became the Booneville Reservoir project.[60] But, as observed by Carl Perkins, all the dam projects in the region, including the Booneville Reservoir, were effectively ended by the Red River Gorge controversy.[61]

Conservationists certainly would have disapproved of the ecological damage that would have resulted from the construction of the Booneville Reservoir. According to a Kentucky Department of Fish and Wildlife report, the construction of the dam would have eliminated twenty-two miles of "high quality" stream habitat. The loss of that habitat would have subsequently killed off various species of fish, including small-mouth bass and muskellunge. While a planned fishery could have potentially offset the loss of native fish species, the success of the fishery was not assured due to acid pollution from coal mining operations in the vicinity of Goose Creek in Clay County. The degradation of fish habitats was problematic for a lake that was supposed to attract fishermen.[62]

The water quality on the South Fork of the Kentucky River was deemed by the Corps of Engineers to be in "viable condition" while it flowed freely as a river, although there were significant pollution problems. Besides the aforementioned acid pollution from coal mining, chemicals used for agricultural purposes were present in the water. The presence of untreated raw sewage was also unmistakable. Another significant pollution problem was the existence of a garbage dump in Clay County where trash, motor oil, and the carcasses of decomposing animals were being dumped directly into the South Fork. The damming of the South Fork of the Kentucky River stood to compound these existent problems since it was inevitable that "accelerated cultural eutrophication" would result.

Without a doubt, Lake Daniel Boone would not have been a safe or pleasant place to swim.[63]

The United States Department of the Interior, reflecting lessons learned as a result of the problems with constructing the dam on the Red River, found the impoundment of the South Fork of the Kentucky River extremely problematic. The department instead proposed that the South Fork be designated a "wild and scenic river." The Department of the Interior was particularly concerned about the acid runoff emanating from Goose Creek in Clay County, noting that in 1957 pollution emanating from that waterway killed all the fish in a sixteen-mile portion of the South Fork of the Kentucky River.[64] The recommendation of the Department of the Interior that the South Fork be maintained as a wild river dovetailed with the goals of the U.S. Forest Service concerning the South Fork of the Kentucky River.

In 1965, the United States Forest Service, using funds appropriated as part of the Appalachian Regional Development Act, had established the Red Bird Purchase Unit. The purchase unit was a 591,000-acre area, comprised primarily of land in Clay, Owsley, and Leslie counties, targeted for purchase as part of a plan to expand the Daniel Boone National Forest. The acreage included the headwaters of the South Fork of the Kentucky River. The initial purchase of land in 1966 included a 60,000-acre tract that had once belonged to the Ford Motor Company.[65]

One of the goals of the Forest Service was to rejuvenate the watershed of the South Fork, which had been depleted by a combination of factors such as strip mining, pollution, and logging. Improving management efforts of the watershed's natural resources held the promise of repairing ecological damage that had been caused by decades of erosion and coal mining. Controlling pollution at the headwaters of the Kentucky River had the added benefit of creating cleaner water for communities such as Lexington, Richmond, and Frankfort that depended in large part on the Kentucky River for their water supply.[66]

Besides the ecological damage, the preconstruction planning by the Corps of Engineers had revealed that one fundamental issue that had existed throughout the dam talk era had not been adequately addressed. Owsley County in 1971 still did not have the required transportation infrastructure to support such a massive construction project.

The Corps of Engineers attempted to remedy the problem by requesting from both the U.S. Department of Transportation and the

Commonwealth of Kentucky Department of Highways that a highway be built to the dam site so that they could get the required building materials onsite. Both agencies opted to decline the request.[67] Without the highway, the engineers could not have built the Booneville Reservoir even if they had so desired.

Although the road problem existed throughout the history of the dam project, the Corps of Engineers apparently never communicated the need to fix the problem to the dam supporters who resided in the South Fork of the Kentucky River region or their congressmen. If the KRDA, MKRADC, or KRADD had been made aware by the Corps of Engineers that it was absolutely essential to construct a road to the dam site, it stands to reason they would have worked with their congressmen to ensure that funding for that road was secured during the preplanning process. The silence on the road issue by the engineers strongly suggests that this was the final ace in the hole that they kept in reserve to ensure that they would never have to construct the Booneville Reservoir.

Despite their knowledge of the issues involving the Red River Gorge, the ecological damage that would have resulted from the construction of the Booneville Reservoir, and the road problem, the Louisville District of the Corps of Engineers announced that a formal public meeting was being held on July 17, 1972, in Booneville. The fact that a "formal" meeting was being held stunned Owsley Countians because that step implied that the Booneville Reservoir was potentially moving towards actual construction. Although the Corps of Engineers invited politicians to the proceedings, they stayed away in droves. Kentucky governor Wendell Ford and his lt. governor, Julian Carroll, did not attend. Congressmen John Sherman Cooper, Marlow Cook, Tim Lee Carter, and Carl D. Perkins also declined invitations to the meeting. Since it was an election year, it was probably a prudent decision.[68]

The Sizemores perceived the meeting as a line in the sand, and thus urged "each and every one of you to attend this meeting and fight for your rights. Don't be afraid to stand up and 'TELL IT LIKE IT IS' for what little worth it will be anyway!"[69] Such strident rhetoric from the Sizemores was curious because they had previously been supporters of the dam project. T.C. Sizemore in 1965 had urged clubs and civic organizations to contact their congressmen to express support for Lake Daniel Boone. At the same time, he had lauded the efforts of his "good friend Colonel Clarence Begley of Beattyville" as the head of the Lake Daniel Boone Dam

Committee to get the Booneville Reservoir constructed. In 1966, Pat Sizemore had stridently gone on record that the failure to construct Lake Daniel Boone was proof that the "War on Poverty" had been lost. Due to their troubles with local politicians refusing to pay for space in *The Peoples Journal*, the Sizemores in 1972 were suddenly fiery leaders against the construction of the dam, so much so that they pretended never to have taken any other stance on the issue.[70]

Colonel John T. Rhett of the Corps of Engineers, Louisville District, began the meeting with a very professional presentation that included maps of Lake Daniel Boone so that everyone knew the parameters of the project. He also spoke of how people would be compensated for any lands that were to be submerged as a result of the dam's construction. He then opened up the floor for questions and comments.[71]

Malcolm Holiday of the KRADD threw a softball question to Colonel Rhett so that the engineer could talk of the 600,000 tourists that Lake Daniel Boone would theoretically attract to the region. Judge Clay Bishop, who served on the bench of the 41st Judicial District, spoke against the tourism justification using his experience with tourists in the vicinity of Buckhorn: "I get letters practically every day from somebody on Buckhorn Lake, Judge why don't you do something about these people coming in here, drunk, stealing, robbing, doing everything under the sun?"[72]

Steven Durbin read a letter on behalf of Judge Bill Brandenburg, Estill County Court. Durbin spoke late in the proceedings and did so reluctantly:

> I don't enjoy one bit being here tonight speaking out in support of this dam; however, I am speaking on behalf of the Estill County Fiscal Court. I must qualify the things that I will make in this written statement. The Court adopted this statement I think after misinterpreting the information we had been given and so for any statements that are made in there that do not actually jibe with what we've heard tonight, then I'm sorry.[73]

Holliday and Durbin were the only individuals to go on record that night in support of the Booneville Reservoir project. Other supporters of the dam who were in attendance at the meeting, including Clarence M. Begley, declined their opportunity to make a case in support of the project to the Corps of Engineers.

Although there were 286 registered attendees at the 3½ hour meeting, the Corps of Engineers estimated the actual attendance to be 500 indi-viduals. Led by T.C. and Pat Sizemore, all other speakers treated the Corps of Engineers brusquely as they went on the record in opposition to the construction of the Booneville Reservoir. Comments were even made con-cerning all of their congressmen who had worked steadfastly, for decades in some cases, for the dam, who were suddenly unavailable for the meet-ing. All of the congressmen were supposedly busy in Washington, DC, despite the fact that the U.S. Congress was officially adjourned at the time.[74]

In the aftermath of this pivotal meeting, each faction attempted to characterize the event to their advantage. *The Beattyville Enterprise* claimed that there were 800 people at the meeting, with the audience split in sup-port of or opposition to the dam. The opposition was portrayed as "low key" and not very vocal. The writer of the article actually claimed that the percentage of Owsley Countians who attended the meeting was low con-sidering how many were going to be personally impacted by the creation of Lake Daniel Boone.[75]

According to the Sizemores, the crowd at the meeting numbered closer to 1,200 as they all had a "hot time in the old town that night." They characterized Col. Rhett as "a lean, grey looking man, who contin-ually shot icy stares at persons asking questions for which he had no answers." The Sizemores congratulated themselves for putting Col. Rhett in an uncomfortable position when they pointed out that Kentucky's con-gressmen weren't in Washington, but in Kentucky due to the congressional recess. In their editorial, the Sizemores addressed the characterizations by other newspapers in the region that the opposition to the dam was low key by posing a question: "Why did only ONE PERSON speak up FOR the Booneville Dam and that person represented the Estill County Fiscal Court at Irvine, Kentucky? This person even halfway apologized for speak-ing FOR the dam." In their question, the Sizemores were suggesting that more people might have spoken for the dam if they had not been so intim-idated by the large number of people expressing themselves loudly in an openly hostile manner. The Sizemores advocated in their newspaper con-tinuing the assault on the pro-dam forces by urging Owsley Countians not already on the record to write letters to the Corps of Engineers in Louisville as they had thirty days from the date of the public meeting to submit their letters for inclusion on the official record.[76]

Neither *The Beattyville Enterprise* nor *The Peoples Journal* provided objective coverage of the meeting. The same cannot be said of *The Courier-Journal*, which had dispatched Frank Ashley to the meeting. Ashley reported that 700 individuals, most of whom opposed constructing the Booneville Reservoir, attended the meeting. He observed that only one person, the representative from Estill County, spoke in favor of the dam. In addition to his coverage of the proceedings, Ashley also conducted a number of interviews with Owsley Countians who were going to be impacted by the proposed dam. Nelson Johnson said he was opposed to the dam because he stood to lose his 200-acre farm. According to Johnson, "For what I'd get for my farm, I couldn't buy enough land to run three head of cattle."[77] Johnson's perspective on the issue was enlightening because his farm was going to be the actual location of the dam. Both Johnson and the Owsley County sheriff, Charley McIntosh, charged that rural Owsley Countians were going to be displaced from their homes so that "businessmen" engaging in land speculation could enrich themselves. MacIntosh alleged that land in certain areas of Owsley County was being purchased by businessmen for as much as $10,000 per acre.[78] This was probably the land that was going to become lakefront property on Lake Daniel Boone.

The damage done at the public meeting was palpable to dam supporters. Bob Morgan, who attended the meeting, called Congressman Tim Lee Carter to tell him of the results. He informed Carter that it was a smart move not to attend the meeting and advised, "We ought to play that thing low key for a while, and not get involved." Morgan stated that there were a lot of people at the meeting and they were "bitter." He even noted that Clarence Begley of Beattyville didn't say anything in support of the dam. In short, it "was a bad meeting."[79]

Like the 1963 meeting held in Irvine, the 1972 meeting in Booneville served to inflame individuals on both sides of the dam issue for no real purpose. Dam construction was not imminent, nor would it ever be. Although the meeting was a setback to pro-dam forces, they continued efforts to regain momentum towards the construction of the Booneville Reservoir.[80]

The Daniel Boone Development Council, Inc., headquartered in Manchester, Kentucky, joined the effort by asking Congressman Perkins to propose that an even larger dam be constructed in Booneville than had ever been proposed. Their justification for the increased size was based on projections made by the Clay County V.I.C.A. Club of the Clay County

Vocational School. According to the high school students in the club, Clay County stood to generate five million dollars a year in revenues derived from the recreational benefits of Lake Daniel Boone. From all indications, Perkins did not act on the request.[81]

Ultimately, after spending a total of $1,038,595 on the preplanning stage of the Booneville Reservoir, the Corps of Engineers finally moved the project to the inactive category in January 1976. The reason given for the move was that the entire project was "economically infeasible." The inactive designation apparently did not mean that all work on the project had ceased, as evidenced by the existence of two Corp of Engineers maps, dated 30 September 1976, of Booneville Lake.[82]

Charles Beach, Jr., was incensed when he found out the Booneville Reservoir had been moved to inactive status. He found it "incomprehensible" that Kentucky's congressmen had allowed the move by the Corps of Engineers in light of all the money that had been spent on the reservoir throughout the preplanning process. Beach urged Congressman Perkins to explore how best to reactivate the Booneville Reservoir project because "the development of our geographical area is highly dependent upon the construction of this dam."[83] Otherwise, the whole preplanning process had been a terrible waste of taxpayer money. While Perkins opted not to act on Beach's request, he did commiserate with his long-time ally by acknowledging, "Flood control projects all over the country are held in great disdain these days by conservationists and those well-meaning folks who have only recently discovered the environment." According to Perkins, the political climate of the mid–1970s was not conducive to reactivating the Booneville Reservoir project because "We live in an age where 'no growth' is an ideal for some people and development is a naughty word. I hope we recover our senses before too much damage is done."[84]

For more than a decade, it appeared that Owsley County's citizens had finally emerged from the shadow of the Booneville Reservoir. But, as had happened throughout the twentieth century, another excuse to construct the Booneville Reservoir briefly emerged. Kentucky in 1988 suffered through a severe drought that had actually begun the year before. It resulted in communities across Kentucky, including Lexington, to ration water. The shortage of water in central Kentucky led to the formation of the Kentucky River Basin Steering Committee, which was charged with finding a solution to the apparent water supply problem. The chairman of the

Kentucky River Basin Steering Committee was Lexington mayor and future U.S. Congressman Scotty Baesler. Other notable members of the committee were future U.S. Congressman Ben Chandler and future Lexington mayor Pam Miller. Representing Lee County on the committee was Charles Beach, Jr.[85]

At a meeting of the Kentucky River Basin Steering Committee meeting held on April 12, 1989, the Booneville Reservoir once again came to the fore. Not surprisingly, it was Charles Beach, Jr., who made the suggestion to construct the dam in order to impound enough water to solve Lexington's water problem. Beach noted that the Booneville Reservoir would not only provide water to central Kentucky, but would also boost revenue in the vicinity of the dam through tourism. Unfortunately for Beach, Jim Duck of the U.S. Army Corps of Engineers was also at the meeting and was familiar with the previous history of the Booneville Reservoir project. Duck reported that the Corps of Engineers had estimated in 1975 that the minimum cost for the construction of the Booneville Reservoir was $60.7 million dollars. Even at the 3.25 percent interest rate that existed at the time, the Louisville District Corps of Engineers had not been able to justify the expense. In 1989 dollars, the cost of the dam stood at 117 million dollars. The costs to construct the dam would actually have been higher than that amount once the high interest rates of the period had been applied to the principal required to construct the Booneville Reservoir. In short, the Booneville Reservoir project was still deemed to be economically infeasible.[86]

The failure to get the Booneville Reservoir constructed had repercussions throughout the Three Forks of the Kentucky River region. Officials in counties throughout the area, especially in Beattyville, had been actively working towards the construction of the Booneville Reservoir since 1951 and had nothing to show for decades of development planning.[87]

Owsley County had spent much of the twentieth century fending off the development ideas of its neighbors rather than charting its own economic improvements. While neighboring counties had been planning toward a tourism industry, Owsley Countians had been putting off development in large areas of the county because it made no sense to spend money to improve areas that were going to be inundated by a lake. Many rural people had not been willing to improve farms that would have been flooded by Lake Daniel Boone. Years of neglect toward the economic infrastructure the county did have only compounded Owsley's problems when the feared lake was not constructed. The end result is that Owsley County begins the twenty-first century in a fashion amazingly similar to where it had been a century before. Owsley County began the twentieth century as one of Kentucky's pauper counties. It is now the second poorest county in the United States of America.[88]

5. Moments of Development

In 1990, Danny Barrett of Owsley County proposed a merger of Owsley, Wolfe, Breathitt, and Lee counties. While he knew his proposal would be met with disdain by the elites of the respective counties, Barrett succeeded in bringing attention to the fact that these counties all had an inadequate tax base to support basic expenses such as county school districts and the salaries of county government officials. Combining the four counties would have allowed for the elimination of duplicate services, thereby saving money that could be used to improve the infrastructure of the economically depressed area. When asked about Barrett's proposal, Owsley County judge-executive Jimmy Herald admitted that there were many obvious economic benefits to consolidating the four counties. At the same time, he made it clear that he was opposed to the idea entirely: "I myself feel, as a representative of the people, that we will bear that extra expense in order to have our own county government; that's a price we pay. ... our pride goes to our county lines."[1] In that statement, Herald embraced the idea that Owsley County was a little kingdom. In his eyes, and those of the elites that preceded him, control of Owsley County represented the American dream. It did not matter how poor the county was in relation to other counties in the United States, it was still their kingdom.

In fairness to Herald, it is understandable why Owsley County elites perceived their community to be a little kingdom. Their power and influence historically extended to the county's borders and went no further. Owsley County elites, with the exception of the Hogg family in the late nineteenth century, were never able to extend their political ties outside of their county in a manner that would have aided Owsley's economic development. Thus, outside of their immediate sphere of influence, Owsley County elites were impotent.

Much to the detriment of Owsley County's general populace, its local elites historically were actively utilizing the county's few resources for their personal empowerment and enrichment. The Estill County elites who created Owsley utilized their control of the county to construct roads in the vicinity of Proctor and Beattyville. During the 1920s, Owsley County elites were able to obtain money from the Commonwealth of Kentucky for the construction of roads and utilized that money for their personal purposes, rather than using the funds for their intended purpose. Owsley County elites never really evolved beyond seeking opportunities within the county to enhance their power and access to county funds. In truth, they did not need to diversify beyond rent-seeking behavior because they controlled both the courthouse and the school system. This provided county elites with the ability to reward their political clients with jobs in a place where employment opportunities were not readily available. This also meant that elites could get these clients to do whatever they wished because they also had the power to dismiss these same individuals from their jobs.

A smaller group of elites within Owsley County held political power through control of Booneville's government apparatus. These elites also desired to enrich themselves through political control but did not get many opportunities to achieve their goal because Booneville did not even generate enough tax revenue to pay all of their local government officials. This situation led Booneville elites, such as Carl Reynolds, to seek other sources of revenue for themselves. They were obviously not receiving many political spoils from the elites who controlled Owsley County's political and economic infrastructure, thus they turned to outside elites from neighboring counties to serve as their political and economic patrons. During the 1960s, Booneville elites were certainly acting as local managers for the interests of Breathitt, Lee, and Estill elites to the detriment of Owsley County's general populace.

Although Owsley County's elites were cognizant that their "pride" ended at their county's boundaries, elites residing outside of Owsley County did not respect the same barrier. From the time Owsley County was first created, elites from neighboring counties engaged in predatory behavior within Owsley's borders. Since Owsley's elites abrogated their responsibility to defend their kingdom, it was left to the general populace of Owsley to oppose the actions of the intruding elites. This meant that the general citizenry were forced to react to the political designs of interlopers residing outside of Owsley County rather than charting their vision of the American dream. The crux of Owsley County's history is that it was shaped not by its inhabitants, but by outside elites who controlled the nondemocratic geopolitical structure centered on the Three Forks of the Kentucky River. Power within this structure was based on the connections made by local elites to their counterparts in Kentucky cities such as Frankfort or Lexington, or to officials in Washington, DC. These connections tended to be short-lived, resulting in brief moments of development benefiting a handful of elites rather than impacting the respective counties over an extended period of time.

The first moment of development within the Three Forks region centered around the salt manufacturing industry of Clay County in the early nineteenth century. During that era, salt manufacturing was such an important component of Kentucky's economy that the general assembly of the Commonwealth of Kentucky went to great lengths to address the economic infrastructure needs of the salt manufacturers. Acts were passed in 1802, 1817, and 1842 that connected Clay County's saltworks to the Wilderness Road, thereby making it much easier to get salt to major markets outside of Eastern Kentucky on overland routes. This road construction also greatly benefited the growth of Manchester, the home community of the salt manufacturers. The state legislature also authorized water traffic improvements, most notably in 1810, 1813, and the late 1830s. By the 1840s, the importance of salt to Kentucky's economy had begun its precipitous decline. Clay County's salt manufacturers obviously lost the support of their political patrons in Frankfort during that period because state money was no longer being spent on infrastructure improvements that aided Clay County entrepreneurs to get their goods to market. With their livelihoods threatened, the major salt manufacturers used their economic power to seize control of Clay County's governmental structure.[2]

Clay County's salt manufacturers unwittingly created a model that would be subsequently emulated by other elites within the Three Forks of the Kentucky River region. They had harvested a local commodity and had utilized an existing river network to get the product to distant markets. The Clay Countians had also managed to utilize the state legislature to obtain legislation designed specifically to improve the roads and waterways around their homes and businesses. Most importantly, the Clay

Countians had demonstrated that it was possible to convert economic power into control of the political and economic infrastructure of one's home county.

The second moment of development within the Three Forks region was the application of the Clay County model by a group of Estill County elites tied together through their business interests in coal mining. These elites secured legislation through the general assembly of the Commonwealth of Kentucky in order to create Owsley County in 1843. In the process of establishing Owsley, these elites took land, along with the taxpayers residing therein, from Breathitt, Clay, and Estill counties. For nearly three decades, these elites utilized their ability to secure legislation from Frankfort to both improve the infrastructure around their homes and businesses in the Proctor/Beattyville area and provide themselves political positions that gave them access to the tax revenue generated by Owsley Countians. The frustration felt by Owsley's general populace over having their county's assets being spent on one locale ultimately cost the former Estill County elites control of the county. This should not be misinterpreted as a victory for Owsley's citizens. The elites centered in Proctor and Beattyville simply utilized their political contacts in Frankfort to create Lee County in 1870.

The creation of Lee County in 1870 halved Owsley County in size. Breathitt, Estill, and Wolfe counties also lost land, and taxpayers, to the creation of Lee. One cannot underestimate the level of loss that resulted from the creation of Lee County to Owsley County's economic potential, because part of the land lost to Lee was the area where the Three Forks came together to form the main course of the Kentucky River. The town located on the confluence of the Three Forks, Beattyville, subsequently became the economic shipping center of Eastern Kentucky into the 1920s. While Lee County boomed, Owsley County stagnated.

The Booneville Reservoir project, especially during the 1950s and 1960s, should also be looked upon as a moment of development that was quite unique for the Three Forks of the Kentucky River region. It represented a cooperative effort on the part of Lee, Estill, Breathitt, Clay, Madison, Franklin, and Fayette elites to create a development moment for Owsley County. Just because that development was not desired within Owsley was immaterial to these outside elites. In truth, the Booneville Reservoir project was never intended to serve the needs of Owsley's populace. Its construction stood to depopulate much of the county. The construction of the reservoir was designed to serve both the needs of central Kentucky communities such as Richmond, Lexington, and Frankfort and the counties arrayed around the Three Forks of the Kentucky River.

Throughout the twentieth century, communities such as Richmond, Lexington, and Frankfort depended on the Kentucky River to supply water to their rapidly growing populations. During times of drought, water was not available in much quantity. Impounding water in Owsley County through the construction of the Booneville Reservoir would have helped ensure that enough water would have been available to sustain the water needs of downriver cities located in central Kentucky.

For elites residing in the county seats surrounding Owsley County, the Booneville Reservoir project in the 1950s initially represented a solution to the significant flooding problems that annually plagued their communities and businesses. This was especially true in Estill and Lee counties. By the 1960s, these same elites began to view the Booneville Reservoir as the solution to both the poverty found throughout the Three Forks region and the related out-migration problem that was depopulating individual counties of taxpayers. They envisioned the resulting lake in both Owsley and Clay counties as the centerpiece of a tourism industry. It was hoped that a tourism industry built around the Daniel Boone theme would create jobs that could be filled by kinfolk returning from cities such as Cincinnati, Ohio, or Detroit, Michigan. In anticipation of the eventual construction of the reservoir, these elites began development planning towards a tourism industry they envisioned, rather than developing the industries that already existed within their communities. While making development decisions around a structure that was never built ultimately proved misguided, it still represented activity towards economic development.

One should be careful not to construe the cooperation of elites in pushing for the construction of the Booneville Reservoir as an indication of a commitment by Three Forks elites to jointly solve mutual problems. The Booneville Reservoir project represented a point in time when the interests of elites throughout the region converged. They all stood to gain economic benefit from the flooding of large portions of Owsley and Clay counties.

The lack of cohesion among these elites most vividly came to the fore during Breathitt County's moment of development in the 1960s. Although the Breathitt County elites centered in Jackson, Kentucky, worked with their counterparts from neighboring counties on the Booneville Reservoir project during the War on Poverty era, they also preyed on them at the same time.

Beginning in 1965, the OEO utilized the MKRADC as the CAP that distributed federal War on Poverty monies intended for Owsley, Wolfe, Lee, and Breathitt counties. Unfortunately for a vast majority of the impoverished inhabitants of the four counties, the MKRADC was under the firm political control of Breathitt County elites. The dominant elite family in Breathitt selected the members of the executive board of the organization, along with its director. The funds sent to the MKRADC flowed through the bank owned by the same family. These elites ensured that most of the money sent to alleviate the chronic poverty in the four-county area they served was actually spent in their home community. During the War on Poverty, the MKRADC built three permanent structures using OEO funds. They were a greenhouse, sorghum mill, and country store. All three facilities were located in Breathitt County. Wolfe, Owsley, and Lee elites bitterly complained, to no avail, that they were being denied their rightful share of money during an era in which the federal government was making a concerted effort to address poverty. Their pleas fell on deaf ears because they were in direct conflict with the most powerful group of elites in the Three Forks region.

The Breathitt Countians acted with impunity because they were well protected by political allies in Frankfort, Kentucky, and Washington, DC. Any Democratic Party candidate in Kentucky desiring to hold a statewide office coveted the support of Breathitt County elites because they could deliver a substantial number of votes in Eastern Kentucky. United States Congressman Carl Perkins was also beholden to the Breathitt Countians because he needed their political support if he wanted to be reelected to his congressional seat. Although Perkins also represented Wolfe and Lee counties, he could hold onto his congressional seat without those voters. He had to have the Breathitt County votes controlled by the Turner family. Perkins' political debts to the Breathitt County faction cannot be understated, because Perkins was a powerful politician in Washington, DC, serving as chair of the United States House of Representatives' Committee on Education and Labor. It was this very committee that was responsible for overseeing the activities of the Office of Economic Opportunity. The Committee on Education and Labor also controlled the OEO's funding, which could always be held hostage by Perkins should the need arise.

One common thread in all these moments of development is that elites in one county were making decisions for their personal benefit that negatively impacted the people residing in other counties. This thread suggests that scholars constructing county studies may be missing key developments in a respective county's history that occurred in a completely different locale, but were nonetheless significant.

Another consistent trend was that these moments of development did not positively impact the respective counties as a whole. Any improvements in physical infrastructure that resulted from these periods were predominantly confined to the respective county seats. Rural areas located on the peripheries of the respective county seats never saw any benefit from the monies flowing into their county's coffers. Not surprisingly, these rural areas became the most impoverished portions of their counties. Since the county seats of the Three Forks of the Kentucky River region are situated along the Kentucky River's forks or main course, the poorest portions of all the counties in the region are contiguous.[3]

Elites throughout the Three Forks of the Kentucky River region have unsuccessfully tried to create other moments of development since the 1970s. Beginning in the 1990s, a number of industrial parks were built in many of the counties situated along the Kentucky River and its tributaries. It was believed that creating industrial spaces would serve as an attraction to companies that were being recruited to relocate to the Three Forks of the Kentucky River region. Unfortunately, this industrial recruiting strategy proved shortsighted because it did not address other factors that would have concerned companies interested in the workspaces, such as the state of local roads and the availability of an educated workforce.

Owsley County began construction of the 91-acre Lone Oak Industrial Park in the mid–1990s using its coal severance funds, which would have ordinarily gone to road construction, and some government grants. The industrial park has two buildings that, as of 2006, have never been occupied. Companies are simply not willing to move to an industrial site that is located approximately 30 miles from a state or federally authorized trucking network. The state of Owsley's roads has also hindered industrial recruitment, since more than 75 percent are still unpaved. Owsley County is not alone in having an empty industrial park. The industrial parks in Lee and Wolfe counties are also empty. Millions of dollars in expenditures have thus far yielded nothing.[4]

A major hindrance to industrial recruiting is the notoriety that the

Three Forks region has gained as a major center of marijuana production. Beginning in the 1970s, many impoverished people who could not find steady jobs turned to growing marijuana in order to make a living. Cultivating marijuana was particularly attractive for individuals who were unemployed because they could make money in the illegal drug trade while also being technically unemployed, thus drawing welfare benefits from the federal government.[5]

By the late 1980s, the Three Forks of the Kentucky River region was well-known nationally for the amount of marijuana being grown in the area. This unwanted attention resulted in state and federal law enforcement officials beginning a campaign to eradicate the area's primary source of income. For instance, in 1989, the Kentucky State Police destroyed 51,098 marijuana plants within Owsley County alone. Owsley led the state in the number of plants destroyed that year, with Nelson County coming in second with 36,146. The following year, CBS News' *48 Hours* produced a segment on Kentucky's illicit marijuana economy that focused primarily on Owsley County. It included footage, broadcast nationally, of the Kentucky State Police arresting the son of Owsley County judge-executive Dale Roberts for cultivating marijuana. It was not just marijuana growers who were targeted by law enforcement officials at the state and federal level but also those who were responsible for maintaining law and order. The sheriffs of Owsley, Lee, Breathitt, and Wolfe counties, along with the police chief of Beattyville, were all indicted on drug-related charges in 1991. All but the Breathitt County sheriff were eventually convicted of crimes in federal court.[6]

One of the reasons that marijuana was able to get a strong foothold in rural counties was the size of the local population. In Owsley County, there were only 3,000 potential jurors to serve on juries in 1989. With such a small population, anonymity was not possible. A vote to convict anyone of a crime would have most likely resulted in retaliation from the individual, their associates, or their kinfolk. Thus, in counties such as Owsley and Lee, it became extremely difficult to get a jury to convict people of drug related offences. If an individual did get convicted of committing a crime, they often received a light penalty. Another problem with getting an unbiased jury seated in these counties was the reality that a significant portion of the population, in many cases indirectly, benefited from the profits made through the cultivation of marijuana.[7] Harold Campbell, president of Farmers State Bank in Owsley County identified the impact of the revenue generated by marijuana growers to the local economy: "They pay off their loans with it. They pay cash for their funerals. They buy groceries. Where they used to run credit from month to month, they pay for it now.... Whether you want to admit to it or not, we all see the effect."[8] The marijuana economy resulted in the legal system throughout the Three Forks area's becoming impotent. It first became very difficult for prosecutors to convict anyone of offenses related to marijuana. Once people discovered that they could traffic in illegal drugs with impunity, they graduated to trafficking harder drugs such as cocaine and OxyContin. Not surprisingly, the prevalence of these harder drugs have led to a great many lives being destroyed through either addiction or the violence that inevitably erupts over their trafficking.[9]

Despite the influx of drug money into the local economy, the Three Forks of the Kentucky River region continued to be among the poorest areas in the United States. The region's well-known illicit industry proved to be a severe handicap in its efforts to attract companies within its borders. For instance, in Owsley County, industrial recruiters had to concede that marijuana cultivation and use was prevalent within the county. The executive director of the Owsley County Industrial Authority observed in 2003 that "It's harder drugs, not pot, that scare off companies and limit the supply of able workers."[10] The continued availability of space in the Lone Oak Industrial Park suggests that companies have been scared off by the prospect of having employees working for them whose senses might be dulled from the use of marijuana.

Since companies will not bring industry into the region, Three Forks elites have once again opted to turn to tourism in order to economically revitalize the region. Owsley County is presently developing a 9-hole golf course as its part of this regional economic revitalization movement. Ironically, the golf course is going to be constructed near the site where the Booneville Dam was going to be built decades ago. Wolfe County is pinning its tourism hopes on a 75-foot steel sculpture that incorporates within its design structure a banjo, a fiddle, and a guitar.[11]

While elites continue to dream about a prosperous future built around tourism, the economic conditions within the entire Three Forks of the Kentucky River region remain depressed. The persistent poverty of this area demonstrates that poverty is not created within individual counties, because poverty does not respect county boundaries any more than have the dominant political elites of Eastern Kentucky.

Tables

TABLE A
INDIVIDUALS INVOLVED IN COAL MINING WITHIN OWSLEY COUNTY IN 1850[1]

Name	Bushels of Coal Produced	Value
Wm Kelly	10,000	$1,000
A.G. Crawford	10,000	$1,000
? H. Cole	20,000	$1,000
Isaac Addison	15,000	$600
? Price	14,000	$1,400
John ?	16,000	$1,600
Hiram McGuire	27,000	$3,000
William Fulkerson	8,000	$800
George Williams	10,000	$1,000
Joseph Davis	8,000	$800
Samuel Baty [sic]	30,000	$3,000
Newberry Day	2,500	$200
Archibald McGuire	8,000	$800
George Patrick	8,000	$800
James McGuire	12,000	$1,200
H. H. Abells	14,000	$1,400
? Phillips	6,000	$600
Decatur Baty [sic]	35,000	$3,000
Wm Gum	12,000	$1,200
John G. McGuire	30,000	$3,000
I. G. Bacon?	30,000	$3,150

TABLE B
Individuals Involved in Coal Mining Within Owsley County in 1860[2]

Name	Bushels of Coal Produced	Value
Decatur Beaty [sic]	65,000	$7,500
Samuel Beaty [sic]	25,000	$3,000
Price Price	40,000	$5,000
John W. Hunter	40,000	$5,000
W. H. Reed	20,000	$2,500
J. G. McGuire	30,000	$3,500
J. C. Howerton	32,000	$4,750
Isaac Congleton	30,000	$4,000
J. B. McGuire	10,000	$1,250
Robert Jimison	40,000	$5,000

TABLE C
Gubernatorial Election Returns for Owsley County and the Commonwealth of Kentucky 1844–1859[3]

Year	Name of Candidate (Party)	Owsley Votes	Kentucky Votes
1844	William Owsley (Whig)	151	59,680
	William O. Butler (Democrat)	216	55,056
1848	John J. Crittenden (Whig)	268	66,466
	Lazarus W. Powell (Democrat)	270	58,045
1851	Lazarus W. Powell (Democrat)	276	54,821
	Archibald Dixon (Whig)	25	54,023
	Cassius M. Clay (Emancipation Anti-Slave State)	61	3,531
1855	Charles Morehead (American)	319	69,816
	Beverley L. Clark (Democrat)	478	65,413
1859	Beriah Magoffin (Democrat)	423	76,187
	Joshua F. Bell (Opposition)	398	67,283

TABLE D
PRESIDENTIAL ELECTION RETURNS FOR OWSLEY COUNTY AND THE COMMONWEALTH OF KENTUCKY 1844–1860[4]

Year	Name of Candidate (Party)	Owsley Votes	Kentucky Votes
1844	James K. Polk (Democrat)	129	52,053
	Henry Clay (Whig)	165	61,167
1848	Zachary Taylor (Whig)	330	67,141
	Lewis Cass (Democrat)	248	49,720
1852	Franklin Pierce (Democrat)	326	53,807
	Winfield Scott (Whig)	294	57,108
	John P. Hale (Free Soil)	0	256
1856	James Buchanan (Democrat)	401	69,509
	John C. Fremont (Republican)	0	314
	Millard Fillmore (American)	355	63,391
1860	Abraham Lincoln (Republican)	1	1,364
	Stephen A. Douglas (Northern Democrat)	5	25,652
	John C. Breckenridge (Southern Democrat)	370	53,143
	John Bell (Constitutional Union)	330	66,058

TABLE E
ROAD MILEAGE IN A SMALL SAMPLE OF KENTUCKY COUNTIES CIRCA 1923[5]

County	Gravel, Macadam or Hard Surfaced Roads	Dirt Roads	County	Gravel, Macadam or Hard Surfaced Roads	Dirt Roads
Allen	75	375	Lincoln	180	380
Anderson	256	75	Lyon	25	250
Bath	250	475	Mason	270	70
Boone	250	150	Nelson	223	215
Caldwell	41	400	Ohio	10	1,200
Campbell	390	40	Owsley	0	250
Clark	180	120	Perry	1.5	400
Gallatin	130	22	Pulaski	110	2,200
Garrard	185	250	Rockcastle	17	425
Harlan	15	175	Rowan	8	1,000
Harrison	333	171	Trimble	100	130
Hart	100	740	Washington	246	256
Henderson	68	558	Woodford	218	60
Lewis	212	400			

TABLE F
Rainfall and River Level in Lee County During the Flood of 1937[6]

Date in January	Amount of Rain in Inches	River Level in Feet	Date in January	Amount of Rain in Inches	River Level in Feet
1	.00	642.0	14	.00	640.2
2	1.70	643.4	15	1.39	643.7
3	.15	649.2	16	.00	647.7
4	.00	646.4	17	.22	646.0
5	.00	642.2	18	2.00	647.1
6	.00	640.7	19	.41	649.2
7	.46	640.2	20	.77	648.4
8	.00	640.2	21	.95	649.3
9	.00	639.8	22	.64	647.8
10	.40	639.5	23	1.21	646.5
11	.46	640.5	24	.39	648.7
12	.11	640.4	25	.66	647.8
13	.00	640.3	26	.00	650.2

TABLE G
Population Trends in Counties with Representation in the KRDA[7]

County	1940	1950	Percentage Change
Breathitt	23,946	19,964	-16.6%
Clark	17,988	18,898	+5.1%
Estill	17,978	14,677	-18.4%
Fayette	78,899	100,746	+27.7%
Jessamine	12,174	12,458	+2.3%
Lee	10,860	8,739	-19.5%
Madison	28,541	31,179	+9.2%
Owsley	8,957	7,324	-18.2%
Perry	47,828	46,566	-2.6%

TABLE H
POPULATION OF COUNTIES IN THE VICINITY OF THE PROPOSED BOONEVILLE RESERVOIR[8]

County	1940	1950	1960	1970
Owsley	8,957	7,324	5,369	5,023
Clay	23,901	23,116	20,748	18,481
Jackson	16,339	13,101	10,677	10,005
Estill	17,978	14,667	12,466	12,752
Lee	10,860	8,739	7,420	6,587
Breathitt	23,946	19,964	15,490	14,221
Perry	47,828	46,566	34,961	25,714
Leslie	14,981	15,537	10,941	11,623

Appendices

APPENDIX A
FARMS IN OWSLEY COUNTY, 1909–1974[1]

Year	Number of Farms	Land in Farms	Average Farm Size
1909	1,408	110,308	78
1919	1,331	110,567	83
1924	1,356	97,520	72
1929	1,351	107,400	80
1934	1,591	102,580	65
1939	1,713	99,077	58
1944	1,353	89,462	66
1949	1,333	92,859	70
1954	1,052	83,018	79
1959	807	71,278	88
1964	843	70,594	84
1969	687	62,264	91
1974	382	38,508	101

APPENDIX B
BURLEY TOBACCO PRODUCTION IN OWSLEY COUNTY, 1935–1975[2]

Year	Production	Owsley Yield per Acre	KY Yield per Acre
1935	392,000	560	765
1940	776,000	1,093	1,040
1945	1,274,000	1,180	1,070
1950	1,473,000	1,169	1,165

Year	Production	Owsley Yield per Acre	KY Yield per Acre
1955	1,259,000	1,415	1,470
1960	1,195,000	1,440	1,625
1965	1,689,000	2,060	2,160
1970	1,632,000	2,400	2,710
1975	1,918,000	2,180	2,320

APPENDIX C
CORN PRODUCTION IN
OWSLEY COUNTY, 1930–1970[3]

Year	Production	Owsley Yield per Acre	KY Yield per Acre
1930	122,000	9.0	10.0
1935	233,000	17.5	21.5
1940	239,000	21.7	24.5
1945	170,000	25.0	32.0
1950	245,000	35.0	37.0
1955	216,000	36.0	41.0
1960	176,000	47.5	48.0
1965	101,000	56.0	69.0
1970	19,600	49.0	50.0

APPENDIX D
TRANSCRIPTION OF SPECIFIC CHARGES
ASSERTED AGAINST MS. TREVA HOWELL
AND THE MKRADC[12]

Memorandum

August 16, 1969.

To: MKRADC active file.
From: Lynn Frazer.
Subject: Henry Raleigh interview.

Richard Oexmann and I met Henry Raleigh, one of four Breathitt county Operation Mainstream supervisors in Powell county. Accompanying Raleigh was Mr. _____ Deaton, also of Breathitt county.

Purpose of the meeting was to interview Raleigh concerning his knowledge of political and administrative inadequacies of the four county Middle Kentucky River Area Development Council, an Office of Economic Opportunity, Department of Labor grantee. Raleigh's interview facts are as follows:

1. Fulltime Operation Mainstream (O/M) enrollees are being paid $1.60 per hour (for 40 hours week) were consistently being given vouchers drawn against MKRADC

Emergency Food and Medical component to allow said enrollees to purchase or supplement their purchasing of Food Stamps. This violates the intent of the emergency component and is done with the express knowledge of the director, Mrs. Treva Howell.

Some of these O/M enrollees are: James Hensley, Fred Turner, Clyde Noble and Frank Turner, all of Breathitt county.

Henry Raleigh, Rebecca Blair and Imogene Evandorf should be interviewed in reference to this point.

Mrs. Blair resigned under pressure after she allowed an interview with Bill Peterson of the Courier-Journal.

Mrs. Blair can testify that Treva instructed EF&M employees to "give them to anyone" before the May 27, 1969, primary election.

Arch Holland, Campton, will testify that he was cut off EF&M before the election after Holland indicated to Steve Rose, a MKRADC employee brought in by Mrs. Howell, that he was opposing a Turner candidate.

2. Charlie (Lester) Burton (referred to in Item #8 of July 8, 1969, Summary Report). Henry Raleigh has more direct knowledge of same. Some on list one year ahead of Burton.

3. Treva Howell said to Henry Raleigh that program guidelines would not permit her to hire close relatives or more than one person per family into various OEO/DOL components she administers.

Treva Howell has employed both Mary Salyers and her niece Lena Salyers. (Second Hand) Mary Salyers supposedly was told that if she would swear in court that she voted for Troy Deaton, a school board candidate in Breathitt in November of 1968, she would get a job opening the Neighborhood Youth Corps program. (The court legation concerned contested votes between Deaton and his opponent, a Turner candidate he defeated.)

Mary Salyers subsequently testified she voted for Deaton and was later employed by Mrs. Howell. The niece is employed in the Concentrated Employment Programs (CEP's) versatile component.

Kevin Charters, deputy director, MKRADC, employed by Mrs. Howell has been working while at the same time his wife has been on the NYC In-School program.

Mr. Howell's son-in-law, Charles Franks, was employed to complete a survey and worked out of the CAA office this summer. (The source of his salary is not known). C.A. Memo 23A, C, section 4c.

4. CEP or O/M enrollees who are MKRADC board members (a highly questionable practice since they owe their job to Mrs. Howell) have allegedly had repairs made to their personal dwellings.

Sam Moore's home was repaired by an O/M crew in July of 1969. A work crew floored the porch, repaired a gutter, poured a concrete basement floor and painted.

Henry Raleigh believes repair work was also done on the home of Letcher Turner, another board member.

The home of the father of the then MKRADC executive committee chairman, Mrs. Marha (Steve) Turner, was repaired by O/M crew.

5. Treva Howell appeared on and was quoted on the family Radio Station, WEKG, Jackson, after Governor's veto was announced and misrepresented the truth, saying the veto meant all Federal programs would be lost including programs not under MKRADC, i.e., food stamps. Boyd Noble of the local Public Assistance office later partially refuted in subsequent issues of Jackson Times. To gain support she and staff preyed on program enrollees and communities continually telling them this (veto) meant they were loosing jobs, county monies and services.

Mrs. Howell had petitions circulated in opposition to the Governor's veto, calling in DOL as well as OEO staff on the July 14 Federal holiday for Moon Landing, telling them to take off a later day to make up.

DOL should investigate this misuse of their Federally funded staff and money. Clyde Combs and Mitchell turned in a days time against the DOL Funds for this day. (Can possibly be verified by record check).

6. OEO staff worker's forged many names to the petitions and told others misrepresentations to secure their signatures.

7. Mrs. Howell sponsored a picnic at Booneville on Friday, May 23, for all DOL programs enrollees. According to Mrs. Howell's instruction the men would receive their paychecks at the picnic.

Men were told by crew chiefs and supervisors they would not be paid for their regular day's work if they did not show up at the picnic.

Benton Gross a crew leader of seven or eight enrollees was handing out soft drinks and stated: "come ahead and drink up if you're for the Turner ticket and if you're not — don't drink" — addressing the enrollees.

8. Mainstream enrollees were shaken down for $10 political contributions by their crew leaders before the May primary.

Bedford Gross's crew was told by him to pay. The crewmen are Claybe McIntosh, Gilford McKinney, Benton Gross (brother of Bedford Gross), Alex Ritchie, Brack Ritchie, Morgan Hardin and Beecher Campbell.

Hugh Johnson, a Breathitt O/M supervisor, just prior to the May 27 election, asked Henry Raleigh if he had gotten up his campaign money yet and showed Raleigh a large roll of big denomination bills. This was in the Jackson CAA office. Immediately after flashing the money he entered Mrs. Howell's office and stayed with her ten or fifteen minutes. Raleigh was with him during the day and did not again see the money in Johnson's possession.

Mrs. Jean Pence heard the conversation and saw the money. She is the secretary to Mitchell Spicer, O/M project director.

Hugh Johnson hit up Will Jett's, Letcher Turner and Richard Vires O/M crews for campaign assessments. He also contacted O/M men assigned to board of Education and Forestry Department. Jesse Salyers is crew leader for the Forestry crew.

Leaving the May 23, 1969, picnic Raleigh was in a car with Mr. and Mrs. Robert Costells, Ervin Raleigh, Sam B. Turner when Claybe McIntosh asked Henry Raleigh, "How much did they tax you for?" (Raleigh asked him what he said and McIntosh repeated with a laugh, "Didn't they tax you boys for no election money?" (Raleigh to Frazer) "No — never heared it mentioned." Subsequent conversation with McIntosh by Raleigh indicated that crew leader Bedford Gross had asked every man for $10 and they all paid.

9. Further irregularities and violations of hiring practices were specifically discussed by Raleigh.

CEP coaches were hired by Lewis Warrix, acting deputy director and O/M project supervisor with the consent of the MKRADC chairman subject to subsequent board approval.

Treva Howell assumed her duties February 1 and sent the new coaches home. The men were later rehired by the board after Martha Turner of Owsley county tried unsuccessfully to comprise [sic] with hiring back only half and allowing Treva to fill the other half remaining with new men of her choosing.

The point is made to emphasize that the board was aware of its role in approving interim personnel actions by the director.

However, Raleigh indicated several instances of her hiring personnel without board review of her actions.

10. Elija Stivers was used to transport friendly witnesses in the Deaton-Little court contest wherein Mrs. Howell's mother, Marie G. Turner (Breathitt school superintendent) was contesting Deaton's election over her candidate, Little.

Stivers was drawing pay from the in-school NYC program on those days.

11. Henry Raleigh was asked to make an ambulance trip to Lexington by Treva for a Jackson funeral home owned by Treva's first cousin in February of 1969. He refused and Hugh Johnson went in his place on DOL payroll time.

Raleigh's sister was denied EF&M voucher. She was told they were out of funds. However, others continued to receive them.

Another sister of Raleigh's was told by Treva to tell Raleigh that he was going to loose his job if he did not quit buying gas at an Ashland station. The Turner family owns another station in Jackson.

Enrollees and staff are told to have their checks cashed at the Citizens Bank by Treva. Same with savings accounts and loans.

12. Breathitt county O/M men are working in an unapproved county, Lee, on home repair (J.C. Lucas's crew).

13. Mrs. Howell continually allowed her name to be directly used in radio commercials by Berta Watts in support of the Turner candidate for circuit judge.

14. An O/M enrollee, twice sent home for drunkenness and thirdly given two week layoff was ordered reinstated by Treva in violation of contract guidelines.

15. Harvey Gross of Will Jett's O/M crew told Granville Deaton that Jett asked him for $10 or he would not work any more on O/M. (Mr. Deaton will testify).

16. Treva held square dances at Old Breathitt gym subsequent to primary and since, charging fifty cents and one dollar admission. These dances were sponsored in the name of the MKRARC. Money was for community clubs and versatile. Raleigh understands money, or a large part, went to Turner campaigning fund. (CAA treasurer's report and bank deposits should check with estimates of attendance.)

17. Before the May primary, Frank Turner worked for O/M. He dropped out to run for magistrate as a third party to pull votes from Turner opponent and then was rehired on O/M.

18. Raleigh reported that Woodrow Moore, a candidate for Democratic nominee as county judge, told Raleigh that Treva called him to run.

I believe Henry Raleigh to be beyond reproach, completely honest. He stuck to those facts of which he had first person knowledge. His reputation in the county is without question.

APPENDIX E
RESPONSES TO CLAIMS MADE BY SIERRA CLUB
MEMBERS AT THE PUBLIC REAL ESTATE
HEARING HELD IN STANTON
ON AUGUST 16, 1967[5]

The following is a list of destructive impacts from the construction of the Red River Reservoir, as claimed by members of the Sierra Club. Answers follow each statement and were assembled by the Kentucky Division of Water from every possible responsible source:

STATEMENT 1: The elimination of the land route along and through the scenic Red River Gorge. This is the most unique and beautiful area of its kind in the eastern United States.

Answer: Estimates of the number of persons who now visit the portion of the Red River Gorge to be flooded by the reservoir range from a low 200 annually to 500. The 200 person estimate was furnished by a resident of the area immediately adjacent to the gorge, and the 500 estimate by a former president of the Kentucky Archery Association. He owns land near the gorge and has repeatedly hunted in the area. Some 14 miles of the upper gorge will be left untouched and access roads and new hiking, riding, and camping trails will be provided to give access to hundreds of thousands.

STATEMENT 2: The elimination of most of the white water which is now being used by Kentuckians and those from adjoining states for canoe travel. This is the best of the few white streams in Kentucky.

Answer: Only about 14 miles of the lower gorge will be covered by the seasonal pool of the reservoir. Some 15 miles of the upper gorge will be left untouched except in seasons of heavy flooding (when canoeing is impractical) and some 11 miles of fast water (at least 115 cubic feet per second) of good canoeing caliber below the dam and downstream to Stanton. The Kentucky Recreation Plan provides for preservation in its natural state of the lower Rockcastle River, which is an excellent white water canoe stream.

STATEMENT 3: The elimination of the beaver population. This is one of the few areas in Kentucky where a high beaver population exists without conflict with farming and access road flooding.

Answer: Most of the beaver population of Red River is located below the sight of Red River Dam. The Beaver population is so large in the lower part of Red River that trapping of beaver is allowed in the winter time.

STATEMENT 4: Elimination of trout fishing in Swift Camp Creek and the Red River above the bridge.

Answer: Trout fishing will continue in the river proper above the 14 miles of the Red River Gorge to be occupied by the seasonal pool of the reservoir, and in a portion of Swift Camp Creek. There will probably be some loss of fishing in the river itself, but it will be more than compensated for by the vast increase in reservoir fishing. Many authorities think the Red River Reservoir may well become an outstanding fishing location.

STATEMENT 5: The elimination of key wildlife habitat component in the form of cleared bottom land soils. This component can't be replaced anywhere in the area.

Answer: If this statement refers to acreage to be inundated, there is very little cleared bottom land in the reservoir area. It is the opinion of wildlife specialists that the majority of existing wildlife will relocate in the vicinity. There will be almost no detrimental effect on cleared bottom lands below the reservoir as far as wildlife is concerned, and farm land which is periodically flooded will be placed in safe and full production as a result of flood protection by the reservoir.

STATEMENT 6: The drastic reduction or elimination of the wild turkey population in the area. This is one of the best in Kentuck [*sic*].

Answer: The reservoir plan, as approved by the Fish and Wildlife departments of the State and Federal Governments, provides for the acquisition of additional, privately owned and isolated acreage in the area, and the reestablishment by these agencies of the turkey population in an agreeable environment where the population will likely increase rather than decrease.

STATEMENT 7: The drastic reduction of quirrel [*sic*], deer and grouse which now habitat the area. The grouse and squirrel hunting in this area is very good.

Answer: It is the opinion of experienced wildlife men that the game in the immediate area of the reservoir would move out in direct proportion to the increased influx of visitors. They feel, however, since the reservoir is located in the Boone National Forest, that there is plenty of other desirable habitat available and they would simply transfer to other areas less susceptible to visitors.

STATEMENT 8: The elimination of what is potentially one of Kentucky's best fishing streams for walleye and muskie, with controlled situation measures enforced.

Answer: The walleye population, according to fish and game authorities, is very small. The muskie population, which is also very small, will likely adapt. In any case the increased availability of lake fishing will be compensatory.

STATEMENT 9: The elimination of one of the finest stretches of wild river left in Kentucky, and a future tourist attraction of far greater potential than any lake that could be built.

Answer: The Kentucky Recreation Plan provides for the continued preservation of three wild rivers in the Commonwealth: Kinniconick Creek in Lewis County, the lower Rockcastle River in Laurel and Pulaski counties and Station Camp Creek in Estill County. Also earmarked for preservation are some 32 stretches of other streams totaling about 1,100 miles. The necessity of providing flood control, pollution abatement, low-flow augmentation, and water supply for the Red River, Kentucky River, and for the cities of Lexington and Frankfort is overriding. As for the comparative value of the Red River Gorge in its wild state and its being developed as planned ... it is now viewed and enjoyed by only a few hundred each year. The Federal Bureau of Outdoor Recreation estimates that the area will attract several millions annually when the reservoir is completed — new access roads will be built — and hiking and riding trails constructed.

STATEMENT 10: The elimination of parts of the most scenic of the hiking trails and the land route to view the scenic Sky Bridge.

Answer: The long-range comprehensive plan for the development of the area provides for the construction of many additional access roads, many miles of hiking and riding trails, rest shelters, and additional facilities which will compensate — many times over — for the small amount lost.

(Note) If another drought equal to the 1930 should occur next year in the Kentucky River, Lexington, Kentucky, would have a shortage of nineteen thousand million gallons per day. The nineteen thousand million gallons per day shortage cannot be supplied from any other source.

Since the year 1937 there have been 65 floods in the Red River Valley. Only four years since 1937 has the Red River Valley been free of floods. The dam in Red River will lower the flood crest at Clay City approximately 6 feet. The dam will insure no further floods of Clay City by Red River.

None of the 15 rock bridges in the vicinity of Red River will be covered by the reservoir at its highest level. One rock bridge known as Hunters Arch or Moon Shiners Arch will be partially covered at extreme high water level but will not be affected at pool stage.

APPENDIX F
STATEMENT OF
SENATOR JOHN SHERMAN COOPER

Before Senate and House Appropriations Subcommittees on Fiscal 1967 Budget Recommendations for Kentucky Corps of Engineers Projects, May 3–4, 1966[6]

Mr. Chairman. I am pleased to come before you and the members of the Subcommittee to give my views on the Budget requests for Corps of Engineers flood control and river improvement projects for my State of Kentucky for the Fiscal Year 1967. As in past years, I am here with the Kentucky Delegation in the Congress to testify on the Budget items and funds affecting these projects, and I thank you for extending this privilege to us.

I support the Budget requests for the following Kentucky projects recommended for construction and planning work in the President's civil works budget for the Fiscal Year 1967. I am not listing the itemized requests for maintenance and operation of projects on which construction has been completed, but in addition to the amounts noted in this statement, I also support the President's request for these necessary funds required to operate facilities that have been built by the Corps of Engineers in Kentucky.

CONSTRUCTION

Project	Amount	Purpose
Barkley Locks & Dam	3,484,000	Complete Construction
Carr Fork Reservoir	4,800,000	Continue Construction
Cave Run Reservoir	4,500,000	Continue Construction
Fishtrap Reservoir	9,600,000	Continue Construction
Grayson Reservoir	7,558,000	Complete Construction
Green No. 2 Reservoir	8,700,000	Continue Construction
Laurel Reservoir	2,500,000	Continue Construction
Frankfort Floodwall	790,000	Continue Construction
Sturgis Local Protection	710,000	Continue Construction
Cannelton Locks & Dam	9,000,000	Continue Construction
Newburgh Locks & Dam	6,070,000	Continue Construction
Uniontown Locks & Dam	9,500,000	Continue Construction
Red River Reservoir	400,000	Initiate Construction

ADVANCED ENGINEERING AND DESIGN

Project	Amount	Purpose
Martins Fork Reservoir	100,000	Initiate AE & D
Paintsville Reservoir	100,000	Initiate AE & D
Mound City Locks & Dam	250,000	Continue AE & D
Smithland Locks & Dam	225,000	Continue AE & D

INVESTIGATIONS

Project	Amount	Purpose
Bluegrass Creek Survey	40,000	Complete Survey
Covington–Rosedale Survey	22,000	Complete Survey
Appalachian Water Resources	1,830,000	Special Investigation
Ohio River Basin Review	285,000	Continue Review
Highland Creek Survey	10,000	Initiate Survey

The projects for which operation and maintenance funds have been requested, and which I support, include Dale Hollow Reservoir, Middlesboro, Kentuc'y [*sic*] local control, Barren River Reservoir, Hickman Harbor, Kentucky River navigation system, Buckhorn Reservoir, Dewey Reservoir, Green and Barren Rivers navigation system, Nolin Reservoir, Rough River Reservoir, Tennessee River navigation system, and general improvement work along the Lower Mississippi River and its tributaries affecting Kentucky.

I recognize that the costs of the war in Vietnam have resulted in the Bureau of the Budget requiring a reduction in expenditures requested by the Corps of Engineers. As a result of the Budget requirements, funds for construction starts on Booneville and Eagle Creek Reservoirs on the Kentucky River were not included in the budget, and no funds were requested by the President to resume planning for the proposed Falmouth Reservoir on the Licking River.

I urge the Bureau of the Budget and the Committees to secure the fullest information from the Corps of Engineers on these projects and on the requirements to protect the areas in which they are located, so that they can be fully considered at this session of the Congress. Also, with the cutback in construction starts and the reduction in existing planning schedules, I would hope that attention will still be given to seeing that overall water resource development proceeds by including funds to begin planning required new flood protection projects.

In Kentucky, the Paintsville Reservoir is budgeted, but it requires the full $200,000 capability for advanced engineering and design work this year, and I urge the full amount. The local protection project for the town of Martin on Beaver Creek, authorized by Congress last year, has a capability of $200,000 to begin planning and to provide additional formulation, and I hope funds will be appropriated for the purpose.

There are other surveys and studies, including the Dayton-Bellevue floodwall restudy, in process and approaching completion in Kentucky. The Corps of Engineers has said that it has adequate funds for the required work on these surveys and studies for the next Fiscal Year, but I do want to say that the Budget requests I have discussed here are essential to assure that flood protection and navigation improvement remain on schedule in Kentucky.

This Committee has always given our Kentucky needs good attention, and our water resource development is going forward in good order. As in years past, I am pleased to join with my fellow Kentucky members of the Congress in making our presentation to you, and for myself and the Delegation, I want to express appreciation to the members of the Committee who are always so kind in giving us this opportunity.

APPENDIX G
Attendees of the Lake Daniel Boone Development Committee Meeting, April 26, 1966[7]

Name	Hometown	Affiliation or Profession
Joe Brown	Campton	MKRADC
Roland Sebastian	Jackson	MKRADC
Carl R. Reynolds	Booneville	City of Booneville
Sam P. Deaton	Jackson	Breathitt County Judge
Sam Johnson	Frankfort	Frankfort Electric & Water Plant Board
J. Wise Deaton, Jr.	Jackson	Breathitt County Planning Developer
King Justice	Beattyville	Buckhorn Scenic Mountain Trail Assoc.
Curtis E. Davis	Beattyville	Business
Fred Callahan	Booneville	Banker
Francis G. Miller	Irvine	Mayor
C.G. Mainous	Lexington	Citizens Union National Bank
Paul Wisegouver	Lexington	Lexington Chamber of Commerce
D. Ray Gillespie	Lexington	Sec., Lexington Chamber of Commerce
Freeman Saylor	Beattyville	Block Company and Readymix
Arco Begley	Beattyville	Business
Clyde Cornelius	Beattyville	Lumber and Supply
William R. Miller	Quicksand	Univ. of KY Resource Development
George Armstrong	Quicksand	Univ. of KY Resource Development
J.W. Flynn	Frankfort	Mayor
G.P. Congleton	Beattyville	Mining and Hardware
Russell Marshall	Frankfort	City Manager
Clarence Begley	Beattyville	Begley Auto Parts

Notes

Introduction

1. U.S. Census Bureau, U.S. Census Bureau State and County QuickFacts: Owsley County, Kentucky. (Database online.) For representations of Owsley County's poverty see "Marijuana Growing and Eradication in the United States," *48 Hours*, CBS, 7 June 1990, 8:00–9:00 P.M. (Database Online), transcript available from LexisNexis; John Voskuhl, "Grim Statistics Nothing New in Owsley," *Courier-Journal*, 15 August 1992, A1; Timothy L. O'Brien, "Pride of Ownership: Making Entrepreneurs of the Poor May Lift Some Off Federal Aid — Agencies Find Business Loans Stir Dreams, Hard Work in Recipients of Welfare — Debt Troubles in Appalachia," *Wall Street Journal*, 22 January 1993, A1; "One Paycheck from Poverty, Part 3 — Small Businesses," *CNN News*, CNN, 10 April 1994, 9:00–9:30 P.M. (Database online), transcript available from LexisNexis; "Town of Mistletoe Thrives During Holidays, Tiny Post Office Stays Alive Through Mailings," *Rocky Mountain News*, 18 December 1994, A28; Richard R. Clayton, *Marijuana in the "Third World": Appalachia, U.S.A.* (Boulder, CO: Lynne Reinner Publishers, Inc., 1995); Carol Jouzaitis, "Still Poor, Appalachia Faces the New Welfare — For 30 Years, Many in Job-Barren Region Have Lived on the 'Draw,'" *Chicago Tribune*, 11 November 1996, 1; "Aid Recipients Get Savings Help — Public, Private Grants Used to Match Poor Person's Cache," *Chicago Tribune*, 15 June 1997, 8; Anne Hull, "Coming Down from Oil Rig Hollow," *St. Petersburg Times*, 12 October 1997, A1; Michael Janofsky, "Pessimism Retains Grip on Appalachian Poor," *New York Times*, 9 February 1998, A1; Hugh B. Price, "To Be Equal: Black Poverty/White Poverty," Copley News Service, 19 February 1998 (Database online), transcript available from LexisNexis; Joe Frolik, "Lack of Job Opportunities Drives Young Workers to Cities," *Plain Dealer*, 4 May 1999, A6; J. Kelly, "40% in the County Said to Grow Weed," *USA Today*, 11 July 1989, 1–2; Mark Ferenchik, and Jill Riepenhoff, "Mountain Money Federal Tax Dollars Miss the Mark in Core Appalachia," *Columbus Dispatch*, 26 September 1999, A1; "Life on Easy Street..." *Columbus Dispatch*, 27 September 1999, A6; "... and Tobacco Row," *Columbus Dispatch*, 27 September 1999, A7; "What Can the Government Do about Poverty in Appalachia?" *Both Sides*, with Jesse Jackson, CNN, 26 March 2000, 5:30 P.M. (Database online), transcript available from LexisNexis; "Golf Plan Baffles Poor County's Leaders," *Augusta Chronicle*, 19 October 2002, B3; "5 Arrested in Theft of Corpse's Jewelry," *Chicago Tribune*, 23 March 2004, 14.

2. Joyce Wilson, *This Was Yesterday: A Romantic History of Owsley County* (Ashland, KY: Economy Printers, 1977); G.L. Bailey, *Early History of Owsley County, Kentucky* (Jackson, KY: Maw & Paw's Printing, 1994); Joe Powlas, *The Church with the Golden Roof* (Detroit: Harlo Press, 1988); James C. Klotter, and Henry Mayer, *A Century of Banking: The Story of Farmers State Bank and Banking in Owsley County 1890–1990* (Booneville, KY: Farmers State Bank, 1989).

3. Berea College Archives and Special Collections, *Burch Family Collection*; *Report of the Adjutant General of the State of Kentucky* vol.

1, *1861–1866* (Frankfort: Kentucky Yeoman Office, 1866), 756.

4. Alice O'Connor, *Poverty Knowledge: Social Science, Social Policy, and the Poor in Twentieth-Century U.S. History* (Princeton: Princeton University Press, 2001), 117.

5. Henry D. Shapiro, *Appalachia on Our Minds: The Southern Mountains and Mountaineers in the American Consciousness, 1870–1920* (Chapel Hill: University of North Carolina Press, 1978); W.G. Frost, "Appalachian America," *Woman's Home Companion* 23 (1896): 3–4, 21; Frost, "Our Contemporary Ancestors in the Southern Mountains," *Atlantic Monthly* 83 (1899): 311–319; Ellen Churchill Semple, "The Anglo-Saxons of the Kentucky Mountains: A Study in Anthropogeography," *Geographical Journal* 17, no. 6 (1901): 588–623; George E. Vincent, "A Retarded Frontier," *The American Journal of Sociology* 4 (1898): 1–20.

6. Michael Harrington, *The Other America: Poverty in the United States* (Baltimore: Penguin Books, 1963).

7. Thomas R. Ford, "The Passing of Provincialism," in *The Southern Appalachian Region*, ed. Thomas R. Ford (Lexington: University of Kentucky Press, 1962), 21, 32; Dwight Billings, "Culture and Poverty in Appalachia: A Theoretical Discussion and Empirical Analysis," *Social Forces* 53, no. 2 (1974): 315–323.

8. Jack Weller, *Yesterday's People: Life in Contemporary Appalachia* (Lexington: University of Kentucky Press, 1965), 7, 161.

9. Richard A. Ball, "A Poverty Case: The Analgesic Subculture of the Southern Appalachians," *American Sociological Review* 33, no. 6 (1968): 886, 890–891.

10. John Fetterman, *Stinking Creek* (New York: E.P. Dutton, 1967), 188.

11. Robert D. Hawkins, "Social Control in the Eastern Kentucky Subculture of Violence," (Ph.D. diss., Sam Houston State University, 1998), 12, 14, 16.

12. David E. Whisnant, *Modernizing the Mountaineer: People, Power, and Planning in Appalachia*, revised ed. (Knoxville: University of Tennessee Press, 1994), 50.

13. Ibid., xxi.

14. Ibid., 117.

15. Ada F. Haynes, *Poverty in Central Appalachia: Underdevelopment and Exploitation* (New York: Garland, 1997), 142.

16. Glen Edward Taul, "Poverty, Development, and Government in Appalachia" (Ph.D. diss., University of Kentucky, 2001), 417–419.

17. Elgin Mannion, "The Method of Growth: Development Models and Income Distribution in Appalachian Kentucky from 1969–2003" (Ph.D. diss., University of Kentucky, 2003), 308, 312.

18. Ibid., 420–428.

19. Harry M. Caudill, *Night Comes to the Cumberlands: A Biography of a Depressed Area* (Boston: Little, Brown, 1962). See also H.M. Caudill, *The Watches of the Night: A New Plea for Appalachia* (Boston: Little, Brown, 1976), and H.M. Caudill, *Theirs Be the Power: The Moguls of Eastern Kentucky* (Urbana: University of Illinois Press, 1983).

20. David Cattell-Gordon, "The Appalachian Inheritance: A Culturally Transmitted Traumatic Stress Syndrome?" *Journal of Progressive Human Services* 1, no. 1 (1990): 41–43, 54–55.

21. Helen M. Lewis and Edward E. Knipe, "The Colonialism Model: The Appalachian Case," in Lewis, Johnson, and Askins, eds., *Colonialism in Modern America: The Appalachian Case* (Boone, NC: The Appalachian Consortium Press, 1978), 16–26; Helen Matthews Lewis, Sue Easterling Kobak, and Linda Johnson, "Family, Religion and Colonialism in Central Appalachia, or Bury My Rifle at Big Stone Gap," in Lewis, Johnson, and Askins, eds., *Colonialism in Modern America: The Appalachian Case* (Boone, NC: The Appalachian Consortium Press, 1978), 117–136.

22. Appalachian Land Ownership Task Force, *Who Owns Appalachia? Landownership and Its Impact* (Lexington: University Press of Kentucky, 1983), 14.

23. John Gaventa, *Power and Powerlessness: Quiescence and Rebellion in an Appalachian Valley* (Urbana: University of Illinois Press, 1980), 98, 161, 206, 236–237.

24. Douglas O'Neil Arnett, "Eastern Kentucky: The Politics of Dependence and Underdevelopment," (Ph.D. diss., Duke University, 1978), 259–265.

25. David Walls, "Internal Colony or Internal Periphery? A Critique of Current Models and an Alternative Formulation," in Lewis, Johnson, and Askins, eds., *Colonialism in Modern America: The Appalachian Case* (Boone, NC: The Appalachian Consortium Press, 1978), 319–350. For an introduction to Wallerstein and world-systems analysis see Immanuel Wallerstein, *The Essential Wallerstein* (New York: New Press, 2000).

26. Ronald D Eller, *Miners, Millhands, and Mountaineers: Industrialization of the Appalachian South, 1880–1930* (Knoxville: University of Tennessee Press, 1982), 60–63.

27. Mary Beth Pudup, "The Limits of Subsistence: Agriculture and Industry in Central Appalachia," *Agricultural History* 64, no. 1 (1990): 61–89.

28. Altina L. Waller, *Feud: Hatfields, Mc-Coys, and Social Change in Appalachia, 1860–1900* (Chapel Hill: University of North Carolina Press, 1988), 233–234.

29. David C. Hsiung, *Two Worlds in the Tennessee Mountains* (Lexington: University Press of Kentucky, 1996), 186–187.

30. Ronald L. Lewis, *Transforming the Appalachian Countryside: Railroads, Deforestation, and Social Change in West Virginia, 1880–1920* (Chapel Hill: University of North Carolina Press, 1988), 211–234.

31. John G. Inscoe, *Mountain Masters: Slavery and the Sectional Crisis in Western North Carolina* (Knoxville: University of Tennessee Press, 1989).

32. Martin Crawford, *Ashe County's Civil War: Community and Society in the Appalachian South* (Charlottesville: University of Virginia Press, 2001), 34, 45, 62, 65, 130–132.

33. Paul Salstrom, *Appalachia's Path to Dependency: Rethinking a Region's Economic History 1730–1940* (Lexington: University Press of Kentucky, 1994), xiii–xix, 1–4, 10, 63–64.

34. Wilma A. Dunaway, *The First American Frontier: Transition to Capitalism in Southern Appalachia, 1700–1860* (Chapel Hill: University of North Carolina Press, 1995), 19, 87–106, 119–121.

35. Wilma A. Dunaway, *Slavery in the American Mountain South* (New York: Cambridge University Press, 2003), 20, 25.

36. Manuscript Census, Owsley County, Kentucky 1850, Schedule 2.

37. Dunaway, *Slavery in the American Mountain South*, 131.

38. Dwight B. Billings and Kathleen Blee, *The Road to Poverty: The Making of Wealth and Hardship in Appalachia* (New York: Cambridge University Press, 2002), 18.

39. Robert S. Weise, *Grasping at Independence: Debt, Male Authority, and Mineral Rights in Appalachian Kentucky 1850–1915* (Knoxville: University of Tennessee Press, 2001), 13, 255–280.

40. Robert M. Ireland, *Little Kingdoms: The Counties of Kentucky, 1850–1891* (Lexington: University Press of Kentucky, 1977).

41. "Public Service or Private Gain? Some Officials Trample on Kentuckians' Trust," *Lexington Herald-Leader*, 1 February 1994, A1; Kit Wagar, "New Cruisers Could be Called Raises on Wheels," *Lexington Herald-Leader*, 2 February 1994, A1; Wagar, "'Disabled' Fayette Deputies Work, Collect Pensions," *Lexington Herald-Leader*, 2 February 1994, A7; "Timeline," *Lexington Herald-Leader*, 2 February 1994, A6; Kit Wagar, "Fayette Deputies' Duties Take Them to Resorts, Beach," *Lex-ington Herald-Leader*, 2 February 1994, A1; Wagar, in Fayette County, Who You Know Still Matters," *Lexington Herald-Leader*, 2 February 1994, A8; Karen Samples, "State Looks Into Rent-Free Housing Given to Perry Chief's Son — Treasurer," *Lexington Herald-Leader*, 2 February 1994, A1; Scott Learn, "Boyd Splurges on Employees' Health Care," *Lexington Herald-Leader*, 2 February 1996, A6; Lee Mueller, "Little Expense Spared for Pike Public Servants: 6 Magistrates Cost Taxpayers $375,000 in Pay, Perks in '93," *Lexington Herald-Leader*, 2 February 1994, A1; Mueller, "Readers Respond to 'Little Kingdoms,'" *Lexington Herald-Leader*, 2 February 1994, A8.

42. Ronald D Eller, with Phil Jenks, Chris Jasparro, and Jerry Napier, *Kentucky's Distressed Communities: A Report on Poverty in Appalachian Kentucky* (Lexington: Appalachian Center, University of Kentucky, 1994), 1–6, 14.

Chapter 1

1. Kentucky Heritage Council, "Kentucky Historic Resources Inventory Files for Lee County," LE-40; Cecil R. Ison, "The Cold Oak Shelter: Providing a Better Understanding of the Terminal Archaic," in Hockensmith, Pollack, and Sanders, eds., *Paleoindian and Archaic Research in Kentucky* (Frankfort: Kentucky Heritage Council, 1988), 205–220.

2. Joyce Wilson, *This Was Yesterday: A Romantic History of Owsley County* (Ashland, KY: Economy Printers, 1977), 1; John Mack Faragher, *Daniel Boone: The Life and Legend of an American Pioneer* (New York: Henry Holt, 1992).

3. Quoted in Arch B. Bowman, "Geographic History and Early Settlement of Owsley County, Kentucky" (unpublished document in Owsley County — History Vertical File), n.pag.

4. Ibid.; I.W. Gabbard, in I.W. Gabbard Collection (Berea College Archives and Special Collections, Hutchins Library, Berea College, Berea, KY), Notebook 3, 49.

5. Stephen Aron, *How the West Was Lost: The Transformation of Kentucky from Daniel Boone to Henry Clay* (Baltimore: Johns Hopkins University Press, 1996), 133–137; Charles Sellers, *The Market Revolution: Jacksonian America, 1815–1846* (New York: Oxford University Press, 1991), 63–65; Craig Thompson Friend, *Along the Maysville Road: The Early American Republic in the Trans-Appalachian*

West (Knoxville: University of Tennessee Press, 2005), 254–261.

6. *Kentucky Acts 1801*, 93; *Kentucky Acts 1810*, 134; *Kentucky Acts 1811*, 113; Mary Verhoeff, *Kentucky River Navigation* (Louisville: The Filson Club, 1917), 153–154.

7. Dwight B. Billings and Kathleen Blee, *The Road to Poverty: The Making of Wealth and Hardship in Appalachia* (New York: Cambridge University Press, 2002), 281–336.

8. Manuscript Census, Owsley County 1850, Schedule 5, Owsley, 1; Manuscript Census, Owsley County 1860, Schedule 5, 1; Oscar Barton Davidson, compiler, *Kentucky Coal Production 1790–1988* (Lexington: Kentucky Geological Survey, 1990), 11, 30–64. See Tables A and B for a list of individuals in Owsley County involved in coal mining in 1850 and 1860.

9. Estill County, Kentucky, Minute/Order Books D–F 1834–1853, 88–89, 96, 149.

10. *Kentucky Acts 1842*, 11–13; G.L. Bailey, *Early History of Owsley County, Kentucky* (Jackson, KY: Maw & Paw's Printing, 1994), 16.

11. "Owsley, William," in *The Kentucky Encyclopedia*, John E. Kleber, ed. (Lexington: University Press of Kentucky, 1992), 702–703; Michael J. Dubin, *United States Gubernatorial Elections 1776–1860: The Official Results by State and County* (Jefferson, NC: McFarland, 2003), 76–80. On voting patterns for both presidential and gubernatorial candidates in Owsley County, see Tables C and D.

12. John H. Long, ed. *Atlas of Historical County Boundaries: Kentucky* (New York: Simon & Schuster, 1995), 377–379.

13. Kentucky, Constitutional Convention, *Official Report of the Proceedings and Debates in the Convention: Assembled at Frankfort, on the Eighth Day of September, 1890, to Adopt, Amend, or Change the Constitution of the State of Kentucky* (Frankfort: E. Polk Johnson, 1890), 395; Robert M. Ireland, *Little Kingdoms: The Counties of Kentucky, 1850–1891* (Lexington: University Press of Kentucky, 1977) 10; R.M. Ireland, *The Kentucky State Constitution: A Reference Guide* (Westport, CT: Greenwood Press, 1999), 9, 70.

14. *Kentucky Acts 1842*, 11–13; *Journal of the Regular Session of the Senate of the Commonwealth of Kentucky 1842–3*, 246. James McGuire, Jr., is the son of Archibald's brother, James McGuire, Sr. James McGuire, Jr., is not to be confused with James McGuire, one of Archibald's sons, who shared the same birth year with James, Jr. See Robert L. Smith, *Owsley County, Kentucky 1860 Census* (Cincinnati: Robert L. Smith, n.d.), 81–82.

15. Ireland, *Little Kingdoms: The Counties of Kentucky, 1850–1891*, 24.

16. Ibid., 1–2; John Alexander Williams, *Appalachia: A History* (Chapel Hill: University of North Carolina Press, 2002), 136–138; Ronald L. Lewis, *Transforming the Appalachian Countryside: Railroads, Deforestation, and Social Change in West Virginia, 1880–1920*, 211–234; Fred W. Gabbard, "Historical Sketches of Owsley County," *The Owsley County Courier*, 7 June 1940, 1.

17. Morris M. Garrett, "Booneville," in *The Kentucky Encyclopedia*, John E. Kleber, ed., 102; Lewis Collins, *Historical Sketches of Kentucky: Embracing Its History, Antiquities, and Natural Curiosities, Geographical, Statistical, and Geological Descriptions; with Anecdotes of Pioneer Life, and More Than One Hundred Biographical Sketches of Distinguished Pioneers, Soldiers, Statesmen, Jurists, Lawyers, Divines, Etc.* (Cincinnati: Lewis Collins, and Mayfield, KY: J. A. & U.P. James, 1848), 492; Ireland, *Little Kingdoms: The Counties of Kentucky, 1850–1891*, 1.

18. James C. Klotter and Henry C. Mayer, *A Century of Banking: The Story of Farmers State Bank and Banking in Owsley County 1890–1990*, 2; Garrett, *The Kentucky Encyclopedia*, 102.

19. *Kentucky Acts 1844*, 217.

20. Michael J. Dubin, *Presidential Elections, 1788–1860: The Official Results by County and State* (Jefferson, NC: McFarland, 2002), 86–87, 103, 123–124, 144, 168–169.

21. Manuscript Census, Owsley County, Kentucky, 1850, Schedule 1; Robert L. Smith, *Owsley County, Kentucky Tax Books 1844–1858* (Cincinnati: Robert L. Smith, n.d.), 2, 8.

22. United States Department of Agriculture, *Soil Survey of Jackson and Owsley Counties, Kentucky* (Washington, DC: United States Department of Agriculture, 1989), 2, 7, 36.

23. Eller, 16–22.

24. Manuscript Census, Owsley County, Kentucky, 1850, Schedule 1; Manuscript Census, Owsley County, Kentucky, Schedule 4, 3–4; Manuscript Census, Owsley County, Kentucky, 1860, Schedule 4, 31–32.

25. Manuscript Census, Owsley County, Kentucky, 1850, Schedule 4, 17–18; Manuscript Census, Owsley County, Kentucky, 1860, Schedule 4, 13–14, 31–32; Kentucky Heritage Council, "Kentucky Historic Resources Inventory Files for Owsley County," OW-2-OW-5; Wilson, *This Was Yesterday*, 25.

26. Marion B. Lucas, *A History of Blacks in Kentucky*, vol. 1, *From Slavery to Segregation, 1760–1891* (Frankfort: Kentucky Historical

Society, 1992), 108; Manuscript Census, Owsley County, Kentucky 1850, Schedule 1, 50, 71; Manuscript Census, Owsley County, Kentucky 1860, Schedule 1; Manuscript Census, Owsley County, Kentucky 1860, Schedule 2; Robert L. Smith, *Owsley County, Kentucky 1850 Census* (Cincinnati: Robert L. Smith, n.d.), 70–71.

27. Pat Trocano, *Lieutenant James McGuire, 1740–August 19, 1782: Reflections on My Fifth Great-grandfather and the Battle of Blue Licks* (Trocano Home Publishing, 1996), 23; Smith, *Owsley County, Kentucky Tax Books 1844–1858*, 6; Manuscript Census, Owsley County, *Kentucky 1850*, Schedule 4; *Manuscript Census, Owsley County 1850*, Schedule 1, 307–308; *Manuscript Census, Owsley County 1850*, Schedule 2, Owsley 1–2.

28. Robert L. Smith, *Owsley County, Kentucky Tax Books 1844–1858*, 16; Manuscript Census, Owsley County, Kentucky 1850, Schedule 4; Manuscript Census, Owsley County 1850, Schedule 1.

29. Rosemary Porter Kilduff and Mary Helen McGuire, *Peoples Exchange Bank 1912–1987* (Beattyville, KY: Peoples Exchange Bank, 1990), 176; Garrett, *The Kentucky Encyclopedia*, 102; Smith, *Owsley County, Kentucky 1850 Census*, 9; Smith, *Owsley County, Kentucky 1860 Census*, 4, 52. Decatur Beatty, age 29, was young enough to be 56-year-old Samuel's son. They were the only two Beatty heads of household in the 1850 census and had business ties that suggested a familial relationship. See Smith, *Owsley County, Kentucky, 1850 Census*, 9.

30. Manuscript Census, Owsley County, 1850, Schedule 4; Manuscript Census, Owsley County 1850, Schedule 5, 1; Manuscript Census, Owsley County 1860, Schedule 5, 1.

31. *Journal of the House of Representatives of the Commonwealth of Kentucky 1851–1852*, 148; *Kentucky Acts 1851*, 461–462, 687; Smith, *Owsley County, Kentucky, 1860 Census*, 33, 82; Klotter and Mayer, *A Century of Banking*, 2.

32. Mary Verhoeff, *Kentucky Mountain Transportation and Commerce 1750–1911: A Study in the Economic History of a Coal Field* (Louisville: John P. Morton, 1911), plate between pages 98–99, 161–166; Leland R. Johnson, and Charles E. Parrish, *Kentucky River Development: The Commonwealth's Waterway* (Louisville: Louisville Engineer District, U.S. Army Corps of Engineers, 1999), 99.

33. *Kentucky Acts 1859*, vol. 2, 8–10.

34. Manuscript Census, Owsley County, Kentucky, 1860, Schedule 1, 81, 83–84, 93, 95; Manuscript Census, Owsley County 1860, Schedule 2, 187.

35. Michael J. Dubin, *Presidential Elections, 1788–1860: The Official Results by County and State*, 86–87, 103, 123–124, 144, 168–169. Owsley Countians voted for Breckenridge because he was a Democrat and they had supported candidates from that party for decades. Their vote was not an endorsement of his views on slavery or secession. See James C. Klotter, *The Breckinridges of Kentucky 1760–1981* (Lexington: University Press of Kentucky, 1986), 117.

36. Wilson, *This Was Yesterday*, 6; Manuscript Census, Owsley County, Kentucky 1860, Schedule 4, 1; Manuscript Census, Owsley County, Kentucky 1860, Schedule 2.

37. Klotter, *The Breckinridges of Kentucky 1760–1981*, 169; James E. Copeland, "Where Were the Kentucky Unionists and Secessionists?" *The Register* 71 (1973): 350, 352; Klotter and Mayer, *A Century of Banking*, 5; Wilson, *This Was Yesterday*, 6.

38. Wilson, *This Was Yesterday*, 12; Jess D. Wilson, ed., *Mountain Men in the Mexican War 1847–1848: A Roster of Soldiers Enrolled for the Mexican War from the Eastern Kentucky Counties of Estill, Owsley, Clay, Laurel and Rockcastle* (McKee, KY: Jackson County Rural Electrical Cooperative, 1975); *Report of the Adjutant General of the State of Kentucky*, vol. 1, *1861–1866* (Frankfort: Kentucky Yeoman Office, 1866), 749–769; Eastern Kentucky University Special Collections and Archives, William Julius Moore Papers, Box 6; Smith, *Owsley County, Kentucky, 1850 Census*, 51–53; Smith, *Owsley County, Kentucky, 1860 Census*, 12, 81–83; Kenneth A. Haffendorfer, *The Battle of Wild Cat Mountain* (Louisville: KH Press, 2003); *Report of the Adjutant General of the State of Kentucky*, vol. 1, *1861–1866* (Frankfort: Kentucky Yeoman Office, 1866), 749–769; Eastern Kentucky University Special Collections and Archives, William Julius Moore Papers, Box 6. Thomas J. and Jonathan McGuire were sons of Archibald McGuire. The Archibald McGuire who enlisted in the Union Army was the son of Hiram McGuire. All the other listed McGuires were the elder Archibald McGuire's grandsons. See Smith, *Owsley County, Kentucky, 1850 Census*, 51–53; Smith, *Owsley County, Kentucky, 1860 Census*, 12, 81–83.

39. On the nature of the Civil War in Appalachia see Kenneth W. Noe and Shannon H. Wilson, *The Civil War in Appalachia: Collected Essays* (Knoxville: University of Tennessee Press, 1997); John C. Inscoe and Gordon B. McKinney, *The Heart of Confederate Appalachia* (Chapel Hill: University of North Carolina Press, 2000); Martin Crawford, *Ashe*

County's Civil War: Community and Society in the Appalachian South (Charlottesville: University of Virginia Press, 2001); Noel C. Fisher, *War at Every Door: Partisan Politics and Guerrilla Violence in East Tennessee, 1860–1869* (Chapel Hill: University of North Carolina Press, 1997); Philip Paludan, *Victims: A True Story of the Civil War* (Knoxville: University of Tennessee Press, 1981); Keith S. Bohannon, "The Northeast Georgia Mountains during the Secession Crisis and the Civil War" (Ph.D. diss., Pennsylvania State University, 2001); Bryan D. McKnight, *Contested Borderlands: The Civil War in Appalachian Kentucky and Virginia* (Lexington: University of Kentucky Press, 2006).

    40. Quoted in Klotter and Mayer, *A Century of Banking*, 5.

    41. *Report of the Adjutant General of the State of Kentucky*, vol. 1, *1861–1866*, 750–752; *Report of the Adjutant General of the State of Kentucky*, vol. 2, *1861–1866* (Frankfort: Kentucky Yeoman Office, 1867), 780–791.

    42. Jess Wilson, *When They Hanged the Fiddler and Other Stories from "It Happened Here" (Including Some Unpublished Work by the Author)* (Berea, KY: Kentucke Imprints, 1978), 75.

    43. *Kentucky Acts 1867*, vol. 1, 396.

    44. D.L. Brewer, comp., *Individuals Representing Owsley County in the Kentucky State Legislature 1843–1900*, http://www.owsleyky-hist.org/individuals_representing_owsley.htm (accessed 26 November 2004); *Journal of the House of Representatives of the Commonwealth of Kentucky, 1869*, 161; *Journal of the Regular Session of the Senate of the Commonwealth of Kentucky, 1869*, 164; *Kentucky Acts 1869*, vol. 1, 14–18; Long, 272, 379. Lee County is not to be confused with a failed proposal to create a county with the same name out of portions of Allen, Barren, and Monroe counties in 1867. See *Journal of the Regular Session of the Senate of the Commonwealth of Kentucky 1867*, 465–468.

    45. *Kentucky Acts 1869*, vol. 1, 14–18.

    46. Lee County, Kentucky, Court Orders, Book 1, 10–12, 71.

    47. Ibid., 27–29, 80–81, 89.

    48. *Kentucky Acts 1871*, vol. 1, 68–70; Ireland, *Little Kingdoms: The Counties of Kentucky, 1850–1891*, 4.

    49. Lee County, Kentucky, Court Orders, Book 1, 97; Dennis L. Brewer, *The Land of Lee: The Formation and County Officials of Lee County, Kentucky, 1870–1983* (Beattyville, KY: Three Forks Heritage Series, 1983), 6–8; Ireland, *Little Kingdoms: The Counties of Kentucky, 1850–1891*, 5.

    50. Klotter and Mayer, *A Century of Bank-*

ing, 8; William E. Ellis, *The Kentucky River* (Lexington: University Press of Kentucky, 2000), 44.

    51. *Annual Report of the Auditor of Public Accounts, of the State of Kentucky for the Fiscal Year Ending October 10, 1871* (Frankfort: Kentucky Yeoman Office, 1871), 62–125; *Biennial Report of the Auditor of Public Accounts of Kentucky* (Frankfort: Kentucky Yeoman Office, 1881), 158–257. The total values for each county reflect the combination of totals for "Whites" and "Negroes." For Lee County in 1871, the "White" value was $466,604, and the "Negro" total was $1,547. The "White" value the same year in Owsley County was $496,687, and the "Negro" total was $90. In 1881, the total valuation for "Whites" in Lee County was $407,395 and $3,045 for "Colored." There were no property values reported for "Colored" in Owsley County in 1881.

    52. Leland R. Johnson and Charles E. Parrish, *Kentucky River Development: The Commonwealth's Waterway* (Louisville: Louisville Engineer District, U.S. Army Corps of Engineers, 1999), 98.

    53. Ibid. John D. White was a member of the Clay County family whose efforts to dominate their home county are detailed in Billings and Blee's *The Road to Poverty: The Making of Wealth and Hardship in Appalachia*.

    54. "The Lock and Dam," *Three Forks Enterprise*, 30 March 1888, 2.

    55. *Prospectus of the Three Forks Investment Company: Its Beattyville Town Site, with Maps, Plats, Illustrations, Etc.*, 5, 10–12; Kilduff and McGuire, *Peoples Exchange Bank 1912–1987*, 1–2, 8–11.

    56. Leland R. Johnson, *The Falls City Engineers: A History of the Louisville District, Corps of Engineers, United States Army, 1970–1983* (Louisville: United States Army Engineer District, 1984), 258–260.

    57. Soldier's Friend, "Our Future Prospects," *Three Forks Enterprise*, 30 January 1884, 2.

    58. "A Plea for Education," *Three Forks Enterprise*, 16 December 1885, 2.

    59. Lucas Moore, *Twelfth Biennial Report of the Bureau of Agriculture, Labor, and Statistics of the State of Kentucky* (Louisville: The Geo. G. Fetter Printing, 1897), 132–133.

    60. Owsley County Deed Book 1, Microfilm at the Kentucky Department of Libraries and Archives. Owsley County land records are incomplete up to 1930 due to the 1929 fire that destroyed the county courthouse and the county records contained therein. Owsley County attempted to reconstruct its land records by having known deeds reregistered.

61. Owsley County Deed Book 5.

62. Robert F. Collins, *A History of the Daniel Boone National Forest, 1770–1970* (Winchester, KY: U.S. Forest Service, 1975), 257.

63. Wilson, *This Was Yesterday*, 53–54; Klotter and Mayer, *A Century of Banking*, 8; Tyrel Gilce Moore, Jr., "An Historic Geography of Economic Development in Appalachian Kentucky, 1800–1930" (Ph.D. diss., University of Tennessee, 1984), 106; Robert M. Rennick, "The Post Offices of Owsley County, Kentucky," *La Posta: A Journal of American Postal History* 35, no. 5 (2004): 57.

64. Klotter and Mayer, *A Century of Banking*, 14; Nicholas McDowell, *Tenth Biennial Report of the Bureau of Agriculture, Labor, and Statistics of the State of Kentucky* (Louisville: The Bradley & Gilbert, Printers and Binders, 1894), 135–137.

65. Klotter and Mayer, *A Century of Banking*, 14–16.

66. Quoted in Kilduff and McGuire, *Peoples Exchange Bank, 1912–1987*, 15.

67. Ibid.; Ron D. Bryant, "Lee County," in *The Kentucky Encyclopedia*, John E. Kleber, ed., 541.

68. Johnson, *The Falls City Engineers: A History of the Louisville District, Corps of Engineers, United States Army, 1970–1983*, 265.

69. Quoted in Ibid.

70. Ibid., 270–275.

71. Ibid.

72. United States Census Bureau, *Kentucky Population of Counties by Decennial Census: 1900 to 1990*, http://www.census.gov/population/cencounts/ky190090.txt (accessed 26 April 2002).

73. Willard Rouse Jillson, *The Oil and Gas Resources of Kentucky: A Geological Review of the Past Development and Present Status of the Industry in Each of the One Hundred and Twenty Counties in the Commonwealth* (Frankfort: Department of Geology and Forestry, 1919), 1–2, 11; W.R. Jillson, *Geology of the Island Creek Oil Pool* (Frankfort: Kentucky Geological Survey, 1927), 52. Some of the Lee County gas logs are located in the Willard Rouse Jillson Collection (Berea College Archives and Special Collections, Hutchins Library, Berea College, Berea, KY), Box 12–1.

74. Owsley County Deed Book 6.

75. Owsley County Deed Book 4.

76. Ibid.; Owsley County Deed Book 1.

77. Owsley County Deed Book 4; "British Get Oil Well in Owsley," *The Courier-Journal*, 1 July 1927, sect. 1, p. 3; "New Gusher is Found in Owsley," *The Courier-Journal*, 3 July 1927, sect. 1, p. 7.

78. David A. Waples, *The Natural Gas Industry in Appalachia: A History from the First Discovery to the Maturity of the Industry* (Jefferson, NC: McFarland, 2005), 116.

79. "The Rainbow in Owsley," *The Courier-Journal*, 11 May 1926, sec. 1, 6; "British Get Oil Well in Owsley;" *The Courier-Journal*; "New Gusher Is Found in Owsley," *The Courier-Journal*.

80. "A Chance for Owsley," *The Courier-Journal*, 1 January 1925, sec. 1, 6.

81. Vance Armentrout, "Protest Heard on Owsley Dam," *The Courier-Journal*, 19 March 1925, sec. 1, n.p.

82. Ibid.

83. Memo on Projects Nos. 389, 539, 540, 566, 604, 700, 729, 904 — Kentucky; and Project No. 728, Tennessee, by the Federal Power Commission, 14 August 1928, Willard Rouse Jillson Collection, Box 8–3.

84. "The Rainbow in Owsley," *The Courier-Journal*; "British Get Oil Well in Owsley," *The Courier-Journal*.

Chapter 2

1. Robert M. Ireland, *Little Kingdoms: The Counties of Kentucky, 1850–1891* (Lexington: University Press of Kentucky, 1977), 3; "26 Pauper Counties Listed in Kentucky," *Pineville Sun*, 12 April 1934.

2. George Peak and J.E. Reeves, "Kentucky County Debts, June 30, 1938," *Bulletin of the Bureau of Business Research* 2, no. 3 (1940): 5–8.

3. Charles Seale, "Nature Has Appointed the Twilight as a Bridge to Pass Out of Night into Day," *The Owsley County News*, 1 September 1950; I.W. Gabbard Collection, Notebook 4, n.pag.

4. *County Government in Kentucky: A Report by the Efficiency Commission of Kentucky* (Frankfort: The State Journal Company, 1923), 68–76.

5. Ibid., 69.

6. Luther M. Ambrose, letter, to President Hutchins of Berea College, 20 September 1926 (Owsley County Vertical File, Berea College Archives and Special Collections).

7. *County Government in Kentucky: A Report by the Efficiency Commission of Kentucky*, 69. See also Table E for road construction statistics from a sample of counties in Kentucky. Some of the hard-surfaced roads found within the listed counties may have been national roads constructed by the U.S. government.

8. Luther M. Ambrose, letter, to President Hutchins of Berea College (Owsley

County Vertical File, Berea College Archives and Special Collections).

9. I.W. Gabbard Collection, Notebook 3, n.p.

10. "Funding Bonds Approved by Fiscal Court; To Total $80,000," *The Owsley County News*, 2 September 1949.

11. *Griffin et al. v. Clay County et al. Burchell v. Same* (Database online), transcript available from LexisNexis.

12. United States Department of Agriculture, *Soil Survey of Jackson and Owsley Counties, Kentucky*, 2, 7, 36; Mary Camille Erwin, "The Vicious Circle: A Study of the Effects of the Depression and New Deal Relief Programs in Eastern Kentucky" (master's thesis, University of Louisville, 1967), 6–7, 40–41.

13. Luther M. Ambrose, letter, to President Hutchins of Berea College (Owsley County Vertical File, Berea College Archives and Special Collections).

14. Kentucky Agricultural Statistics Service, *Owsley County, Kentucky: Agricultural Statistics: 1909–1999*, http://www.nass.usda.gov/ky/Coa/coa.htm (accessed July 15, 2005); Paul Salstrom, *Appalachia's Path to Dependency: Rethinking a Region's Economic History, 1730–1940*, 101.

15. Ibid. For statistics on the number of farms and their size in Owsley County, see Appendix A.

16. *Biennial Report of the Department of Agriculture, Labor, and Statistics, 1934–1935* (Frankfort: The Department of Agriculture, Labor, and Statistics, 1935), 146; Kentucky Agricultural Statistics Service, *Owsley County, Kentucky: Agricultural Statistics: 1909–1999*. See Appendices A, B, and C for agricultural statistics showing the changes in Owsley County's agricultural sector.

17. Erwin, "The Vicious Circle: A Study of the Effects of the Depression and New Deal Relief Programs in Eastern Kentucky," 102–105; Salstrom, *Appalachia's Path to Dependency: Rethinking a Region's Economic History, 1730–1940*, 101. For statistics on corn production in Owsley County, see Appendix C.

18. Ibid. For statistics on burley tobacco production in Owsley County, see Appendix B.

19. Jerry Bruce Thomas, *An Appalachian New Deal: West Virginia in the Great Depression* (Lexington: University Press of Kentucky, 1998), 166; Salstrom, *Appalachia's Path to Dependency: Rethinking a Region's Economic History, 1730–1940*, 94–105; Ronald D Eller, "Modernization," in *High Mountains Rising: Appalachia in Time and Place*, Richard A. Straw and H. Tyler Blethen, eds. (Urbana:

University of Illinois Press, 2004), 197–200; David E. Hamilton, *From New Day to New Deal: American Farm Policy From Hoover to Roosevelt, 1928–1933* (Chapel Hill: University of North Carolina Press, 1991), 238–250. See also Van L. Perkins, *Crisis in Agriculture: The Agricultural Adjustment Administration and the New Deal, 1993* (Berkeley: University of California Press, 1969); Theodore Saloutos, *The American Farmer and the New Deal* (Ames, IA: Iowa State University Press, 1982).

20. Erwin, "The Vicious Circle: A Study of the Effects of the Depression and New Deal Relief Programs in Eastern Kentucky," 118–120, 143–150.

21. *Griffin et al. v. Clay County et al. Burchell v. Same.*

22. Ibid.; *Farmers State Bank et al. v. Owsley County et al.* (Database online), transcript available from LexisNexis.

23. *Griffin et al. v. Clay County et al. Burchell v. Same.*

24. *Farmers State Bank et al. v. Owsley County et al.; Griffin et al. v. Clay County et al. Burchell v. Same.*

25. Quoted in *Farmers State Bank et al. v. Owsley County et al.*

26. Alan Maimon, "East Kentucky Poverty Dashes Industrial Hopes: As Business Park Falters, Owsley Co. Looks to Tourism for Salvation," *The Courier-Journal*, 22 December 2005, A1, A4.

27. Johnson, *The Falls City Engineers: A History of the Louisville District, Corps of Engineers United States Army, 1970–1983*, 154.

28. Johnson and Parrish, *Kentucky River Development*, 137–138.

29. Quoted in Ibid., 141.

30. Ibid.

31. United States Corps of Engineers, Louisville District, *Booneville Lake Ohio River Basin South Fork Kentucky River Kentucky Memorandum No. 4* (Louisville: Louisville Corps of Engineers, 1972), 19–2.

32. "January Rainfall 11 More Than 5 Months in 1936," *The Beattyville Enterprise*, 28 January 1937, 1. See Table F for the rainfall levels in Lee County in January 1937.

33. Ellis, 107–112; "Flood of 1937," in *The Kentucky Encyclopedia*, John E. Kleber, ed., 327–328; Jerry Hill, *Kentucky Weather* (Lexington: University Press of Kentucky, 2005), 58, 74–79; "Ohio Valley, Kentucky Lies Stricken: Louisville, Frankfort, Paducah and Many Kentucky Cities Devastated by Greatest Flood in History," *The Beattyville Enterprise*, 28 January 1937, 1.

34. United States Corps of Engineers, Louisville District, *Booneville Reservoir Ohio*

River Basin South Fork Kentucky River Kentucky, Design Memorandum No. 3: Structure, Site Selection (Louisville: United States Army Engineer District, Louisville, 1970), 1–1; Johnson and Parrish, *Kentucky River Development*, 151.

35. Johnson and Parrish, *Kentucky River Development*, 153.

36. Ibid.; United States Congress, House of Representatives, *Kentucky River and Tributaries, Kentucky*, 87th Cong., 2nd Session (Washington, DC: Government Printing Office, 1962), 93.

37. United States Congress, House of Representatives, *Creation of Pioneer National Monument, KY*, 73rd Cong., 2nd Session (Washington, DC: Government Printing Office, 1934), n.p.; J.T. Dorris, letter, to Judge Wilson, November 24, 1945 (Eastern Kentucky University Library, Special Collections, Eastern Kentucky University, Richmond, KY), *Pioneer National Monument Association & Fort Boonesborough State Park Association Records, 1926–1976*, Box 1; C. Frank Dunn, letter, to Tom Wallace, August 19, 1946, Tom Wallace Papers (Filson Historical Society, Louisville, KY).

38. C. Frank Dunn, letter, to Tom Wallace, August 19, 1946, Tom Wallace Papers; Resolution No. 9, Kentucky Society Daughters of the American Revolution, *Pioneer National Monument Association & Fort Boonesborough State Park Association Records, 1926–1976*, Box 1; Statement of Cassius M. Clay, of Paris, Kentucky, *Pioneer National Monument Association & Fort Boonesborough State Park Association Records, 1926–1976*, Box 2.

39. United States Corps of Engineers, Louisville District, *Booneville Lake, General Design Memorandum* (Louisville: U.S. Army Engineer District, Louisville, 1972), 1; United States Congress, House of Representatives, *Kentucky River and Tributaries, Kentucky*, 49.

40. C.H. Chorpening (assistant chief of engineers for Civil Works), letter, to Carl D. Perkins, August 22, 1951, Carl D. Perkins Papers, 1949–1984, Box D3 (Eastern Kentucky University Library, Special Collections, Eastern Kentucky University, Richmond, KY); Senator Earle C. Clements, letter, to Major General Lewis A. Pick, July 13, 1951, Carl D. Perkins Papers, 1949–1984, Box D3; "House Resolution No. 36," February 1, 1952, Carl D. Perkins Papers, 1949–1984, Box D3; C.H. Chorpening, letter, to Carl D. Perkins, February 25, 1952, Carl D. Perkins Papers, 1949–1984, Box D3; "River Flood Control Study Seen by Milne," *The Owsley County News*, 30 July 1951, 1; "Pledged Support by Sen. Cooper

of River Development Association, *The Owsley County News*, 6 November 1957, 1; Ellis, *The Kentucky River*, 30; Pioneer National Monument Association Minutes, November 18, 1954, *Pioneer National Monument Association & Fort Boonesborough State Park Association Records, 1926–1976*, Box 1. The Corps of Engineers did not officially deactivate the Jessamine Creek Dam until 1962. See Johnson and Parrish, *Kentucky River Development*, 160. On Thomas D. Clark and his influence in Kentucky, see Kleber, ed. *Thomas D. Clark of Kentucky: An Uncommon Life in the Commonwealth* (Lexington: University Press of Kentucky, 2003); Thomas D. Clark, *My Century in History: Memoirs* (Lexington: University Press of Kentucky, 2006).

41. Ellis, *The Kentucky River*, 30; "Ky. River Development Body Lays Plans at Beattyville Meeting," *The Owsley County News*, 14 August 1953, 1; "Kentucky River Development Association Sets Meeting at Natural Bridge State Park," *The Owsley County News*, 25 September 1953, 1; "Pledged Support by Sen. Cooper of River Development Association," "River Development Association Schedules Meeting at Jackson," *The Owsley County News*, 4 December 1953, 1. See Table G for the population trends in counties represented by the KRADA.

42. Ellis, *The Kentucky River*, 31.

43. Ibid.

44. "Examination of House Document 85, 73rd Congress, 1st Session: Committee Report to the Kentucky River Development Association," Carl D. Perkins Papers, 1949–1984, Box D3; C.H. Chorpening, letter, to Carl D. Perkins, February 13, 1952, Carl D. Perkins Papers, 1949–1984, Box D3; Ellis 117–118, 138–139; Hill, 71.

45. Quoted in Clennie Holon, "Ramblin through Williba," *The Owsley County News*, 25 December 1953, 2.

46. "River Development Association Recommends 11-Point Program," *The Owsley County News*, 11 December 1953, 1.

47. Johnson and Parrish, *Kentucky River Development*, 160.

48. Ibid.

49. "A Resume of Facts Leading Up to the Approval by Congress of the Red River Dam," John Sherman Cooper Collection, 1927–1972, Box 97 (University of Kentucky Libraries, Special Collections and Archives, University of Kentucky, Lexington, KY).

50. "Delegation Presses for River Flood and Navigation Projects: Arterberry and Reynolds Make Appearance before Subcommittee Urging Passage of Control Measure for East-

ern Kentucky," *Owsley County News*, 23 April 1954, 4. See Table H for the population trends between 1940 and 1970 for counties in the vicinity of the proposed Booneville Reservoir.

51. "Board of Engineers Requested to Review Reports with Idea for Improvement of Kentucky River: Senator Cooper Pledges Assistance on Dam Project," *Owsley County News*, 24 April 1953, 1.

52. Richard C. Smoot, "John Sherman Cooper: The Paradox of a Liberal Republican in Kentucky Politics," (Ph.D. diss., University of Kentucky, 1988), 118, 145, 147, 170–171, 183–185.

53. Ibid.

54. Cassius M. Clay, letter to editor, n.d., Thruston B. Morton Collection, 1933–1969, Box 188.

55. "No Opposition on River Program," *Owsley County News*, 28 May 1954, 1; "Delegation Presses for River Flood and Navigation Projects: Arterberry and Reynolds Make Appearance before Subcommittee Urging Passage of Control Measure for Eastern Kentucky," *Owsley County News*; "Delegation Presses for River Flood and Navigation Projects: Arterberry and Reynolds Make Appearance before Subcommittee Urging Passage of Control Measure for Eastern Kentucky," *The Beattyville Enterprise*, 22 April 1954, 1; "River Development Prospects Look Good," *The Beattyville Enterprise*, 10 June 1954, 1; "River Development Prospects Look Good," *Owsley County News*, 11 June 1954, 1.

56. "Petition of Objection to the Proposed Reservoir to Be Built in the South Fork of the Kentucky River Near Booneville, Kentucky," John Sherman Cooper Collection, 1927–1972, Box 2.

57. Gerald Griffin, "Reservoir Plan Draws Protest in Owsley," *Courier-Journal*, 14 June 1954, sect. 2, 1.

58. "Public Meeting for Review of the Status of the Authorized Booneville Reservoir in the Kentucky River Basin," Thruston Ballard Morton Collection, 1933–1969, Box 4. (University of Kentucky Libraries, Special Collections and Archives, University of Kentucky, Lexington, KY).

59. Leonie Barger, letter, to Eugene Siler, February 6, 1959, Tim Lee Carter Collection 1955–1983, Box 607 (Western Kentucky University Library, Special Collections, Western Kentucky University, Bowling Green, KY).

60. "Army Engineers Offer Sound Advice," *The Lexington Herald*, 8 January 1963; Statement from Congressman Siler dated January 21, 1964, Tim Lee Carter Collection, 1955–1983, Box 607; William F. Cassidy, letter, to

Eugene Siler, April 18, 1961, Tim Lee Carter Collection, 1955–1983, Box 607; John Sherman Cooper, letter, to Corrbet Baker, December 9, 1961, John Sherman Cooper Collection, 1927–1972, Box 46; "Notice of Review Report for Flood Control and Allied Purposes on the Kentucky River and Its Tributaries, Kentucky," Carl D. Perkins Papers, 1949–1984, Box D16.

61. William F. Cassidy, letter, to Eugene Siler, April 18, 1961. Senator Cooper also mentioned the requirement for "concrete evidence." See Letter from John Sherman Cooper to Corrbet Baker, December 9, 1961.

62. United States Congress, House of Representatives, *Kentucky River and Tributaries, Kentucky*, xxvii, 9, 60, 87, 97.

63. King Justice, letter, to John Sherman Cooper, January 3, 1961, John Sherman Cooper Collection, 1927–1972, Box 46; United States Census Bureau, *Kentucky Population of Counties by Decennial Census: 1900 to 1990*.

64. Lucian Burch, Wm. M. Hopper, and Denver Farmer, letter, to John Sherman Cooper, March 5, 1962, John Sherman Cooper Collection, 1927–1972, Box 46.

65. Mr. and Mrs. L.L. Mainous, letter, to John Sherman Cooper, March 22, 1962, John Sherman Cooper Collection, 1927–1972, Box 46.

66. Clay and Laura Thomas, letter, to John Sherman Cooper Collection, 1927–1972, Box 46.

67. P.S. Turner, letter, to John Sherman Cooper, March 14, 1962, John Sherman Cooper Collection, 1927–1972, Box 46.

68. King Justice, letter, to John Sherman Cooper, March 9, 1961, John Sherman Cooper Collection, 1927–1972, Box 46; G.P. Congleton, letter, to John Sherman Cooper, March 30, 1962, John Sherman Cooper Collection, 1927–1972, Box 46; G.D. Beach, letter, to John Sherman Cooper, April 17, 1962, John Sherman Cooper Collection, 1927–1972, Box 46. Many of these Beattyville elites had ties to the Peoples Exchange Bank of Beattyville, Kentucky. The Beach family had been involved as officers of the Peoples Bank since 1912. G.D. Beach was the bank's vice president from 1963 to 1964. Charles Beach, Jr., began serving as a bank officer in 1951. G.P. Congleton became a member of the bank's board of directors in 1948. G.A. Begley, who was C.M. Begley's brother, began his affiliation with the Peoples Exchange Bank in 1951. See Kilduff and McGuire, *Peoples Exchange Bank, 1912–1987*, 224–225.

69. Joe Powlas, letter, to John Sherman Cooper, March 8, 1962, John Sherman Cooper

Collection, 1927–1972, Box 46.

70. Van H. Reneau, letter, to Carl D. Perkins, May 1, 1957, Carl D. Perkins Papers, 1949–1984, Box D12.

71. King Justice, letter, to Congressman Eugene Siler, October 16, 1962, Tim Lee Carter Collection, 1955–1983, Box 607.

72. Secretary, letter, to King Justice, October 19, 1962, Tim Lee Carter Collection, 1955–1983, Box 607.

73. John Sherman Cooper, letter, to Pleasant Amis, March 20, 1962, *John* Sherman Cooper Collection, 1927–1972, Box 46.

74. Pleasant Amis, letter, to John Sherman Cooper, March 14, 1962, John Sherman Cooper Collection, 1927–1972, Box 46.

75. Ibid.

76. P.S. Turner, letter, to John Sherman Cooper, March 11, 1962, John Sherman Cooper Collection, 1927–1972, Box 46.

77. King Justice, letter, to John Sherman Cooper, October 16, 1962, John Sherman Cooper Collection, 1927–1972, Box 46.

78. "Delegation Asks Siler to Reopen Booneville Dam Project in Region," Tim Lee Carter Collection, 1955–1983, Box 607.

79. Ibid.

80. Ibid.

81. Transcript of telephone call from Eugene Siler to the Corps of Engineers, Louisville District, dated December 6, 1962, Tim Lee Carter Collection, 1955–1983, Box 607; Eugene Siler, letter, to Colonel James L. Lewis, December 6, 1962, Tim Lee Carter Collection, 1955–1983, Box 607; Eugene Siler, letter, to Mayor E.P. Rice, Manchester, Kentucky, G.P. Congleton, Beattyville, Kentucky, and Carl R. Reynolds, Booneville, Kentucky, December 6, 1962, Tim Lee Carter Collection, 1955–1983, Box 607; Major David Carter, letter, to Eugene Siler, December 11, 1962, Tim Lee Carter Collection, 1955–1983, Box 607.

82. "Resolution of the Jackson Kiwanis Club," Thruston Ballard Morton Collection, 1933–1969, Box 4.

83. "Resolution Favoring Construction of Booneville Dam," Tim Lee Carter Collection, 1955–1983, Box 607.

84. Mart V. Mainous, letter, to Eugene Siler, December 26, 1962, Tim Lee Carter Collection, 1955–1983, Box 607.

85. "Public Meeting for Review of the Status of the Authorized Booneville Reservoir in the Kentucky River Basin," Thruston Ballard Morton Collection, 1933–1969, Box 4.

86. Ibid., 10–11.

87. Ibid.

88. Ibid., 17–19.

89. Ibid., 20.

90. Ibid., 23.

91. Ibid.

92. Ibid., 24.

93. Ibid., 22–25.

94. Ibid., 31–32.

95. Quoted in "Army Engineers Offer Sound Advice," *The Lexington Herald*, 8 January 1963.

96. "Public Meeting for Review of the Status of the Authorized Booneville Reservoir in the Kentucky River Basin," Thruston Ballard Morton Collection, 1933–1969, Box 4, 27–28.

97. Ibid., 30–31.

98. Quoted in "Sharp Protests Evidenced at Public Hearing Friday Concerning Booneville Dam: Minister Charges 'Lying' in Reopening Dam Project," Tim Lee Carter Collection, 1955–1983, Box 607.

99. "Army Engineers Offer Sound Advice," *The Lexington Herald*, 8 January 1963; Fred W. Luigart, Jr., "Owsley, Clay County Groups Clash Over Proposal for Booneville Dam," Tim Lee Carter Collection, 1955–1983, Box 607. The tag line to Luigart's article states that he worked for the *Courier-Journal*, East Frankfort Bureau.

100. Frankfort Chamber of Commerce, "A Resolution Endorsing the Construction of a Dam at Booneville, Kentucky, by the United States Government," Tim Lee Carter Collection, 1955–1983, Box 607.

101. George Long, letter, to Eugene Siler, January 7, 1963, Tim Lee Carter Collection, 1955–1983, Box 607.

102. Joe Powlas, interview by author, 12 January 2006, Booneville, KY, tape recording in the possession of the author.

Chapter 3

1. Ronald D Eller, "Modernization, 1940–2000," in *High Mountains Rising: Appalachia in Time and Place*, Richard A. Straw and H. Tyler Blethen, eds., 197–200. On the outmigration from Appalachia, see Chad Berry, *Southern Migrants, Northern Exiles* (Urbana: University of Illinois Press, 2000); Kathryn M. Borman, and Phillip J. Obermiller, eds., *From Mountain to Metropolis: Appalachian Migrants in American Cities* (Westport: Bergin and Garvey, 1994); Phillip J. Obermiller, Thomas E. Wagner, and Bruce Tucker, eds., *Appalachian Odyssey: Historical Perspectives on the Great Migration* (Westport: Praeger, 2000); William Philliber, *Appalachian Migrants in*

Urban America (Westport: Praeger, 1981); William W. Philliber, and Clyde B. McCoy, eds., *The Invisible Minority: Urban Appalachians* (Lexington: University Press of Kentucky, 1981).

2. Quote in Taul, 43.

3. Ibid., 42–90.

4. Quote in Ronald D Eller, "Modernization, 1940–2000," 201–202.

5. Quotes from "Back to the Beginnings in Eastern Kentucky," *The Louisville Courier-Journal*, 19 March 1963, 6; Eller, "Modernization, 1940–2000," 205; "One Dead, Thousands Homeless as Flooding Brings More Misery to Eastern Kentucky: Weekend Rains Hit as Area Recovering from Earlier Damage," *The Lexington Herald*, 18 March 1963, 1; Michael Harrington, *The Other America: Poverty in the United States* (Baltimore: Penguin Books, 1963); Harry M. Caudill, *Night Comes to the Cumberlands: A Biography of a Depressed Area* (Boston: Little, Brown, 1962); Jack Weller, *Yesterday's People: Life in Contemporary Appalachia* (Lexington: University of Kentucky Press, 1965).

6. "State of the Union Address, Lyndon B. Johnson, January 8, 1964," in Gwendolyn Mink and Alice O'Connor, eds., *Poverty in the United States* (Denver: ABC-Clio, 2004), 778–779.

7. Council of Economic Advisors, *Economic Report of 1964* (Washington, DC: Government Printing Office, 1964), 55.

8. Robert Dallek, *Flawed Giant: Lyndon Johnson and His Times, 1961–1973* (New York: Oxford University Press, 1998), 74.

9. Thomas J. Kiffmeyer, "From Self-Help to Sedition: The Appalachian Volunteers in Eastern Kentucky, 1964–1970," *The Journal of Southern History* 64 (1998): 67; Ronald D Eller, "Modernization, 1940–2000," 207–210; "100 Million Expected in Federal Funds," *The Beattyville Enterprise*, 13 January 1966, 1.

10. "Economic Justification for Grant and Loan to Finance Water Treatment Plant, Water Distribution System, Water Storage Tanks, Sewage Treatment Plant and Sewage Collection System for Town of Booneville, Kentucky," John Sherman Cooper Collection, 1927–1972, Box 127.

11. "The Application for the Program Development Grant for Owsley County Community Action Committee Inc," September 1965," Carl D. Perkins Papers, 1949–1984, Box D47; Douglas O'Neil Arnett, "Eastern Kentucky: The Politics of Dependency and Underdevelopment" (Ph.D. diss., Duke University, 1978), 188. The origin of the claim that Owsley County was the second poorest

county in the United States cannot be determined, though it appeared regularly within the county during the 1960s; see letter from T.C. Sizemore to Carl D. Perkins, October 1, 1965, Carl D. Perkins Papers, 1949–1984, Box D47; Pat Sizemore, "War on Poverty Lost!" *The Peoples Journal*, 7 April 1966, 1. According to the United States Census Bureau's 1960 Census of Population, the ten poorest counties in the United States were: (1) Wade-Hampton, Alaska (2) Wolfe, Kentucky (3) Magoffin, Kentucky (4) Fayette, Tennessee (5) Owsley, Kentucky (6) Webster, Georgia (7) Hancock, Tennessee (8) Leslie, Kentucky (9) Jefferson, Mississippi (10) Issaquena, Mississippi. See United States Census Bureau, *1960 Census of Population: Supplementary Reports, Nos. 36–56* (Washington, DC: Government Printing Office, 1963). According to the United States Department of Agriculture's Economic Research Service, the ten poorest counties in the United States in 1960 were: (1) Wade-Hampton, Alaska (2) Issaquena, Mississippi (3) Leslie, Kentucky (4) Starr, Texas (5) Mora, New Mexico (6) Jefferson, Mississippi (7) McCreary, Kentucky (8) Wilcox, Alabama (9) Carroll, Mississippi (10) Greene, Alabama. Owsley County appeared in the ranking at number 26; see Robert Gibbs, USDA Economic Research Service, *RE: 10 Poorest U.S. Counties in 1960*, personal e-mail (12 September 2005).

12. "The Application for the Program Development Grant for Owsley County Community Action Committee Inc, September 1965;" T.C. Sizemore, letter, to Carl D. Perkins, October 1, 1965, Carl D. Perkins Papers, 1949–1984. Sizemore used the term "Appalachian Program" to describe both the OEO and Appalachian Regional Commission.

13. Ibid.

14. "Owsley Loses Neighborhood Youth Corps, Courthouse Repairs, Grants," *The Peoples Journal*, 24 February 1966, 1.

15. T.C. Sizemore, Western Union telegram, to Carl D. Perkins, October 15, 1965, Carl D. Perkins Papers, 1949–1984, Box D47.

16. "Office of Economic Opportunity: Breathitt, Lee, Wolfe and Owsley Counties, Kentucky," Carl D. Perkins Papers, 1949–1984, Box D47; "Middle Kentucky River Council Wins U.S. Development Grant: Four-County Area Will Receive Funds," *The Jackson Times*, 10 February 1966, 1.

17. Joe Creason, "Sheriff on the Spot: His Car Blown Up Twice, Clay County's T.C. Sizemore Says He Will Continue Crusade — Even if It Kills Him," *Louisville Courier-Journal*, 1 March 1959 (*Louisville Courier-*

Journal clipping file, the *Courier-Journal* library).

18. Quoted in "Clay Sheriff's Home Hit by Blast, Fire," *Louisville Courier-Journal*, 29 March 1960 (*Louisville Courier-Journal* clipping file, the *Courier-Journal* library).

19. Quoted in Creason, "Sheriff on the Spot: His Car Blown Up Twice, Clay County's T.C. Sizemore Says He Will Continue Crusade — Even if It Kills Him," *Louisville Courier-Journal*.

20. "Clay Sheriff's Home Hit by Blast, Fire;" Creason, "Sheriff on the Spot," *Louisville Courier-Journal*; "Blast Link to Raids Is Hinted," *Louisville Courier-Journal*, 5 April 1958 (*Louisville Courier-Journal* clipping file, the *Courier-Journal* library); "Probers Seek Dynamiters of Clay Sheriff's Car: Auto Blasted at Manchester while Officer Was Absent; News Offices Also Damaged," *Louisville Courier-Journal*, 5 April 1958 (*Louisville Courier-Journal* clipping file, the *Courier-Journal* library; "Clay Sheriff Presses Drive on Bootlegging: Despite Dynamiting of His Car, Officer Jails 35 — An All Time High — After Raids," *Louisville Courier-Journal*, 8 April 1958 (*Louisville Courier-Journal* clipping file, the *Courier-Journal* library; "Blast Rips Sheriff's Automobile: Clay Officer Narrowly Escapes Death," *Louisville Courier-Journal*, 4 February 1959 (*Louisville Courier-Journal* clipping file, the *Courier-Journal* library; "3 Indicted in Dynamiting of Sheriff's Car," *Louisville Courier-Journal*, 7 February 1959 (*Louisville Courier-Journal* clipping file, the *Courier-Journal* library).

21. Creason, "Sheriff on the Spot," *Louisville Courier-Journal*.

22. "Owsley Oracle Leads County Astray," *The Jackson Times*, 20 January 1966, 1; "Owsley Oracle Leads County Astray," *The Beattyville Enterprise*, 27 January 1966, 1.

23. United States Congress, House of Representatives, *Administration and Conduct of Antipoverty Programs: Hearings before the Committee on Education and Labor*, 91st Cong., 1st Session (Washington, DC: Government Printing Office, 1969), 70, 76–77; "Jackson Banker to Head Council For Development in 4 Counties: Whisman Addresses Beattyville Confab," *The Jackson Times*, 7 October 1965, 1; Eve Edstrom, "OEO Overrides Nunn's Veto," *The Washington Post*, October 8, 1969, A8.

24. United States Congress, House of Representatives, *Administration and Conduct of Antipoverty Programs: Hearings before the Committee on Education and Labor*, 20.

25. Ibid., 76–77; 134, 165.

26. Quoted in Tom Loftus, "Treva Turner

Howell, 1923–2004: Breathitt Political Heir Dies Following Surgery," *Louisville Courier-Journal*, 4 September 2004, B1.

27. Malcolm E. Jewell and Everett W. Cunningham, *Kentucky Politics* (Lexington: University of Kentucky Press, 1968), 54–55; Arnett, "Eastern Kentucky: The Politics of Dependence and Underdevelopment," 70–72; Bill Estep, "Daughter Continued Parents' Legacy of Working to Improve Breathitt County," *Lexington Herald-Leader*, 31 December 2004, B7.

28. "Nation's Magazine Disgraces Neighboring County," *The Peoples Journal*, 10 February 1966, 1; "Jeff Howell Elected Bank's Executive," *The Jackson Times*, 8 February 1968, 1; "Feud in the Hills," *Time*, September 12, 1969, 21; United States Congress, House of Representatives, *Administration and Conduct of Antipoverty Programs: Hearings before the Committee on Education and Labor*, 257–259; John Ed Pearce, "A Dynastic Family at the Crossroads," *Louisville Courier-Journal & Times Magazine*, 30 August 1970, 8–15; Arnett, "Eastern Kentucky: The Politics of Dependence and Underdevelopment," 71–72.

29. United States Census Bureau, *Kentucky Population of Counties by Decennial Census: 1900–1990*, http://www.census.gov/population/cencounts/ky190090.txt (accessed April 26, 2002).

30. "Mrs. Johnson Visits Poverty Area: In Hills of Kentucky, She Discusses Relief Plans," *New York Times*, 22 May 1964, 16; "Nation's Magazine Disgraces Neighboring County, *The Peoples Journal*;" William F. Haddad, "Mr. Shriver and the Savage Politics of Poverty," *Harper's*, December 1965, 48.

31. William F. Haddad, "Mr. Shriver and the Savage Politics of Poverty," *Harper's*, December 1965, 48.

32. Ibid.; "Nations Magazine Disgraces Neighboring County, *The Peoples Journal*, 1.

33. The "Happy Pappies" program was authorized by the Economic Opportunity Act of 1965 and was designed to provide a salary and job training to unemployed men who had children; see Carol Crowe-Carraco, "Happy Pappies," in John E. Kleber, ed., *The Kentucky Encyclopedia*.

34. "Owsley Loses Neighborhood Youth Corps, Courthouse Repairs, Grants," *The Peoples Journal*; Pat Sizemore, "Water and Sewer First," *The Peoples Journal*, 20 January 1966, 1.

35. "Humphrey, Breathitt Assure Owsley Needs Top Priority," *The Peoples Journal*, 6 January 1966, 1; "Owsley Loses Neighborhood Youth Corps, Courthouse Repairs, Grants,"

The Peoples Journal; "Booneville Dam Must Be Built," *The Lexington Herald,* 22 March 1966; "Congressman Ford Asks GOP to Look into Misuse of OEO Funds Locally," *The Peoples Journal,* 14 April 1966, 1; "We Like Gov. Breathitt's Concept of the Local OEO," *The Peoples Journal,* 5 May 1966, 1; "Gov. Breathitt Urges Owsley Re-Organize OEO Group," *The Peoples Journal,* 5 May 1966, 1; "$25,000 Grant Announced for Area," *The Peoples Journal,* 8 December 1966; "Area Development vs. Red-Tape Politics," *The Courier-Journal,* 30 April 1972, reprinted in *The Peoples Journal,* 4 May 1972, 3.

36. Ibid.

37. Quoted in "We Like Gov. Breathitt's Concept of the Local OEO," *The Peoples Journal.*

38. T.C. Sizemore, "Out on a Limb: Lake Daniel Boone," *The Peoples Journal,* 8 December, 1965 1; Pat Sizemore, "Regardless of the Consequences," *The Peoples Journal,* 30 June 1966, 1; The positive relationship between the parties is evident in most 1964–1965 issues of *The Peoples Journal.*

39. Pat Sizemore, "Are They Pocketing Your Money?" *The Peoples Journal,* 15 September 1966, 1; "Attorney General Matthews Rules City, County, Schools Publish Financial Statement," *The Peoples Journal,* 20 October 1966, 1; T.C. Sizemore, telephone interview by the author, 2 January 2006.

40. Pat Sizemore, "Regardless of the Consequences," *The Peoples Journal.* Pat Sizemore capitalized certain words for emphasis.

41. "Dr. Sparks Says VISTA May Use School," *The Peoples Journal,* 14 July 1966, 2; "Letter to the Editor from Sargent Shriver," *The Peoples Journal,* 30 June 1966, 1; Quote in "We'll Teach Under the Trees, VISTA Students Say," *The Courier-Journal,* 29 June 1966, A1; "Owsley Refuses Schools for Poverty Programs," *The Courier-Journal,* 27 June 1966, A19. On the experiences of the VISTA volunteers in Eastern Kentucky, see Thomas J. Kiffmeyer, "From Self-Help to Sedition: The Appalachian Volunteers in Eastern Kentucky, 1964–1970," *The Journal of Southern History* 64 (1998), 65–94.

42. Quoted in "We'll Teach Under the Trees, VISTA Students Say," *The Courier-Journal.*

43. Ibid.; "Dr. Sparks Says VISTA May Use School," *The Peoples Journal;* "Owsley Refuses Schools for Poverty Programs," *The Courier-Journal.*

44. Jim Hampton, "City without Water: Owsley County Courthouse Is Destroyed by Fire," *The Courier-Journal,* 6 January 1967.

45. Ibid.; T.C. Sizemore, "Editorial Comment," *The Peoples Journal,* 21 October 1971, 6.

46. Pat Sizemore, "What's the Clique Up to Now?" *The Peoples Journal,* 26 January 1967, 1; "No Chance Owsley Will Be Divided," *The Peoples Journal,* 9 February 1967, 1.

47. "Morton Says Government Aid for Building Courthouse Slim," *The Peoples Journal,* 19 January 1967, 1.

48. "Judge A.M. Bell Raps Courthouse Revenue Bond," *The Peoples Journal,* 7 October 1971, 1.

49. "Courthouse Discussed Here by Citizens," *The Beattyville Enterprise,* 17 October 1968, 6; "Businessmen Support Owsley County Courthouse Bond Vote," *The Beattyville Enterprise,* 24 October 1968, 1; "Bonds Only Way for Courthouse," *The Beattyville Enterprise,* 24 October 1968, 2.

50. "Special Circuit Judge to Hear Courthouse Bond Contest," *The Peoples Journal,* 9 January 1969, 1.

51. "Judge A.M. Bell Opposes Courthouse Revenue Bond," *The Peoples Journal,* 9 October 1969, 1.

52. Ibid.; "An Editorial," *The Peoples Journal,* 25 September 1969, 1.

53. "Judge A.M. Bell Opposes Courthouse Revenue Bond," *The Peoples Journal;* "Owsley Plans New High School Building," *The Peoples Journal,* 20 November 1969, 1; Pat Sizemore, "Are They Pocketing Your Money?" *The Peoples Journal;* "Attorney General Matthews Rules City, County, Schools Publish Financial Statement," *The Peoples Journal;* "New Judge, Court Shuffle," *The Peoples Journal.*

54. "New Judge, Court Shuffle," *The Peoples Journal.*

55. "An Editorial," *The Peoples Journal,* 22 October 1970, 1. The words were capitalized in the editorial.

56. Ibid.

57. "Voters — Let's Face Facts," *The Peoples Journal,* 29 October 1970, 1.

58. "Federal Grant of $200,000 Is Being Processed to Build New Courthouse Here," *The Peoples Journal,* 28 October 1971, 1; Elijah Campbell, letter, to John Sherman Cooper, March 24, 1972, John Sherman Cooper Collection, 1927–1972, Box 127.

59. Pat Sizemore, "War on Poverty Lost," *The Peoples Journal;* "Carl R. Reynolds Heads Owsley Group Asking Funds for Booneville Dam," *The Peoples Journal,* 5 May 1966, 1; United States Congress, House of Representatives, *Administration and Conduct of Antipoverty Programs: Hearings before the Committee on Education and Labor,* 77.

60. "Carter Disappointed," *The Peoples*

Journal, 24 February 1966, 1. Reprints undated letter from Tim Lee Carter to Sargent Shriver. Based on the contents of the letter, it was written sometime between February 10 and February 24, 1966.

61. "War on Poverty Lost," *The Peoples Journal,* 1.

62. T.C. Sizemore, letter, to Gene Siler, Jr., April 25, 1966, Tim Lee Carter Collection, 1955–1983, Box 193.

63. Ibid.; Telephone message from Carl Reynolds, May 26, 1966, Tim Lee Carter Collection, 1955–1983, Box 193; "Carter Carries Owsley by 18 Votes, Cooper — Brown Wins in Landslide," *The Peoples Journal,* 26 May 1966, 1; T.C. Sizemore, letter, to Tim Lee Carter, January 15, 1968, Tim Lee Carter Collection, 1955–1983, Box 193.

64. "Congressman Ford Asks GOP to Look into Misuse of OEO Funds Locally," *The Peoples Journal,* 14 April 1966, 1.

65. Quoted in "Washington O.E.O. Sharply Criticizes MKRADC," *The Peoples Journal,* 3 August 1967, 1.

66. William Greider, "Wrath of Rep. Perkins Saves Four Counties' Poverty Funds," *Louisville Courier-Journal,* 6 March 1968, 1.

67. Quoted in Arnett, "Eastern Kentucky: The Politics of Dependence and Underdevelopment," 248.

68. Greider, "Wrath of Rep. Perkins Saves Four Counties' Poverty Funds," *Louisville Courier-Journal,* 1; Arnett, "Eastern Kentucky: The Politics of Dependence and Underdevelopment," 248.

69. United States Congress, House of Representatives, *Administration and Conduct of Antipoverty Programs: Hearings before the Committee on Education and Labor,* 227; "Area Council Has Interim Director," *The Jackson Times,* 5 December 1968, 1; "Area Council Cans Director," *The Beattyville Enterprise,* 5 December 1968, 1.

70. United States Congress, House of Representatives, *Administration and Conduct of Antipoverty Programs: Hearings before the Committee on Education and Labor,* 76–77; "MKR Board Votes to Hire Treva Howell as Director," *The Jackson Times,* 23 January 1969, 1; William Turner, Jerry Reynolds, Wise Turner, Viola Harold and Virginia Reynolds, letter, to John Sherman Cooper, January 28, 1969, John Sherman Cooper Collection, 1927–1972, Box 253; "Poverty: Feud in the Hills," *Time,* 12 September, 1969, 21.

71. "MKR Board Votes to Hire Treva Howell as Director," *The Jackson Times,* 1; "Poverty: Feud in the Hills," *Time,* 21.

72. "Nunn Vetoes OEO Funds," *The Peo-*

ples Journal, 10 July 1969, 3; "Poverty: Feud in the Hills," *Time,* 21; Bill Peterson, "4-County Poverty Panel Funds Vetoed by Nunn," *The Courier-Journal,* 19 July 1969, A1; "Breathitt Feud Can Only Hurt the Poor," *The Courier-Journal,* 23 July 1969, A6; "U.S. Officials Arrive to Start Anti-Poverty Probe," *The Peoples Journal,* 31 July 1969, 1; John Herbers, "Nixon Faces Struggle in House Over Shift in Poverty Program," *The New York Times,* 16 March 1969, 42; Edward C. Burks, "Perkins Asks a 5-Year Extension of Federal Poverty Program," *The New York Times,* 25 March 1969, 28; United States Congress, House of Representatives, *Administration and Conduct of Antipoverty Programs: Hearings before the Committee on Education and Labor,* 11–12, 29, 70–72.

73. "Poverty: Feud in the Hills," *Time,* 21; "Nunn Vetoes OEO Funds," *Peoples Journal*; "U.S. Officials Arrive to Start Anti-Poverty Probe," *The Peoples Journal,* 1; Herbers, "Nixon Faces Struggle in House Over Shift in Poverty Program," *The New York Times,* 42; Burks, "Perkins Asks a 5-Year Extension of Federal Poverty Program," *The New York Times,* 28.

74. United States Congress, House of Representatives, *Administration and Conduct of Antipoverty Programs: Hearings before the Committee on Education and Labor,* 227–228; "Officials Arrive to Start Anti-Poverty Probe," *The Courier Journal,* 29 July 1969, B22; Bill Peterson, "OEO Moves to Settle Breathitt Controversy," *The Courier-Journal,* 24 July 1969, C1; Statement by Gov. Louie B. Nunn Regarding Middle Kentucky River OEO Project, 28 July 1969 (University of Kentucky Libraries, Special Collections and Archives, University of Kentucky, Lexington, KY), Governor Louie B. Nunn Records, Box 61. Mr. Cheney is currently vice president of the United States of America.

75. Bill Peterson, "U.S. Officials Overrule Gov. Nunn's Fund Cutoff to 4-County Poverty Unit," *The Courier-Journal,* 4 October 1969, A1.

76. Quoted in United States Congress, House of Representatives, *Administration and Conduct of Antipoverty Programs: Hearings before the Committee on Education and Labor,* 30.

77. Quoted in Edstrom, "OEO Overrides Nunn's Veto," *The Washington Post,* A8.

78. Quoted in United States Congress, House of Representatives, *Administration and Conduct of Antipoverty Programs: Hearings before the Committee on Education and Labor,* 2.

79. Ibid., 2–65.

80. Ibid., 11–12, 69. The use of guns by supporters of the Turner family was not a new phenomenon in the 1960s; see John Ed Pearce,

Divide and Dissent: Kentucky Politics 1930–1963 (Lexington: University Press of Kentucky, 1987), 50. See also Appendix D for a transcription of the detailed charges that Governor Nunn entered into the official record of the hearings.

81. Quoted in United States Congress, House of Representatives, *Administration and Conduct of Antipoverty Programs: Hearings before the Committee on Education and Labor,* 87.

82. Ibid., 134.

83. Ibid., 12, 30.

84. Ibid., 252–257; "The Sweet Aroma of Molasses Making Permeates Air in Vancleve Area," *The Jackson Times,* 10 October 1968, 1.

85. United States Congress, House of Representatives, *Administration and Conduct of Antipoverty Programs: Hearings before the Committee on Education and Labor,* 250–252.

86. Ibid., 251.

87. Quoted in Ibid., 252.

88. Michael Janofsky, "Pessimism Retains Grip on Appalachian Poor," *The New York Times,* 9 February 1998, A13.

Chapter 4

1. "Economic Justification for Grant and Loan to Finance Water Treatment Plant, Water Distribution System, Water Storage Tanks, Sewage Treatment Plant and Sewage Collection System for Town of Booneville Kentucky," John Sherman Cooper Collection, 1927–1972, Box 127.

2. Ibid.

3. Ibid.

4. "Preliminary Report and Estimate of Costs of Water Treatment Plant, Water Distribution System Water, Storage Tanks, Sewage Treatment Plant and Sewage Collection System for Town of Booneville Kentucky," John Sherman Cooper Collection, 1927–1972, Box 127.

5. Ibid.; "Booneville Water-Sewer Construction Starts," *The Jackson Times,* 8 February 1968, 6; "$152,000 EDA Check Comes to Booneville," *The Jackson Times,* 2 May 1968, 4; "Booneville Water and Sewer System Beginning to Take Form," *The Jackson Times,* 9 May 1968, 6.

6. Ross B. Manley, letter, to Charles E. Long, July 20, 1970, John Sherman Cooper Collection, 1927–1972, Box 127.

7. Ibid.; Charles E. Long, letter, to Ross B. Manley, August 20, 1970, John Sherman Cooper Collection, 1927–1972, Box 127; Charles E. Long, letter, to Robert A. Podesta,

August 20, 1970, John Sherman Cooper Collection, 1927–1972, Box 127; Charles E. Long, letter, to John Sherman Cooper, August 20, 1970, John Sherman Cooper Collection, 1927–1972, Box 127; Thomas P. Dunne, letter, to John Sherman Cooper, September 22, 1970, John Sherman Cooper Collection, 1927–1972, Box 127.

8. "Carl R. Reynolds Heads Owsley Group Asking Funds for Booneville Dam," *The Peoples Journal*; "Gov. Breathitt Urges Owsley Re-Organize OEO Group," *The Peoples Journal.*

9. *General Design Memorandum Booneville Lake, Ohio River Basin, South Fork Kentucky River, Kentucky, Design Memorandum No. 4,* 1–3, 3–1–3–2; Charles E. Long, letter, to Tim Lee Carter, April 30, 1966, Tim Lee Carter Collection, 1955–1983, Box 310; United States Congress, House of Representatives, Public Works Appropriation Bill, 1965, 88th Cong., 2nd Session (Washington, DC, Government Printing Office, 1964), 18; United States Congress, House of Representatives, Public Works Appropriation Bill, 1966, 89th Cong., 1st Session (Washington, DC, Government Printing Office, 1965), 17.

10. *General Design Memorandum Booneville Lake, Ohio River Basin, South Fork Kentucky River, Kentucky, Design Memorandum No. 4,* 3–1; "Council Seeks Change to 'Daniel Boone Lake,'" *The Jackson Times,* 9 December 1965, 1; "House Resolution No. 36," January 26, 1966, Tim Lee Carter Collection, 1955–1983, Box 310.

11. Ibid.

12. "Owsley Loses Neighborhood Youth Corps, Courthouse Repairs, Grants," *The Peoples Journal.*

13. Tim Lee Carter, letter, to R.S. Bowman, February 7, 1966, John Sherman Cooper Collection, *1927–1972,* Box 46.

14. "Owsley Loses Neighborhood Youth Corps, Courthouse Repairs, Grants," *The Peoples Journal*; "Rep. Perkins Says He Will Fight to Get Lake Daniel Boone O'Ked," *The Peoples Journal,* 17 February 1966, 1.

15. "Booneville Dam Awaits Federal Funds; Much Depends on Vietnam," *Lexington Leader,* 18 February 1966; "Construction of the Booneville Dam Contingent upon Viet Nam War: Area Impoundment Would Dwarf Buckhorn," *The Jackson Times,* 24 February 1966, 1; Clarence M. Begley, letter, to John Sherman Cooper, February 28, 1966, John Sherman Cooper Collection, 1927–1972, Box 46.

16. John Sherman Cooper, file copy of letter, April 15, 1966, John Sherman Cooper Collection, 1927–1972, Box 46; "Lake Daniel

Boone Development Committee," 26 April 1966, John Sherman Cooper Collection, 1927–1972, Box 46; D. Ray Gillespie, letter, to John Sherman Cooper, April 26, 1966, John Sherman Cooper Collection, 1927–1972, Box 46; "Carl R. Reynolds Heads Owsley Group Asking Funds for Booneville Dam: Col. Begley Represents Lee County," *The Peoples Journal*; Charles Long, letter, to Tim Lee Carter, April 30, 1966, Tim Lee Carter Collection, 1955–1983, Box 310; Fred Callahan, letter, to Tim Lee Carter, April 30, 1966, Tim Lee Carter Collection, 1955–1983, Box 310. See Appendix G for a list of the attendees at the April 26, 1966, meeting.

17. "Carl R. Reynolds Heads Owsley Group Asking Funds for Booneville Dam: Col. Begley Represents Lee County," *The Peoples Journal*.

18. Ibid.

19. Ibid.

20. Ibid.

21. "Statement of Senator John Sherman Cooper before Senate and House Appropriations Subcommittees on Fiscal 1967 Budget Recommendations for Kentucky Corps of Engineers Projects, May 3–4, 1966," Thruston Ballard Morton Collection, 1933–1969, Box 10. See Appendix F for the transcription of Senator Cooper's statement.

22. Ibid.

23. For examples see the letter from Monroe E. Barrett to John S. Cooper, February 10, 1966, John Sherman Cooper Collection, 1927–1972, Box 46; Kenneth Marshall, letter, to Tim Lee Carter, May 8, 1968, Tim Lee Carter Collection, 1955–1983, Box 310.

24. Agnes Peters, letter, to Hon. J.S. Cooper, March 4, 1966, John Sherman Cooper Collection, 1927–1972, Box 46.

25. Letter from D.L. Measel to John Sherman Cooper, December 12, 1966, John Sherman Cooper Collection, 1927–1972, Box 46.

26. James F. Bowman, letter, to John Sherman Cooper, March 16, 1967, John Sherman Cooper Collection, 1927–1972, Box 46.

27. John Sherman Cooper, letter, to Honorable Oakley Wilson, May 5, 1967, John Sherman Cooper Collection, 1927–1972, Box 46; C. Beach, Jr., letter, to Carl D. Perkins, May 2, 1968, Carl D. Perkins Papers, 1949–1984, Box D56; Malcolm H. Holliday, Jr., letter, to Carl D. Perkins, December 9, 1968, Carl D. Perkins Papers, 1949–1984, Box D56.

28. Kilduff and McGuire, 135–136.

29. *Kentucky River Area Development District, Honoring Our Pioneers and Recognizing*

Our Leaders: Twentieth Annual Meeting (Hazard, Kentucky River Area Development District: n.p., 1988); "Eight Counties Combine Forces to Form Development Board," *The Jackson Times*, 16 May 1968, 1; "Holliday Accepts Kentucky River District Development Post," *The Jackson Times*, 29 August 1968, 1.

30. *Kentucky River Area Development District, Honoring Our Pioneers and Recognizing Our Leaders: Twentieth Annual Meeting*; Malcolm H. Holliday, Jr., letter, to John Sherman Cooper, December 9, 1968, John Sherman Cooper Collection, 1927–1972, Box 46; John Sherman Cooper, letter, to Thomas W. Eversole, March 16, 1967, John Sherman Cooper Collection, 1927–1972, Box 46; "Senate Approves $230,000 for Booneville Dam Planning," *The Peoples Journal*, 4 December 1969, 1; U.S. Congress, House of Representatives, *Public Works Appropriation, 1970*, 91st Cong., 1st Session (Washington, DC: Government Printing Office, 1969), 8.

31. Joe Powlas, letter, to John Sherman Cooper, January 5, 1970, John Sherman Cooper Collection, 1927–1972, Box 46.

32. "Statement by Kentucky River Area Development District, Inc., Booneville-Owsley County Planning Commission, Jackson-Breathitt County Planning Commission, Campton-Wolfe County Planning Commission, City of Beattyville Planning Commission, Prepared for the Subcommittee on Public Works Appropriations, United States Senate, May 6, 1970," John Sherman Cooper Collection, 1927–1972, Box 46. See also letter from Jerry F. Howell to John Sherman Cooper, May 1, 1970, John Sherman Cooper Collection, 1927–1972, Box 46.

33. "$245,000 in '72 Budget for Booneville Lake," *The Peoples Journal*, 25 February 1971, 4.

34. Collins, *A History of the Daniel Boone National Forest, 1770–1970*, 270–279; "A Resume of Facts Leading Up to the Approval by Congress of the Red River Dam," John Sherman Cooper Collection, 1927–1972, Box 97. For images of the Red River Gorge's natural beauty, see Eliot Porter, "The Red River Gorge — One Final Look," *Audubon* 70, no. 5 (September/October 1968): 58–70; Wendell Berry, *The Unforeseen Wilderness: Kentucky's Red River Gorge* (San Francisco: North Point Press, 1991); John W. Snell, *Red River Gorge: The Eloquent Landscape* (Morley, MO: Acclaim Press, 2006).

35. United States Congress, House of Representatives, *Kentucky River and Tributaries, Kentucky*, 87th Cong., 2nd Session; Colonel James L. Lewis, letter, February 15, 1963, John

Sherman Cooper Collection, 1927–1972, Box 97.

36. James Crowe, letter, to Honorable John Sherman Cooper, April 25, 1966, John Sherman Cooper Collection, 1927–1972, Box 97; Vandetta L. Derickson, letter, to John Sherman Cooper, January 22, 1964, John Sherman Cooper Collection, 1927–1972, Box 97; R. Foster Adams, letter, to Senator John Sherman Cooper, July 27, 1962, John Sherman Cooper Collection, 1927–1972, Box 97; House Resolution No. 81, Regular Session 1962, John Sherman Cooper Collection, Box 97.

37. Summary of Public Meeting at Stanton, Kentucky, 15 March 1963, Red River Reservoir, John Sherman Cooper Collection, Box 97.

38. For information on the Sierra Club's efforts to save the Hetch Hetchy Valley, see John Warfield Simpson, *Dam!: Water, Power, Politics, and Preservation in Hetch Hetchy and Yosemite National Park* (New York: Pantheon Books, 2005), and Robert W. Righter, *The Battle Over Hetch Hetchy: America's Most Controversial Dam and the Birth of Modern Environmentalism* (New York: Oxford University Press, 2005).

39. Mark W.T. Harvey, "Echo Park, Glen Canyon, and the Postwar Wilderness Movement," *The Pacific Historical Review* 60, no. 1 (February 1991): 43–67. See also Michael P. Cohen, *The History of the Sierra Club, 1892–1970* (San Francisco: Sierra Club Books, 1988), and Mark Harvey, *Symbol of Wilderness: Echo Park and the American Conservation Movement* (Albuquerque: University of New Mexico Press, 1994).

40. Harvey, "Echo Park, Glen Canyon, and the Postwar Wilderness Movement," 43–67. On the Glen Canyon Dam, see Jared Farmer, *Glen Canyon Dammed: Inventing Lake Powell and the Canyon Country* (Tucson: University of Arizona Press, 1999).

41. *We Have Come So Far....*, http://www.kentucky.sierraclub.org/newsletter/text/news0100.asp (accessed May 24, 2006).

42. Johanna Henn, letter, to Harry Caudill, April 19, 1967 (University of Kentucky Libraries, Special Collections and Archives, University of Kentucky, Lexington, KY), Anne and Harry Caudill Collection, Box 18; Harry Caudill, letter, to James E. Kowalsky, November 20, 1967, Anne and Harry Caudill Collection, Box 18. Examples of the letters written by Harry Caudill on behalf of the Sierra Club can be found in Box 18 of the Anne and Harry Caudill Collection.

43. "A Resume of Facts Leading Up to the Approval by Congress of the Red River Dam," John Sherman Cooper Collection, 1927–1972, Box 97; "Red River Reservoir Land Buying Slated: Army Engineer Corps Prints Pamphlet; Public Hearing at Stanton Set Aug. 16," *Clay City Times*, 10 August 1967, 1; United States Army Corps of Engineers, Louisville District, *Red River Reservoir Land Acquisition Procedure* (Louisville: United States Army Engineer District, Louisville, 1967). See Appendix E for information about the allegations put forth by the Sierra Club members at the public meeting.

44. "Conservationists Begin Fight to Hold Up Dam," *Courier-Journal*, 2 September 1967; clipping of article is located in the John Sherman Cooper Collection, 1927–1972, Box 99.

45. "Udall Enters Dam Tiff," *Kentucky Post*, 26 October 1967; clipping of the article is located in the John Sherman Cooper Collection, 1927–1972, Box 99.

46. Ray Harm (naturalist and artist), letter, November 1, 1967, Anne and Harry Caudill Collection, Box 18. The underlining of words is a reflection of the manner in which the words appeared on the original letter.

47. "Delay Will Kill Red River Dam Project," *Lexington Herald*, October 28, 1967; clipping of the article is located in the John Sherman Cooper Collection, 1927–1972, Box 99.

48. John Sherman Cooper, letter, to Stewart L. Udall, November 15, 1967, John Sherman Cooper Collection, 1927–1972, Box 99; John Sherman Cooper, letter, to Orville S. Freeman, November 15, 1967, John Sherman Cooper Collection, 1927–1972, Box 99; William Greider, "Cooper Asks for Review of Red River Project," *Courier-Journal*, November 16, 1967, John Sherman Cooper Collection, 1927–1972, Box 99.

49. Fred Luigart, "Red River Hike: Justice Douglas Calls Gorge Unique Heritage," *Courier-Journal*, 19 November 1967, 1; B. Franklin, "Conservationists Rallying Against a Dam in Kentucky," *The New York Times*, 20 November 1967, 49; "Dam Nonsense in Kentucky," *The New York Times*, 27 December 1967, 36; Jim Kowalsky, letter, to Harry M. Caudill, December 13, 1967, Anne and Harry Caudill Collection, Box 18.

50. "Water Supply for Lexington, Kentucky, in Relation to the Kentucky River," Anne and Harry Caudill Collection, Box 18; Dudley C. Martin, letter, to John C. Watts, February 18, 1968 (University of Kentucky Libraries, Special Collections and Archives, University of Kentucky, Lexington, KY), Red

River Gorge Papers, 1958–1978, loose folders; Carl M. Clark, "Kentucky's Red River Valley: A Brochure Presented in Behalf of the Preservation of the North Gorge As Wilderness," Red River Gorge Papers, 1958–1978, loose folders; William R. Holstein, letter, to Anne Van Tyne, undated, Red River Gorge Papers, 1958–1978, Box 1.

51. Office of the Chief of Engineers, *Red River Reservoir Kentucky Reconnaissance Study* (Washington, DC: U.S. Army Corps of Engineers, 1968).

52. United States Congress, Senate, *Public Works Appropriation for Fiscal Year 1969: Friday, March 15, 1968*, 90th Cong., 2nd Session (Washington, DC: United States Government Printing Office, 1968), 929, 936–938.

53. Ibid., 924–947.

54. William R. Holstein, letter, to Anne Van Tyne, undated, Red River Gorge Papers, 1958–1978, Box 1; Statement by William R. Holstein, May 7, 1968, Red River Gorge Papers, 1958–1978, Box 1; Statement by: Carroll Tichenor to House Subcommittee on Public Works, May 7, 1968, Red River Gorge Papers, 1958–1978, Box 1.

55. Ibid.

56. William R. Holstein, letter, to Anne Van Tyne, undated, Red River Gorge Papers, 1958–1978, Box 1; Statement of Senator John Sherman Cooper on Red River Reservoir, July 15, 1968, Anne and Harry Caudill Collection, Box 18; Statement of Senator John Sherman Cooper on Red River Reservoir following the meeting on July 24 of the Senate-House Conference on the Public Works Appropriations Bill for Fiscal 1969, July 24, 1968, John Sherman Cooper Collection, 1927–1972, Box 100.

57. Harry M. Caudill, "A Wild River That Knew Boone Awaits Its Fate," *Audubon* 70, no. 5 (September/October 1968): 71–75; "Daniel Boone's River," *Time* (11 April 1969): 28; Alton Marsh, "Daniel Boone's Wilderness May be Tamed by a Lake," *Smithsonian* 6 (September 1975): 56–62; Alton Marsh, "Last Stand at Red River Gorge," *National Parks and Conservation Magazine* 48 (August 1974): 18–24; William H. Martin, "The Red River Gorge Controversy in Kentucky: A Case Study in Preserving a Natural Area," *The ASB Bulletin (The Official Quarterly Publication of The Association of Southeastern Biologists)* 23, no. 3 (July 1976): 163–167; Eliot Porter, "The Red River Gorge — One Final Look," *Audubon* 70, no. 5 (September/October 1968): 58–70; Glenn O. Rutherford, "The Saga of the Red River Gorge," *American Forests* (February 1972): 20–23; Edwin Shrake, "Operation Build and Destroy," *Sports Illustrated* (1 April 1968): 46–49;

Mary Euginia Wharton, "Red River Dam Controversy," *AAAS Bulletin* (June 1969); Dael Wolfe, "The Only Earth We Have," *Science* 159, no. 3811 (12 January 1968): 155; Wendell Berry, "Engineering the Red River Gorge," *Sierra Club Bulletin* 59 (July/August 1974): 34–38; Wendell Berry, *The Unforeseen Wilderness: Kentucky's Red River Gorge* (Lexington: University Press of Kentucky, 1971); Branley A. Branson and Donald L. Batch, *Fishes of the Red River Drainage, Eastern Kentucky* (Lexington: University Press of Kentucky, 1974); Marilyn L. Andreason, and W. Hardy Eshbaugh, "Solidago Albopilosa Braun, A Little Known Goldenrod from Kentucky," *Castanea: The Journal of the Southern Appalachian Botanical Club* 38, no. 2 (June 1973): 117–132.

58. United States Congress, House of Representatives, *Kentucky River and Tributaries, Kentucky*; Statement by Elvis J. Stahr, president, National Audubon Society, on the Red River Gorge and Proposed Red River Reservoir, Kentucky, February 5, 1969, *Anne and Harry Caudill Collection, Box 18.*

59. "Text of Governor's Statement Yesterday Concerning Red River Reservoir, February 26, 1969," John Sherman Cooper Collection, 1927–1972, Box 96; Richard Nixon, letter, to John Sherman Cooper, March 21, 1969, Anne and Harry Caudill Collection, Box 18; Louie Nunn, letter, to Lt. General William F. Cassidy, March 28, 1969, John Sherman Cooper Collection, 1927–1972, Box 96.

60. C. Beach Jr., letter, to Carl Perkins, November 6, 1973, Carl D. Perkins Papers, 1949–1984, Box D101; C. Beach Jr., letter, to Carl Perkins, February 3, 1976, Carl D. Perkins Papers, 1949–1984, Box D119; *General Design Memorandum Booneville Lake, Ohio River Basin, South Fork Kentucky River, Kentucky, Design Memorandum No. 4*, n.p.

61. Carl D. Perkins, letter, to C. Beach Jr., February 9, 1976, Carl D. Perkins Papers, 1949–1984, Box D119.

62. United States Corps of Engineers, Louisville District, *Booneville Lake: Land Requirements Plan, Public Use Draft Design Memorandum No. 5* (United States Corps of Engineers, Louisville District, 1971), 6.

63. Ibid., 7; *General Design Memorandum Booneville Lake, Ohio River Basin, South Fork Kentucky River, Kentucky, Design Memorandum No. 4*, 8–2.

64. United States Corps of Engineers, Louisville District, *Booneville Lake: General Design Memorandum Appendix 3 Recreational and Environmental Resources* (United States

Corps of Engineers, Louisville District, 1972), Exhibit 2, Exhibit 3.

65. Robert S. Weise, "Remaking Red Bird: Isolation and the War on Poverty in a Rural Appalachian Locality," in *The Countryside in the Age of the Modern State: Political Histories of Rural America,* Catherine McNicol Stock, and Robert D. Johnston, eds. (Ithaca: Cornell University Press, 2001), 265–266; Collins, *A History of the Daniel Boone National Forest, 1770–1970,* 256–258.

66. Ibid.

67. *General Design Memorandum Booneville Lake, Ohio River Basin, South Fork Kentucky River, Kentucky, Design Memorandum No. 4,* n.p.

68. "Announcement of Public Meeting on Booneville Lake South Fork Kentucky River Ohio River Basin Kentucky, July 17, 1972," John Sherman Cooper Collection, 1927–1972, Box 46.

69. "Why the Dam?" *The Peoples Journal,* 13 July 1972, 1, 6.

70. T.C. Sizemore, "Lake Daniel Boone," *Peoples Journal;* "War on Poverty Lost!" *Peoples Journal;* "Why the Dam?" *Peoples Journal.*

71. "Transcript of Public Meeting on Booneville Lake South Fork Kentucky River Ohio River Basin Kentucky, 17 July 1972," United States Corps of Engineers Planning Division, Louisville District Files, 27.

72. Ibid.

73. Ibid., 29.

74. Ibid.

75. "Opposition Low Key at Booneville Dam Hearing," *The Beattyville Enterprise,* 20 July 1972, 1.

76. "I Tell It Like It Is," *The Peoples Journal,* 27 July 1972, 6.

77. Quoted in "Last-ditch Fight Vowed Against the Booneville Dam Project," *The Courier-Journal,* 19 July 1972, B1.

78. Ibid.

79. Telephone message from Bob Morgan to Tim Lee Carter, July 21, 1972, Tim Lee Carter Collection, 1955–1983, Box 310.

80. Paul T. Townes, letter, to Carl D. Perkins, May 24, 1974, Carl D. Perkins Papers, 1949–1984, Box D101.

81. Henry J. Garrison, letter, to Congressman Carl D. Perkins, May 11, 1973, Carl D. Perkins Papers, 1949–1984, Box D101.

82. United States Corps of Engineers, Louisville District, "Booneville Lake" (document at Buckhorn Lake, USACE, 1986), Booneville F/C 91–2–91–5.

83. C. Beach Jr., letter, to Carl Perkins, February 3, 1976, Carl D. Perkins Papers, 1949–1984, Box D119.

84. Ibid.; Carl D. Perkins, letter, to C. Beach Jr., February 9, 1976, Carl D. Perkins Papers, 1949–1984, Box 119.

85. Hill, *Kentucky Weather,* 107; "Kentucky River Basin Steering Committee 'Minutes,' April 12, 1989" (document at Buckhorn Lake, USACE, 1986), 1.

86. "Kentucky River Basin Steering Committee 'Minutes,' April 12, 1989" (document at Buckhorn Lake, USACE, 1986), 11–13.

87. On development planning as an impediment to actual development, see Vivek Chibber, *Locked in Place: State-Building and Late Industrialization in India* (Princeton, N.J.: Princeton University Press, 2003).

88. "Kentucky Counties Among the Poorest—'03 Census Data Ranks Median Income, Poverty Rates," *Lexington Herald-Leader,* 30 November 2005, A1.

Chapter 5

1. Quoted in Lee Mueller, "Owsley Man Proposes Merger of 4 Counties," *Lexington Herald-Leader,* 29 November 1990, B1.

2. Dwight B. Billings and Kathleen Blee, *The Road to Poverty: The Making of Wealth and Hardship in Appalachia* (New York: Cambridge University Press, 2002), 61–78.

3. This observation is partially corroborated by Ronald Eller, who utilized 1990 United States Census data at the subcounty level to identify distressed communities in Eastern Kentucky. One of the four clusters of census tracts he identified as having a poverty rate ranging from 46 to 63 percent encompassed adjacent portions of Owsley, Clay, and Breathitt counties; see Ronald D Eller, Phil Jenks, Chris Jasparro, and Jerry Napier, *Kentucky's Distressed Communities,* 14.

4. "Driving Past the Job Sites—If We Build It, Business Might Not Come in Rural Kentucky, Industrial Parks Sit Empty Win, Lose, or Draw: Gambling for Jobs," *Lexington Herald-Leader,* 20 November 2005, A1; "Poor Investment—Jobs Bypassing Nearly Empty Industrial Parks," *Lexington Herald-Leader,* 23 November 2005, A14; Alan Maimon, "East Kentucky Poverty Dashes Industrial Hopes: As Business Park Falters, Owsley Co. Looks to Tourism for Salvation," *The Courier-Journal,* 22 December 2005, A1; *Booneville, Kentucky, Owsley County Site 189–001,* http://www.kradd.org/CommunityAndED/Lone_oak.pdf (accessed January 26, 2006). Owsley County's road problems are not going

to be addressed by the state of Kentucky to any great degree in the near future. Between 2005 and 2010, Owsley County is slated to have one bridge replaced and to have a road that it shares with Jackson County moved; see *Key to Interpreting the Information Presented for Recommended FY 2005-FY 2010 Six-Year Highway Plan Projects*, http://www.kradd.org/CommunityAndED/FY05CEDSUPDAT E/six%20year%20road%20plan%20fede rally%20funded%20projects.pdf (66), (accessed January 26, 2006).

5. "Moonshine Again," *The Economist*, 20 October 1990, 25–26; Francis X. Clines, "Reaping Marijuana in Hills Emptied of Stills," *New York Times*, 4 June 2000, 16; Richard R. Clayton, *Marijuana in the "Third World": Appalachia, U.S.A.*

6. "Moonshine Again," *The Economist*; "Marijuana Raid Arouses Anger in Owsley County," *Lexington Herald-Leader*, 12 February 1988, C1; Lee Mueller, "Owsley's Marijuana Industry Under Scrutiny — CBS Show Tonight Causes Anxiety after Increased Pot Growth Reported," *Lexington Herald-Leader*, 12 October 1988, A1; "Marijuana Growing and Eradication in the United States," *48 Hours*; Chris Poore, "Lawmen's Lawyers to Give Closing Arguments Today," *Lexington Herald-Leader*, 13 August 1991, B1; "5 E. Kentucky Lawmen Convicted: Officers Stunned by Guilty Verdict," *Lexington Herald-Leader*, 17 August 1991, A1; "490 Arrested in State-Wide Drug Operation, Sons of Owsley, Lee Ex-Sheriffs Are Charged," *Lexington Herald-Leader*, 18 February 1993, B1; Clayton, *Marijuana in the "Third World": Appalachia, U.S.A*; Bill Estep, "Special Units Taking Down Marijuana Authorities Step Up Crackdown Efforts in September, A Major Harvest Time for Outdoor Crops," *Lexington Herald-Leader*, 3 September 2001, A1; "Government Corruption Widespread, Studies Say — Eastern Kentucky's Recent Past Supports Conclusion," *Lexington Herald-Leader*, 29 January 2003; Tom Lasseter and Bill Estep, "Wrong Interpretation of Law Leads to 40 Cases' Dismissal — Owsley County," *Lexington Herald-Leader*, 2 February 2003, B7; Bill Estep, "Court Backs UNITE — Drug Task Force's Authority Is Upheld — Implications for 29 Counties," *Lexington Herald-Leader*, 4 December 2004, B1; "Police Investigate Grand Jury — May Have Tampered with Fraud Case," *Lexington Herald-Leader*, 26 March 2005, B8; Phil Tursic, "Appalachia HIDTA Assesses Threat to Region," *Kentucky Law Enforcement News*, March 2005, 29–31; High-Intensity Drug Trafficking Areas, Office of National Drug Control Policy, *Appalachia HIDTA Kentucky*, http://www.whitehouse drugpolicy.gov/hidta/ky.html (accessed January 26, 2006). The ultimate irony about the campaign by state and federal law enforcement agencies is that far more money has been expended to wage war on Owsley County's marijuana growers than has ever been spent by state or federal officials for economic infrastructure improvements within the county's borders. See also Tom Loftus, "Breathitt Man Fights Pot Tax of 1.16 Million," *Courier-Journal*, 4 June 2000, A1; Alan Maimon, "Convicted Ex-Sheriff Seeks to Regain Post," *Courier-Journal*, 30 January 2002, B3.

7. "Local Businesses Reap Crop's Cash," *Lexington Herald-Leader*, 14 December 1992; "Pot Tolerated as Economic Necessity," *Lexington Herald-Leader*, 14 December 1992, A1; "Owsley's Marijuana Industry Under Scrutiny — CBS Show Tonight Causes Anxiety after Increased Pot Growth Reported," *Lexington Herald Leader*; "Marijuana Raid Arouses Anger in Owsley County," *Lexington Herald Leader*; Francis X. Clines, "Kentucky Journal: Fighting Appalachia's Top Cash Crop, Marijuana," *New York Times*, 28 February 2001, 10; Jim Warren and Lee Mueller, "Drug Crimes May Create New Risks for Rural Sheriffs — 'Just Unbelievable the Danger That There Is Out There Today,'" *Lexington Herald-Leader*, 18 April 2002, A1; Tom Lasseter and Bill Estep, "Pushing For Justice — When Drug Cases Finally Reach Court in Beattyville, There Are No Guarantees," *Lexington Herald-Leader*, 27 January 2003, A1; "Trying Public Trust — Special Report: Prescription for Pain Punishment of Drug Offenders Varies Widely, Eastern Kentucky Fares Poorly in Statewide Analysis," *Lexington Herald-Leader*, 2 February 2003; B1; "Violent Warnings–Some Jurors Simply Refuse to Convict People, Have Lost Faith in the System, and High-Profile Slayings Help Keep Them Quiet, 'Moonshine Mentality,' Close Ties to Defendants, Fear of Government Scuttle Cases," *Lexington Herald-Leader*, 3 February 2003, A8; Tom Lasseter and Bill Estep, "A Climate of Fear, Mistrust — Man's Killing Sends a Message in Letcher — Eastern Kentucky's Drug Culture Is So Pervasive That Some Foes Cower in Silence," *Lexington Herald-Leader*, 3 February 2003, A1; Tom Lasseter and Bill Estep, "Drugs, Violence: A Family History — For the Newtons of Lee County, So Many Crimes Bring So Little Time," *Lexington Herald-Leader*, 3 February 2003, A9; Bill Estep, "Drug Plea Bargains Weakened by Judge Reducing Sentences," *Lexington Herald-*

Leader, 20 April 2003, A1; Bill Estep, "Raids Net a Familiar Suspect — Drug Roundup in Lee, Owsley Area: Residents Say Light Sentences Make Enforcement Less Effective," *Lexington Herald-Leader,* 12 December 2003, A1; "State Prosecutor Hired for Drug Cases," *Lexington Herald-Leader,* 9 March 2004, B2; Bill Estep, "Judge Sent to Ease Case Backlog — Will Help with Criminal Cases in 23rd Circuit," *Lexington Herald-Leader,* 16 June 2004, A1; "37 People Arrested in Drug-Trafficking Roundup," *Lexington Herald-Leader,* 1 September 2005, B3; Lee Mueller, "Clay County Abuzz Over Federal Drug Inquiry — Politicians Are Implicated — People Wonder Who's Next," *Lexington Herald-Leader,* 18 September 2005, B1; Alan Maimon, "Court Watchers Keep Tabs on Clay County Drug Cases," *Courier-Journal,* 17 October 2005, A1; Lee Mueller, "Drug Case Has Clay County Riveted — Vote-Buying, Staged Shooting, Fixed Court Cases Alleged," *Lexington Herald-Leader,* 23 October 2005, B1; Lee Mueller, "Ex-Clay Co. Clerk Pleads Guilty — Was Part of Drug Ring That Moved Tons of Marijuana Through Eastern Kentucky," *Lexington Herald-Leader,* 26 October 2005, A1.

8. Quoted in "Local Businesses Reap Crop's Cash," *Lexington Herald-Leader.*

9. "Roundup in Lee Nets 32 Alleged Drug Dealers — OxyContin Involved in Many Arrests — Total of 49 Sought," *Lexington Herald-Leader,* 19 December 2001, B1; "Addicted and Corrupted — Drug Trade Infects Eastern Kentucky from Living Room to Courtroom — As Ruined Lives Multiplied, Beattyville Tried to Fight Back," *Lexington Herald-Leader,* 26 January 2003, A1; Tom Lasseter, "Homecoming Queen-Turned-Addict Found Slain — Lee Countian was Featured in Drug Series," *Lexington Herald-Leader,* 13 November 2003, A1; "Drug Supply Has Family Connection — Dad Runs Nursing Home, Daughter Leads Pharmacy," *Lexington Herald-Leader,* 29 February 2004, A14; "Meet the Directors," *Lexington Herald-Leader,* 29 February 2004, A14; "Overmedication, Poor Record Keeping," *Lexington Herald-Leader,* 29 February 2004, A14.

10. Quoted in "'Just Growing Marijuana' — Some Say Anti-Pot Money Should Be Spent Elsewhere," *Lexington-Herald Leader,* 29 January 2003, A9.

11. Roger Alford, "Golf Course Under Debate in Booneville — Some Call Plan for Mine Land Ridiculous," *Lexington Herald-Leader,* 19 October 2002, C1; Maimon, "East Kentucky Poverty Dashes Industrial Hopes: As Business Park Falters, Owsley Co. Looks to Tourism for Salvation, *Courier-Journal;*" Maimom, "Heritage, Recreation Among Region's Strong Points," *Courier-Journal,* 22 December 2005, A4.

Tables

1. Manuscript Census, Owsley County 1850, Schedule 5, Owsley 1.

2. Manuscript Census, Owsley County 1860, Schedule 5, 1.

3. Data in chart located in Dubin, *United States Gubernatorial Elections, 1776–1860: The Official Results by State and County,* 76–80.

4. Data in chart located in Dubin, *United States Presidential Elections, 1788–1860: The Official Results by County and State,* 86–87, 103, 123–124, 144, 168–169.

5. *County Government in Kentucky: A Report by the Efficiency Commission of Kentucky* (Frankfort: The State Journal Company, 1923), 69.

6. "January Rainfall 11 More Than 5 Months in 1936," *The Beattyville Enterprise,* 1.

7. Data from U.S. Congress, House of Representatives, *Kentucky River and Tributaries, Kentucky,* 25–26.

8. *General Design Memorandum Booneville Lake Ohio River Basin South Fork Kentucky River Design Memorandum No. 4,* 4–2.

Appendices

1. Data from Kentucky Agricultural Statistics Service, *Owsley County, Kentucky: Agricultural Statistics: 1909–1999.* Acre is the unit of measurement for both land in farms and average farm size.

2. Data from Kentucky Agricultural Statistics Service, *Owsley County, Kentucky: Agricultural Statistics: 1909–1999,* and *Kentucky: Agricultural Statistics: 1909–1999,* http://www. nass.usda.gov/ky/Coa/coa.htm (accessed July 15, 2005). Pound is the unit of measurement for yield per acre.

3. Data from Ibid. Bushel is the unit of measurement for yield per acre.

4. Transcript of memo inserted into the record for hearings held on November 6, 1969; see United States Congress, House of Representatives, *Administration and Conduct of Antipoverty Programs: Hearings before the Com-*

mittee on Education and Labor, 70–72. The apparent spelling and grammar errors were transcribed as they appeared in the record.

5. Transcription included in "A Resume of Facts Leading Up to the Approval by Congress of the Red River Dam," John Sherman Cooper Collection, 1927–1972, Box 97.

6. Transcription of "Statement of Senator John Sherman Cooper before Senate and House Appropriations Subcommittees on Fiscal 1967 Budget Recommendations for Kentucky Corps of Engineers Projects, May 3–4, 1966," Thruston Ballard Morton Collection, 1933–1969, Box 10.

7. "Lake Daniel Boone Development Committee, 26 April 1966," John Sherman Cooper Collection, 1927–1972.

Bibliography

Primary Sources

PUBLISHED WORKS

Annual Report of the Auditor of Public Accounts, of the State of Kentucky for the Fiscal Year Ending October 10, 1871. Frankfort: Kentucky Yeoman Office, 1871.

Biennial Report of the Auditor of Public Accounts of Kentucky. Frankfort: Kentucky Yeoman Office, 1881.

Biennial Report of the Auditor of Public Accounts of Kentucky. Frankfort: Capital Office, 1893.

Biennial Report of the Department of Agriculture, Labor, and Statistics, 1934–1935. Frankfort: The Department of Agriculture, Labor, and Statistics, 1935.

Booneville, Kentucky, Owsley County Site 189–001. http://www.kradd.org/CommunityAndED/Lone_oak.pdf (accessed January 26, 2006).

Brewer, D.L., compiler. *Individuals Representing Owsley County in the Kentucky State Legislature, 1843–1900,* http://www.owsleykyhist.org/individuals_representing_owsley.htm (accessed November 26, 2004).

Clark, Thomas D. *My Century in History: Memoirs.* Lexington: University Press of Kentucky, 2006.

Clayton, Richard M. *Marijuana in the "Third World": Appalachia, U.S.A.* Boulder, CO: Lynne Rienner Publishers, 1995.

CNN News. "One Paycheck from Poverty, Part 3—Small Businesses." CBS, 10 April 1994, 9:00–9:30 P.M. Transcript available from LexisNexis.

Council of Economic Advisors. *Economic Report of 1964.* Washington, DC: Government Printing Office, 1964.

County Government in Kentucky: A Report by the Efficiency Commission of Kentucky. Frankfort: The State Journal Company, 1923.

"Daniel Boone's River." *Time,* April 11, 1969.

Davidson, Oscar Barton, compiler. *Kentucky Coal Production, 1790–1988.* Lexington, KY: Kentucky Geological Survey, 1990.

Dubin, Michael J. *Presidential Elections, 1788–1860: The Official Results by County and State.* Jefferson: McFarland, 2002.

_____. *United States Congressional Elections, 1788–1997: The Official Results.* Jefferson, NC: McFarland, 1998.

_____. *United States Gubernatorial Elections, 1776–1860: The Official Results by State and County.* Jefferson: McFarland, 2003.

Farmers State Bank et al. v. Owsley County et al. Transcript available from Lexis-Nexis.

Griffin et al. v. Clay County et al. Burchell v. Same. Transcript available from Lexis Nexis.

High-Intensity Drug Trafficking Areas, Office of National Drug Control Policy. *Appalachia HIDTA Kentucky.* http://

www.whitehousedrugpolicy.gov/hidta. ky.html (accessed January 26, 2006).

Jackson, Jesse, and John Bisney. "What Can the Government Do about Poverty in Appalachia?" *Both Sides,* with Jesse Jackson, CNN, 26 March 2000. Transcript available from LexisNexis.

Jillson, Willard Rouse. *Geology of the Island Creek Pool.* Frankfort: Kentucky Geological Survey, 1927.

_____. *The Oil and Gas Resources of Kentucky: A Geological Review of the Past Development and the Present Status of the Industry in Each of the One Hundred and Twenty Counties in the Commonwealth.* Frankfort: Department of Geology and Forestry, 1919.

Johnston, J. Stoddard, ed. *First Explorations of Kentucky.* Louisville: Standard Printing Company, 1898.

Journal of the House of Representatives of the Commonwealth of Kentucky. Frankfort, 1792 —.

Journal of the Regular Session of the Senate of the Commonwealth of Kentucky. Frankfort, 1792 —.

Kentucky Acts. Frankfort, 1792 —.

Kentucky. Adjutant-General's Office. *Report of the Adjutant General of the State of Kentucky.* Vol. 1. *1861–1866.* Frankfort: Kentucky Yeoman Office, 1866.

_____. *Report of the Adjutant General of the State of Kentucky.* Vol. 2. *1861–1866.* Frankfort: Kentucky Yeoman Office, 1867.

Kentucky Agricultural Statistics Service. *Kentucky: Agricultural Statistics, 1909–1999.* http://www.nass.usda.gov/ky/Coa/coa.htm (accessed July 15, 2005).

_____. *Owsley County, Kentucky: Agricultural Statistics, 1909–1999.* http://www. nass.usda.gov/ky/Coa/coa.htm (accessed July 15, 2005).

Kentucky Constitutional Convention. *Official Report of the Proceedings and Debates in the Convention: Assembled at Frankfort, on the Eighth Day of September, 1890, to Adopt, Amend, or Change the Constitution of the State of Kentucky.* Frankfort: E. Polk Johnson, 1890.

_____. *Report of the Debates and Proceedings of the Convention for the Revision of the Constitution of the State of Kentucky.* Frankfort: A.G. Hodges, 1849.

Kentucky River Area Development District. *Honoring Our Pioneers and Recognizing Our Leaders: Twentieth Annual Meeting.* Hazard, KY: Kentucky River Area Development District, 1988.

Key to Interpreting the Information Presented for Recommended FY 2005–FY 2010 Six-Year Highway Plan Projects. http://www. kradd.org/CommunityAndED/FY 05CEDSUPDATE/six%20year%20 road%20plan%20federally%20funded %20projects.pdf (accessed January 26, 2006).

"Marijuana Growing and Eradication in the United States," *48 Hours,* CBS, 7 June 1990, 8:00–9:00 P.M. Transcript available from LexisNexis.

McDowell, Nicholas. *Tenth Biennial Report of the Bureau of Agriculture, Labor, and Statistics of the State of Kentucky.* Louisville: Bradley & Gilbert, Printers and Binders, 1894.

Moore, Lucas. *Twelfth Biennial Report of the Bureau of Agriculture, Labor, and Statistics of the State of Kentucky.* Louisville: Geo. G. Fetter Printing, 1897.

Myers, Will S., Jr., John L. Johnson, and James W. Martin. "Kentucky Income Payments by Counties, 1939, 1947, 1950, and 1951." *Bulletin of the Bureau of Business Research* 26 (1953): 1–37.

Office of the Chief of Engineers. *Red River Reservoir, Kentucky: Reconnaissance Study.* Washington, DC: U.S. Army Corps of Engineers, 1968.

Peak, George, and J.E. Reeves. "Kentucky County Debts, June 30, 1938." *Bulletin of the Bureau of Business Research* 2, no. 3 (1940): 1–62.

"Poverty: Feud in the Hills." *Time,* September 12, 1969, 21.

Price, Hugh B. "To Be Equal: Black Poverty/White Poverty." Copley News Service, 19 February 1998. Transcript available from LexisNexis.

Prospectus of the Three Forks Investment Company: Its Beattyville Town Site, with Maps, Plats, Illustrations, Etc. Louisville: Courier-Journal Printing, 1889.

Quindry, Kenneth E. *Local Revenue in Kentucky.* Lexington: Bureau of Business Research, University of Kentucky, 1963.

Report of the Mississippi Valley Committee of the Public Works Administration. Washington, DC: Government Printing Office, 1934.

Sierra Club v. Morton, Secretary of the Interior et al., No. 70–34 Supreme Court of the United States. Transcript available from LexisNexis.

"State of the Union Address, Lyndon B. Johnson, January 8, 1964." In *Poverty in the United States: An Encyclopedia of History, Politics, and Policy*, edited by Gwendolyn Mink and Alice O'Connor. Denver: ABC-Clio, 2004.

United States Census Bureau. *Kentucky Population of Counties by Decennial Census: 1900 to 1990*. http://www.census.gov/population/cencounts/ky190090.txt (accessed April 26, 2002).

_____. *1960 Census of Population: Supplementary Reports*. Nos. 36–56. Washington, DC: Government Printing Office, 1963.

_____. *U.S. Census Bureau State and County Quickfacts: Owsley County, Kentucky*, http://quickfacts.census.gov/qfd/states/21/21189.html (accessed January 26, 2003).

United States Army Corps of Engineers, Louisville District. *Booneville Lake: General Design Memorandum*. Louisville: United States Army Engineer District, Louisville, 1972.

_____. *Booneville Lake: Land Requirements Plan Public Use Draft Design Memorandum No. 5*. Louisville: United States Corps of Engineers, Louisville District, 1971.

_____. *Booneville Lake Ohio River Basin South Fork Kentucky River Kentucky: Design Memorandum No. 4*. Louisville: Louisville Corps of Engineers, 1972.

_____. *Booneville Reservoir Ohio River Basin South Fork Kentucky River Kentucky: Design Memorandum No. 3: Structure Site Selection*. Louisville: United States Army Engineer District, Louisville, 1970.

_____. *Final Environmental Impact Statement: Red River Lake Project, Kentucky*. Louisville: United States Army Engineer District, Louisville, 1974.

_____. *General Design Memorandum Appendix 3: Recreational and Environmental Resources*. United States Corps of Engineers, Louisville District, 1972.

_____. *Red River Lake, Kentucky: Response to the Council on Environmental Quality, Letter Dated 24 January 1975*. Louisville: United States Army Engineer District, Louisville, 1975.

_____. *Red River Reservoir Land Acquisition Procedure*. Louisville: United States

Army Engineer District, Louisville, 1967.

_____. *Response to Comments by the Council on Environmental Quality on the Final Environmental Impact Statement: Red River Lake Project, Kentucky*. 2 vols. Louisville: United States Army Engineer District, 1974.

_____. *Review Report on Kentucky River and Tributaries for Flood Control and Allied Purposes*. Louisville: Louisville District, Corps of Engineers, U.S. Army, 1958.

_____. *Special Report on Environmental Considerations for Red River Lake: Design Memorandum 16*. Louisville: United States Army Engineer District, Louisville, 1972.

United States Congress, House of Representatives. *Administration and Conduct of Antipoverty Programs: Hearings before the Committee on Education and Labor*. 91st Cong., 1st Session. Washington, DC: Government Printing Office, 1969.

_____. *Appalachian Regional Development Act of 1964*. 88th Cong., 2nd Session. Washington, DC: United States Government Printing Office, 1964.

_____. *Creation of Pioneer National Monument, KY*. 73rd Cong., 2nd Session. Washington, DC: Government Printing Office, 1934.

_____. *Kentucky River and Tributaries, Kentucky*. 78th Cong., 2nd Session. Washington, DC: United States Government Printing Office, 1944.

_____. *Kentucky River and Tributaries, Kentucky*. 87th Cong., 2nd Session. Washington, DC: Government Printing Office, 1962.

_____. *National Environmental Policy Act of 1969*. 91st Cong., 1st Session. Washington, DC: United States Government Printing Office, 1969.

_____. *Poverty in the U.S.* 88th Cong., 2nd Session. Washington, DC: United States Government Printing Office, 1964.

_____. *Poverty: Message from the President of the United States Relative to Poverty, and a Draft of a Bill to Mobilize the Human and Financial Resources of the Nation to Combat Poverty in the United States*. 88th Cong., 2nd Session. Washington, DC: Government Printing Office, 1964.

_____. *Public Works Appropriation Bill, 1965*. 88th Cong., 2nd Session. Washington, DC: Government Printing Office, 1964.

_____. *Public Works Appropriation Bill, 1966.* 89th Cong., 1st Session. Washington, DC: Government Printing Office, 1965.

_____. *Public Works Appropriation Bill, 1970.* 91st Cong., 1st Session. Washington, DC: Government Printing Office, 1969.

United States Congress, Senate. *Appalachian Regional Development Act of 1964.* 88th Cong., 2nd Session. Washington, DC: United States Government Printing Office, 1964.

_____. *Economic Opportunity Act of 1964.* 88th Cong., 2nd Session. Washington, DC: United States Government Printing Office: 1964.

_____. *Public Works Appropriation for Fiscal Year 1969: Friday, March 15, 1968.* 90th Cong., 2nd Session. Washington, DC: United States Government Printing Office, 1968.

_____. *Senate Hearings before the Committee on Appropriations: Public Works for Water and Power Development and Energy Research Appropriations Fiscal Year 1976.* 94th Cong., 1st Session. Washington, DC: United States Government Printing Office, 1975.

_____. *Senate Hearings before the Senate Select Subcommittee on Poverty, Committee on Labor and Public Welfare: Economic Opportunity Act of 1964.* 88th Cong., 2nd Session. Washington, DC: United States Government Printing Office, 1964.

_____. "Senator Cooper of Kentucky Speaking on the Red River Reservoir." 90th Cong., 2nd Session. *Congressional Record* (20 July 1968): 9083–9085.

_____. *War on Poverty: Economic Opportunity Act of 1964.* 88th Cong., 2nd Session. Washington, DC: United States Government Printing Office, 1964.

United States Department of Agriculture. *Soil Survey of Jackson and Owsley Counties, Kentucky.* Washington DC, 1989.

United States Department of Agriculture, Bureau of Agricultural Economics. *Economic and Social Problems and Conditions of the Southern Appalachians.* Washington, DC: USDA Miscellaneous Publication 205, 1935.

United States Engineer Office. *Flood Control Survey: Kentucky River and Tributaries, Kentucky.* Cincinnati: U.S. Engineer Office, 1940.

_____. *Preliminary Examination on Kentucky River and Its Tributaries, Kentucky.* Cincinnati: U.S. Engineer Office, 1939.

United States General Accounting Office. *Environmental and Economic Issues of the Corps of Engineers' Red River Lake Project in Kentucky.* Washington, DC: Government Printing Office, 1975.

We Have Come So Far.... http://www.kentucky.sierraclub.org/newsletter/text/news0100.asp (accessed May 24, 2006).

UNPUBLISHED WORKS

Berea College Archives and Special Collections: Burch Family Collection; I.W. Gabbard Collection; Owsley County Vertical File; Willard Rouse Jillson Collection.

Courier-Journal Library.

Courier-Journal Clipping File.

Eastern Kentucky University Special Collections and Archives: Carl D. Perkins Papers, 1949–1984; McGuire Family File; Pioneer National Monument Association & Fort Boonesborough State Park Association Records, 1926–1976; William Julius Moore Papers.

Estill County, Kentucky: Minute/Order Books D-F 1834–1853.

The Filson Historical Society: Map of Owsley County, Kentucky; Tom Wallace Papers, 1925–1960.

Gibbs, Robert. USDA Economic Research Service. "RE: 10 Poorest U.S. Counties in 1960." Personal e-mail (12 September 2005).

Kentucky Department of Libraries and Archives: Owsley County Deed Books.

Kentucky Heritage Council.

Kentucky Historic Resources Inventory Files for Lee County.

Kentucky Historic Resources Inventory Files for Owsley County.

Lee County, Kentucky: Court Orders, Book 1.

Powlas, Joe. Interview by author, 12 January 2006. Booneville, Kentucky. Tape recording in possession of the author.

Sizemore, T.C. Telephone interview by author, 2 January 2006.

Thomas D. Clark Library, Kentucky Historical Society: Owsley County — History Vertical File.

United States Bureau of the Census: Manuscript Census: Estill County, Kentucky, 1840; Manuscript Census: Lee County, Kentucky, 1870; Manuscript Census: Owsley County, Kentucky, 1850; Manuscript Census: Owsley County, Kentucky, 1860; Manuscript Census: Owsley County, Kentucky, 1870.

United States Corps of Engineers, Louisville District: Buckhorn Lake, USACE; Planning Division Files.

University of Kentucky Special Collections & Archives: Appalachian Regional Commission Archives; Earle C. Clements Collection, 1922–1970s; Governor Louie B. Nunn Records; John Sherman Cooper Collection, 1927–1972; Kentucky Conservationists Oral History Project; Red River Gorge Papers, 1958–1978; Thruston B. Morton Collection, 1933–1969.

Western Kentucky University Library and Special Collections: Tim Lee Carter Collection, 1955–1983.

NEWSPAPERS

Augusta Chronicle (Augusta, Georgia), 2002.
Beattyville Enterprise (Beattyville, Kentucky), 1932–1975.
Booneville Sentinel (Booneville, Kentucky), 1976–2000.
Chicago Tribune (Chicago, Illinois), 1996 to present.
Columbus Dispatch (Columbus, Ohio), 1999.
Jackson Times (Jackson, Kentucky), 1963–1970.
Lexington Herald-Leader (Lexington, Kentucky), 1983 to present.
Louisville Courier-Journal (Louisville, Kentucky), 1926 to present.
New York Times (New York City, New York), 1960 to present.
Owsley County Courier (Booneville, Kentucky), 1932–1943.
Owsley County News (Booneville, Kentucky), 1942–1958.
The People's Journal (Booneville, Kentucky), 1966–1975.
Pineville Sun (Pineville, Kentucky), 1934.
Plain Dealer (Cleveland, Ohio), 1999.
Rocky Mountain News (Denver, Colorado), 1994.
St. Petersburg Times (St. Petersburg, Florida), 1997.
Three Forks Enterprise (Beattyville, Kentucky), 1884–1888.

USA Today (Washington, DC), 1989.
Wall Street Journal (New York City, New York), 1993.
Washington Post (Washington, DC), 1969.
Wayne County (KY) *Outlook*, 1967.

Secondary Sources

PUBLISHED WORKS

Abramson, Rudy, and Jean Haskell, eds. *Encyclopedia of Appalachia.* Knoxville: University of Tennessee Press, 2006.

Ackerman, Bruce, and James Sawyer. "The Uncertain Search for Environmental Policy: Scientific Fact-Finding and Rational Decision-Making Along the Delaware River." *University of Pennsylvania Law Review* 120 (1972): 419–503.

Albert, Richard C. *Damming the Delaware: The Rise and Fall of Tocks Island Dam.* 2nd ed. University Park, PA: Penn State University Press, 2005.

Anderson, James E. "Poverty, Unemployment, and Economic Development: The Search for a National Antipoverty Policy." *The Journal of Politics* 29, no. 1 (February 1967): 70–93.

Andreasen, Marilyn L., and W. Hardy Eshbaugh. "Solidago Albopilosa Braun: A Little Known Goldenrod from Kentucky." *Castanea: The Journal of the Southern Appalachian Botanical Club* 38, no. 2 (June 1973): 117–132.

Andrews, Richard N. *Managing the Environment, Managing Ourselves: A History of American Environmental Policy.* New Haven: Yale University Press, 1999.

Anglin, Mary K. "Lessons from Appalachia in the 20th Century: Poverty, Power, and the 'Grassroots.'" *American Anthropologist* 104, no. 2 (June 2002): 565–582.

Appalachian Land Ownership Task Force. *Who Owns Appalachia? Landownership and Its Impact.* Lexington: University Press of Kentucky, 1983.

Arnold, Joseph L. *The Evolution of the 1936 Flood Control Act.* Fort Belvoir, VA: Corps of Engineers, United States Army, 1988.

Aron, Stephen. *How the West Was Lost: The Transformation of Kentucky from Daniel Boone to Henry Clay.* Baltimore: Johns Hopkins University Press, 1996.

Badger, Anthony. *Prosperity Road: The New Deal, Tobacco, and North Carolina.* Chapel Hill: University of North Carolina Press, 1980.

Bailey, G.L. *Early History of Owsley County, Kentucky.* Jackson, KY: Maw & Paw's Printing, 1994.

Ball, Richard A. "A Poverty Case: The Analgesic Subculture of the Southern Appalachians." *American Sociological Review* 33, no. 6 (1968): 885–895.

Batteau, Allen. "Rituals of Dependence in Appalachian Kentucky." In *Appalachia and America: Autonomy and Ritual Dependence,* edited by Allen Bateau. Lexington: University Press of Kentucky, 1983.

Bauman, John F., and Thomas H. Coode. *In the Eye of the Great Depression: New Deal Reporters and the Agony of the American People.* DeKalb, IL: Northern Illinois University Press, 1998.

_____. *The Invention of Appalachia.* Tucson: University of Arizona Press, 1990.

Baxter, R.M. "Environmental Effects of Dams and Impoundments." *Annual Review of Ecology and Systematics* 8 (1977): 255–283.

Beach, Damian. *Civil War Battles, Skirmishes, and Events in Kentucky.* Louisville: Different Drummer Books, 1995.

Beaver, Patricia Duane. *Rural Community in the Appalachian South.* Lexington: University Press of Kentucky, 1986.

Benhart, John, Jr. *Appalachian Aspirations: The Geography of Urbanization and Development in the Upper Tennessee River Valley, 1865–1900.* Knoxville: University of Tennessee Press, 2007.

Benke, Arthur C., and Colbert E. Cushing. *Rivers of North America.* New York: Elsevier, 2005.

Berry, Chad. *Southern Migrants and Northern Exiles.* Urbana: University of Illinois Press, 2000.

Berry, Wendell. "Engineering the Red River Gorge." *Sierra Club Bulletin* 59 (July/August 1974): 34–38.

_____. *The Unforeseen Wilderness: Kentucky's Red River Gorge.* Lexington: University Press of Kentucky, 1971.

_____. *The Unforeseen Wilderness: Kentucky's Red River Gorge.* San Francisco: North Point Press, 1991.

Billings, Dwight B. "Culture and Poverty in Appalachia: A Theoretical Discussion and Empirical Analysis." *Social Forces* 53, no. 2 (1974): 315–323.

Billings, Dwight B., and Ann Tickameyer. "Uneven Development in Appalachia." In *Forgotten Places: Uneven Development in Rural America,* edited by Thomas Lyson, and William Falk. Lawrence: University Press of Kansas, 1993.

Billings, Dwight B., and Kathleen M. Blee. *The Road to Poverty: The Making of Wealth and Hardship in Appalachia.* New York: Cambridge University Press, 2000.

Blakey, George T. *Hard Times & New Deal in Kentucky 1929–1939.* Lexington: University Press of Kentucky, 1986.

Blee, Kathleen, and Dwight B. Billings. "Race Differences in the Origins and Consequences of Chronic Poverty in Rural Appalachia." *Social Science History* 20, no. 3 (Autumn 1996): 345–373.

_____. "Reconstructing Daily Life in the Past: An Hermeneutical Approach to Ethnographic Data." *Sociological Quarterly* 27 (Winter 1986): 443–462.

Borman, Kathryn M., and Phillip J. Obermiller, eds. *From Mountain to Metropolis: Appalachian Migrants in American Cities.* Westport, CT: Bergin and Garvey, 1994.

Boyer, Paul S., ed. *The Oxford Companion to United States History.* New York: Oxford University Press, 2001.

Bradshaw, Michael. *The Appalachian Regional Commission: Twenty-five Years of Government Policy.* Lexington: University of Kentucky Press, 1992.

Branson, Branley A., and Donald L. Batch. *Fishes of the Red River Drainage, Eastern Kentucky.* Lexington: University Press of Kentucky, 1974.

Brauer, Carl M. "Kennedy, Johnson, and the War on Poverty." *Journal of American History* 69, no. 1 (1982): 98–119.

Brewer, Dennis L. *The Land of Lee: The Formation and County Officials of Lee County Kentucky 1870–1983.* Beattyville, KY: Three Forks Heritage Series, 1983.

_____. *"Upon This Rock I...": A Short History of the New Hope Baptist Church.* Unknown publisher, 1968.

Brown, James Stephen. *Beech Creek: A Study of a Kentucky Mountain Neighborhood.* Berea, KY: Berea College Press, 1988.

Bryant, Ron D. "Lee County." *The Kentucky Encyclopedia.* Lexington: University Press of Kentucky, 1992.

_____. *Kentucky History: An Annotated Bibliography*. Westport, CT: Greenwood Press, 2000.

Buckley, Geoffrey L. "The Environmental Transformation of an Appalachian Valley, 1850–1906." *Geographical Review* 88, no. 2 (April 1998): 175–198.

Burch, John Russell, Jr. "19th-Century Politics in the Formation of Appalachian Kentucky Counties: The McGuires and the Creation of Owsley and Lee Counties." *Journal of Appalachian Studies* 11, nos. 1 and 2 (Spring/Fall 2005): 226–242.

Bussiere, Elizabeth. *(Dis)Entitling the Poor: The Warren Court, Welfare Rights, and the American Political Tradition*. University Park: Pennsylvania State University Press, 1997.

Campbell, John C. *The Southern Highlander and His Homeland*. Lexington: University Press of Kentucky, 1969.

Cattell-Gordon, David. "The Appalachian Inheritance: A Culturally Transmitted Traumatic Stress Syndrome?" *Journal of Progressive Human Services* 1, no. 1 (1990): 41–57.

Caudill, Bernice Calmes. *Remembering Lee County (A Story of the Early Days)*. Danville, KY: Bluegrass Printing, n.d.

Caudill, Harry M. "A Wild River That Knew Boone Awaits Its Fate." *Audubon* 70, no. 5 (September/October 1968): 71–75.

_____. *Night Comes to the Cumberlands: A Biography of a Depressed Area*. Boston: Little, Brown, 1962.

_____. *My Land is Dying*. New York: E.P. Dutton, 1971.

_____. *The Watches of the Night: A New Plea for Appalachia*. Boston: Little, Brown, 1976.

_____. *Theirs Be the Power: The Moguls of Eastern Kentucky*. Urbana: University of Illinois Press, 1983.

Chibber, Vivek. *Locked in Place: State-Building and Late Industrialization in India*. Princeton, NJ: Princeton University Press, 2003.

Clark, Thomas D. "Salt, a Factor in the Settlement of Kentucky." *Filson Club History Quarterly* 12 (1938): 42–52.

Cohen, Michael P. *The History of the Sierra Club, 1892–1970*. San Francisco: Sierra Club Books, 1988.

Coleman, J. Winston, Jr. *A Bibliography of Kentucky History*. Lexington: University of Kentucky Press, 1949.

Collins, Lewis. *Collins' Historical Sketches of Kentucky. History of Kentucky: By the Late Lewis Collins, Judge of the Mason County Court. Revised, Enlarged Four-fold, and Brought Down to the Year 1874, by His Son, Richard H. Collins, A.M., LL.B. Embracing Pre-historic, Annals for 331 Years, Outline, and by Counties, Statistics, Antiquities and Natural Curiosities, Geographical and Geological Descriptions, Sketches of the Court of Appeals, the Churches, Freemasonry, Odd Fellowship, and Internal Improvements, Incidents of Pioneer Life, and Nearly Five Hundred Biographical Sketches of Distinguished Pioneers, Soldiers, Statesmen, Jurists, Lawyers, Surgeons, Divines, Merchants, Historians, Editors, Artists, Etc., Etc.* Covington, KY: Collins, 1882.

_____. *Historical Sketches of Kentucky: Embracing Its History, Antiquities, and Natural Curiosities, Geographical, Statistical, and Geological Descriptions; with Anecdotes of Pioneer Life, and More Than One Hundred Biographical Sketches of Distinguished Pioneers, Soldiers, Statesmen, Jurists, Lawyers, Divines, Etc.* Maysville, KY: Lewis Collins; Cincinnati: J.A. & U.P. James, 1848.

Collins, Robert F. *A History of the Daniel Boone National Forest, 1770–1970*. Winchester, KY: U.S. Forest Service, 1975.

Collins, Timothy, Ronald D Eller, and Glen Edward Taul. *Kentucky River Area Development District: Historic Trends and Geographic Patterns*. Lexington: Appalachian Center, University of Kentucky, 1996.

Coode, Thomas H., and John F. Bauman. "'Dear Mr. Hopkins': A New Dealer Reports From Eastern Kentucky." *Register of the Kentucky Historical Society* 78, no. 1 (1980): 55–63.

Copeland, James E. "Where were the Kentucky Unionists and Secessionists?" *The Register* 71 (1973): 344–363.

Couto, Richard A. *An American Challenge: A Report on Economic Trends and Social Issues in Appalachia*. Dubuque, IA: Kendall-Hunt, 1994.

Coward, Joan Wells. *Kentucky in the New Republic: The Process of Constitution Making*. Lexington: University Press of Kentucky, 1979.

Coy, Fred E., Jr., et al. *Rock Art of Kentucky.* Lexington: University Press of Kentucky, 1997.

Crawford, Martin. *Ashe County's Civil War: Community and Society in the Appalachian South.* Charlottesville: University Press of Virginia, 2001.

_____. "Mountain Farmers and the Market Economy: Ashe County during the 1850s." *North Carolina Historical Review* 71 (1994): 430–450.

_____. "Slaveholding and Power in the New River Valley: Ashe County, North Carolina in 1860." *The New River Symposium* 84: 30–35.

Crofts, Daniel W. *Reluctant Confederates: Upper South Unionists in the Secession Crisis.* Chapel Hill: University of North Carolina Press, 1989.

Crowe-Carraco, Carol. "Happy Pappies." *The Kentucky Encyclopedia.* Lexington: University Press of Kentucky, 1992.

Dallek, Robert. *Flawed Giant: Lyndon Johnson and His Times, 1961–1973.* New York: Oxford University Press, 1998.

"Daniel Boone's River." *Time,* 11 April 1969, 28.

Danziger, Sheldon H., and Daniel H. Weinberg, eds. *Fighting Poverty: What Works and What Doesn't.* Cambridge: Harvard University Press, 1986.

Davies, Gareth. *From Opportunity to Entitlement: The Transformation and Decline of Great Society Liberalism.* Lawrence: University Press of Kansas, 1996.

Davis, Donald Edward. *Where There Are Mountains: An Environmental History of the Southern Appalachians.* Athens: University of Georgia Press, 2000.

De Young, Alan J. "Economic Development and Educational Status in Appalachian Kentucky." *Comparative Education Review* 29, no. 1 (February 1985): 47–67.

Dix, Keith. *What's a Miner to Do? The Mechanization of Coal Mining.* Pittsburgh: University of Pittsburgh Press, 1998.

Douglas, William O. *Nature's Justice: Writings of William O. Douglas.* Corvallis: Oregon State University Press, 2000.

Drake, Richard B. *A History of Appalachia.* Lexington: University Press of Kentucky, 2001.

Dunaway, Wilma A. *The First American Frontier: Transition to Capitalism in Southern Appalachia, 1700–1860.* Chapel Hill: University of North Carolina Press, 1996.

_____. *Slavery in the American Mountain South.* New York: Cambridge University Press, 2003.

_____. *The African-American Family in Slavery and Emancipation.* New York: Cambridge University Press, 2003.

Duncan, Cynthia M. *Worlds Apart: Why Poverty Persists in Rural America.* New Haven: Yale University Press, 1999.

Dunn, Durwood. *Cades Cove: The Life and Death of an Appalachian Community.* Knoxville: University of Tennessee Press, 1988.

Edwards, Grace Toney, JoAnn Aust Asbury, and Ricky L. Cox, eds. *A Handbook to Appalachia.* Knoxville: University of Tennessee Press, 2006.

Eller, Ronald D. *Miners, Millhands, and Mountaineers: Industrialization of the Appalachian South, 1880–1930.* Knoxville: University of Tennessee Press, 1982.

_____. "Modernization, 1940–2000." In *High Mountains Rising: Appalachia in Time and Place,* edited by Richard A. Straw, and H. Tyler Blethen. Urbana: University of Illinois Press, 2004.

Eller, Ronald D, Phil Jenks, Chris Jasparro, and Jerry Napier. *Kentucky's Distressed Communities: A Report on Poverty in Appalachian Kentucky.* Lexington: Appalachian Center, University of Kentucky, 1994.

Ellis, William E. *The Kentucky River.* Lexington: University Press of Kentucky, 2000.

Emerson, Thomas I. "Justice Douglas and Lawyers with a Cause." *The Yale Law Journal* 89, no. 4 (March 1980): 616–623.

Eslinger, Ellen. "The Shape of Slavery on the Kentucky Frontier, 1775–1800." *Register of the Kentucky Historical Society* 92 (1994): 1–23.

Evans, Peter. *Embedded Autonomy: States & Industrial Transformation.* Princeton: Princeton University Press, 1995.

Faragher, John Mack. *Daniel Boone: The Life and Legend of an American Pioneer.* New York: Henry Holt, 1992.

Farmer, Jared. *Glen Canyon Dammed: Inventing Lake Powell and the Canyon Country.* Tucson: University of Arizona Press, 1999.

Feather, Carl E. *Mountain People in a Flat Land: A Popular History of Appalachian Migration to Northeast Ohio, 1940–1965*. Athens: Ohio University Press, 1998.

Ferejohn, John A. *Pork Barrel Politics: River and Harbors Legislation, 1947–1968*. Stanford: Stanford University Press, 1974.

Fetterman, John. *Stinking Creek*. New York: E.P. Dutton, 1967.

Fisher, Noel C. *War at Every Door: Partisan Politics and Guerrilla Violence in East Tennessee, 1860–1869*. Chapel Hill: University of North Carolina Press, 1997.

Fisher, Stephen. *Fighting Back in Appalachia: Traditions of Resistance and Change*. Philadelphia: Temple University Press, 1993.

Ford, Thomas R. "The Passing of Provincialism." In *The Southern Appalachian Region: A Survey*, edited by Thomas R. Ford. Lexington: University of Kentucky Press, 1962.

Fowler, John D. "Appalachia's Agony: A Historiographical Essay on Modernization and Development in the Appalachian Region." *Filson Club History Quarterly* 72, no. 3 (1998): 305–328.

Fradkin, Phillip. *A River No More: The Colorado River and the West, Expanded and Updated Edition*. Berkeley: University of California Press, 1996.

Friend, Craig Thompson. *Along the Maysville Road: The Early American Republic in the Trans-Appalachian West*. Knoxville: University of Tennessee Press, 2005.

Frost, W.G. "Appalachian America." *Woman's Home Companion* 23 (1896): 3–4, 21.

_____. "Our Contemporary Ancestors in the Southern Mountains." *Atlantic Monthly* 83 (1899): 311–319.

Garrett, Morris M. "Booneville." *The Kentucky Encyclopedia*. Lexington: University Press of Kentucky, 1992.

Gaventa, John. *Power and Powerlessness: Quiescence and Rebellion in an Appalachian Valley*. Urbana: University of Illinois Press, 1980.

Gaventa, John, Barbara Ellen Smith, and Alex Willingham, eds. *Communities in Economic Crisis: Appalachia and the South*. Philadelphia: Temple University Press, 1990.

Germany, Kent B. *New Orleans after the Promises: Poverty, Citizenship, and the Search for the Great Society*. Athens: University of Georgia Press, 2007.

Gilens, Martin. "Race and Poverty in America: Public Misperceptions and the American News Media." *The Public Opinion Quarterly* 60, no. 4 (Winter 1996): 515–541.

Gillette, Michael L., ed. *Launching the War on Poverty: An Oral History*. New York: Twayne, 1996.

Glasmeier, Amy. *An Atlas of Poverty in America: One Nation, Pulling Apart, 1960–2003*. New York: Routledge, 2005.

Glasmeier, Amy K., and Tracey L. Farrigan, "Poverty, Sustainability, and the Culture of Despair: Can Sustainable Development Strategies Support Poverty Alleviation in America's Most Environmentally Challenged Communities?" *Annals of the American Academy of Political and Social Science* 590 (November 2003): 131–149.

Glen, John. "The War on Poverty in Appalachia — A Preliminary Report." *Register of the Kentucky Historical Society* 87 (Winter 1989): 40–57.

_____. "The War on Poverty in Appalachia: Oral History from the 'Top-Down' and the 'Bottom-Up.'" *Oral History Review* 22 (Summer 1995): 67–93.

Godden, Richard, and Martin Crawford, eds. *Reading Southern Poverty between the Wars, 1918–1939*. Athens: University of Georgia Press, 2006.

Graham, Frank, Jr. *The Audubon Ark: A History of the National Audubon Society*. Austin: University of Texas Press, 1992.

Haddad, William F. "Mr. Shriver and the Savage Politics of Poverty." *Harper's* (December 1965): 43–50.

Haffendorfer, Kenneth A. *The Battle of Wild Cat Mountain*. Louisville: KH Press, 2003.

Hall, Van Beck. "The Politics of Appalachian Virginia, 1790–1830." In *Appalachian Frontiers: Settlement, Society & Development in the Pre-Industrial Era*, edited by Robert D. Mitchell. Lexington: University Press of Kentucky, 1991.

Halperin, Rhoda H. *The Livelihood of Kin: Making Ends Meet "the Kentucky Way."* Austin: University of Texas Press, 1990.

Hamilton, David E. *From New Day to New Deal: American Farm Policy from Hoover to Roosevelt, 1928–1933*. Chapel Hill: University of North Carolina Press, 1991.

Hammon, Neal O. "Land Acquisition on the Kentucky Frontier." *Register of the*

Kentucky Historical Society 78 (1980): 297–321.

Harrington, Michael. *The Other America: Poverty in the United States.* Baltimore: Penguin Books, 1963.

Harvey, Mark. *Symbol of Wilderness: Echo Park and the American Conservation Movement.* Albuquerque: University of New Mexico Press, 1994.

Harvey, Mark W.T. "Echo Park, Glen Canyon, and the Postwar Wilderness Movement." *The Pacific Historical Review* 60, no. 1 (February 1991): 43–67.

Haynes, Ada F. *Poverty in Central Appalachia: Underdevelopment and Exploitation.* New York: Garland, 1997.

Hays, Samuel P. *A History of Environmental Politics.* Pittsburgh: University of Pittsburgh Press, 2000.

Herman, Daniel J. "The Other Daniel Boone: The Nascence of a Middle-Class Hunter Hero, 1784–1860." *Journal of the Early Republic* 18, no. 3 (Autumn 1998), 429–457.

Hill, Jerry. *Kentucky Weather.* Lexington: University Press of Kentucky, 2005.

Holt, Michael F. *Political Crisis of the 1850s.* New York: W.W. Norton, 1983.

Hsiung, David C. *Two Worlds in the Tennessee Mountains.* Lexington: University Press of Kentucky, 1996.

Inscoe, John C. *Mountain Masters: Slavery and the Sectional Crisis in Western North Carolina.* Knoxville: University of Tennessee Press, 1989.

Inscoe, John C., and Gordon B. McKinney. *The Heart of Confederate Appalachia.* Chapel Hill: University of North Carolina Press, 2000.

Ireland, Robert M. *The County Courts in Antebellum Kentucky.* Lexington: University Press of Kentucky, 1972.

_____. *The County in Kentucky History.* Lexington: University Press of Kentucky, 1976.

_____. *The Kentucky State Constitution: A Reference Guide.* Westport, CT: Greenwood Press, 1999.

_____. *Little Kingdoms: The Counties of Kentucky, 1850–1891.* Lexington: University of Kentucky Press, 1977.

Ison, Cecil R. "The Cold Oak Shelter: Providing a Better Understanding of the Terminal Archaic." In *Paleoindian and Archaic Research in Kentucky,* edited by Charles Hockensmith, David Pollack,

and Thomas Sanders. Frankfort: Kentucky Heritage Council, 1988.

Jewell, Malcolm E., and Everett W. Cunningham. *Kentucky Politics.* Lexington: University of Kentucky Press, 1968.

Johnson, Leland R. *The Falls City Engineers: A History of the Louisville District, Corps of Engineers, United States Army.* Louisville: United States Army Corps of Engineers, 1974.

_____. *The Falls City Engineers: A History of the Louisville District, Corps of Engineers, United States Army, 1970–1983.* Louisville: United States Army Engineer District, 1984.

Johnson, Leland R., and Charles E. Parrish. *Kentucky River Development: The Commonwealth's Waterway.* Louisville: Louisville Engineer District, U.S. Army Corps of Engineers, 1999.

Katz, Michael B. *The Undeserving Poor: From the War on Poverty to the War on Welfare.* New York: Pantheon Books, 1989.

Kennedy, David M. *Freedom from Fear: The American People in Depression and War, 1929–1945.* New York: Oxford University Press, 1999.

Khagram, Sanjeev. *Dams and Development: Transnational Struggles for Water and Power.* Ithaca: Cornell University Press, 2004.

Kierkendall, Richard S. *Social Scientists and Farm Politics in the Age of Roosevelt.* Columbia, MO: University of Missouri Press, 1967.

Kiffmeyer, Thomas J. "From Self-Help to Sedition: The Appalachian Volunteers in Eastern Kentucky, 1964–1970." *The Journal of Southern History* 64 (1998): 65–94.

Kilduff, Rosemary Porter, and Mary Helen McGuire. *Peoples Exchange Bank 1912–1987.* Beattyville, KY: Peoples Exchange Bank, 1990.

Kilty, Keith M., and Elizabeth A. Segal, eds. *Rediscovering the Other America: The Continuing Crisis of Poverty and Inequality in the United States.* New York: Haworth Press, 2003.

Kleber, John E., ed. *The Kentucky Encyclopedia.* Lexington: University Press of Kentucky, 1992.

_____. *Thomas D. Clark of Kentucky: An Uncommon Life in the Commonwealth.* Lexington: University Press of Kentucky, 2003.

Klotter, James C. *The Breckinridges of Kentucky, 1760–1981.* Lexington: University Press of Kentucky, 1986.

Klotter, James C., and Henry C. Mayer. *A Century of Banking: The Story of Farmers State Bank and Banking in Owsley County, 1890–1990.* Booneville, KY: Farmers State Bank, 1989.

Kodras, Janet E. "The Changing Map of American Poverty in an Era of Economic Restructuring and Political Realignment." *Economic Geography* 73, no. 1 (January 1997), 67–93.

Kohl, Lawrence Frederick. *Politics of Individualism: Parties and American Character in the Jacksonian Era.* New York: Oxford University Press, 1989.

Lane, Leon, and David G. Anderson. "Paleoindian Occupations of the Southern Appalachians: A View from the Cumberland Plateau of Kentucky and Tennessee." In *Archaeology of the Appalachian Highlands*, edited by Lynne P. Sullivan and Susan C. Prezzano. Knoxville: University of Tennessee Press, 2001.

Leslie, Jacques. *Deep Water: The Epic Struggle Over Dams, Displaced People, and the Environment.* New York: Farrar, Straus and Giroux, 2005.

Lewis, Helen M. "Fatalism or the Coal Industry." *Mountain Life and Work* 46 (1970): 4–15.

Lewis Helen M., and Edward E. Knipe. "The Colonialism Model: The Appalachian Cast." In *Colonialism in Modern America: The Appalachian Case*, edited by Helen M. Lewis, Linda Johnson, and Donald Askins. Boone, NC: The Appalachian Consortium Press, 1978.

Lewis, Helen M., Linda Johnson, and Donald Askins, eds. *Colonialism in Modern America: The Appalachian Case.* Boone, NC: The Appalachian Consortium Press, 1978.

Lewis, Helen Matthews, Sue Easterling Kobak, and Linda Johnson. "Family, Religion and Colonialism in Central Appalachia, or Bury My Rifle at Big Stone Gap." In *Colonialism in Modern America: The Appalachian Case*, edited by Helen Matthews Lewis, Linda Johnson, and Donald Askins. Boone, NC: The Appalachian Consortium Press, 1978.

Lewis, R. Berry, ed. *Kentucky Archaeology.* Lexington: University Press of Kentucky, 1996.

Lewis, Ronald L. *Transforming the Appalachian Countryside: Railroads, Deforestation, and Social Change in West Virginia, 1880–1920.* Chapel Hill: University of North Carolina Press, 1998.

Lindstrom, Matthew J., and Zachary A. Smith. *National Environmental Policy Act: Judicial Misconstruction, Legislative Indifference, and Executive Neglect.* College Station: Texas A&M University Press, 2002.

Lomuscio, James. *Village of the Dammed: The Fight for Open Space and the Flooding of a Connecticut Town.* Hanover: University Press of New England, 2005.

Long, John H., ed. *Atlas of Historical County Boundaries: Kentucky.* New York: Simon & Schuster, 1995.

Lowry, William R. *Dam Politics: Restoring America's Rivers.* Washington, DC: Georgetown University Press, 2003.

Lucas, Marion B. *A History of Blacks in Kentucky.* Vol. 1. *From Slavery to Segregation, 1760–1891.* Frankfort: Kentucky Historical Society, 1992.

Lyson, Thomas A., and William W. Falk, eds. *Forgotten Places: Uneven Development and the Loss of Opportunity in Rural America.* Lawrence: University Press of Kansas, 1993.

Mallalieu, W.C. "Owsley, William." In *Dictionary of American Biography (Mills-Platner, vol. 7)*, edited by Dumas Malone. New York: Scribner's, 1934.

Marsh, Alton. "Daniel Boone's Wilderness May Be Tamed by a Lake." *Smithsonian* 6 (September 1975): 56–62.

_____. "Last Stand at Red River Gorge." *National Parks and Conservation Magazine* 48 (August 1974): 18–24.

Martin, William H. "The Red River Gorge Controversy in Kentucky: A Case Study in Preserving a Natural Area." *The ASB Bulletin (The Official Quarterly Publication of the Association of Southeastern Biologists)* 23, no. 3 (July 1976): 163–167.

Matusow, Allen J. *The Unraveling of America: A History of Liberalism in the 1960s.* New York: Harper and Row, 1984.

McCullough, David G. *Brave Companions: Portraits in History.* New York: Simon & Schuster, 1992.

McKinney, Gordon B. "Preindustrial Jackson County and Economic Development." *Journal of the Appalachian Studies Association* 2 (1990): 1–10.

_____. *Southern Mountain Republicans, 1865–1900*. Chapel Hill: University of North Carolina Press, 1978.

McKnight, Brian D. *Contested Borderland: The Civil War in Appalachian Kentucky and Virginia*. Lexington: University Press of Kentucky, 2006.

Melish, Joanne Pope. *Disowning Slavery: Gradual Emancipation and "Race" in New England, 1780–1860*. Ithaca: Cornell University Press, 1998.

Milkis, Sidney M., and Jerome M. Mileur, eds. *The Great Society and the High Tide of Liberalism*. Boston: University of Massachusetts Press, 2005.

Mink, Gwendolyn, and Alice O'Connor, eds. *Poverty in the United States: An Encyclopedia of History, Politics, and Policy*. Denver: ABC-Clio, 2004.

Mitchell, Robert D., ed. *Appalachian Frontiers: Settlement, Society, & Development in the Preindustrial Era*. Lexington: University Press of Kentucky, 1991.

"Moonshine Again." *The Economist* 317 (20 October 1990): 25–26.

Moore, Tyrel G. "Economic Development in Appalachian Kentucky, 1800–1860." In *Appalachian Frontiers: Settlement, Society & Development in the Preindustrial Era*, edited by Robert D. Mitchell. Lexington: University Press of Kentucky, 1991.

Murray, Charles. *Losing Ground: American Social Policy, 1950–1980*. New York: Basic Books, 1984.

Nimz, Dale E. "Damming the Kaw: The Kiro Controversy and Flood Control in the Great Depression." *Kansas History* 26, no. 1 (2003): 14–31.

Noe, Kenneth W. *Southwest Virginia's Railway: Modernization and Sectional Crisis*. Urbana: University of Illinois Press, 1994.

Noe, Kenneth W., and Shannon H. Wilson. *The Civil War in Appalachia: Collected Essays*. Knoxville: University of Tennessee Press, 1997.

Nordin, Dennis S., and Roy V. Scott. *From Prairie Farmer to Entrepreneur: The Transformation of Midwestern Agriculture*. Bloomington: University of Indiana Press, 2005.

Obermiller, Phillip J., and Michael E. Maloney, eds. *Appalachia: Social Context Past and Present*. 4th ed. Dubuque: Kendall-Hunt, 2002.

Obermiller, Phillip J., Thomas E. Wagner, and Bruce Tucker, eds. *Appalachian Odyssey: Historical Perspectives on the Great Migration*. Westport: Praeger, 2000.

O'Conner, Alice. *Poverty Knowledge: Social Science, Social Policy, and the Poor in the Twentieth-Century*. Princeton: Princeton University Press, 2001.

Office of History, U.S. Army Corps of Engineers. *The History of the U.S. Army Corps of Engineers*. Honolulu: University Press of the Pacific, 2004.

O'Neill, Karen M. *Rivers by Design: State Power and the Origins of U.S. Flood Control*. Durham: Duke University Press, 2006.

Palmer, Tim. *Endangered Rivers and the Conservation Movement*. Berkeley: University of California Press, 1986.

Paludan, Philip. *Victims: A True Story of the Civil War*. Knoxville: University of Tennessee Press, 1981.

"Participation of the Poor: Section 202(a) (3) Organizations Under the Economic Opportunity Act of 1964." *Yale Law Journal* 75, no. 4 (March 1966): 599–629.

Patterson, James T. *America's Struggle Against Poverty, 1900–1994*. Cambridge, MA: Harvard University Press, 1994.

Pearce, John Ed. *Divide and Dissent: Kentucky Politics 1930–1963*. Lexington: University Press of Kentucky, 1987.

Pearcy, Matthew T. "After the Flood: A History of the 1928 Flood Control Act." *Journal of the Illinois State Historical Society* 95, no. 2 (2002): 172–201.

Pearson, Byron E. *Still the Wild River Runs: Congress, the Sierra Club, and the Fight to Save Grand Canyon*. Tucson: University of Arizona Press, 2002.

Perkins, Van L. *Crisis in Agriculture: The Agricultural Adjustment Administration and the New Deal, 1933*. Berkeley: University of California Press, 1969.

Perry, Huey. *"They'll Cut Off Your Project": A Mingo County Chronicle*. New York: Praeger, 1972.

Philliber, William. *Appalachian Migrants in Urban America*. Westport: Praeger, 1981.

Philliber, William W., and Clyde B. McCoy, eds. *The Invisible Minority: Urban Appalachians*. Lexington: University Press of Kentucky, 1981.

Plunkett, H. Dudley. "Modernization Reappraised: The Kentucky Mountains

Revisited and Confrontational Politics Reassessed." *Comparative Education Review* 22, no. 1 (February 1978): 134–142.

Plunkett, H. Dudley, and Mary Jean Bowman. *Elites & Change in the Kentucky Mountains.* Lexington: University Press of Kentucky, 1973.

Porter, Eliot. "The Red River Gorge — One Final Look." *Audubon* 70, no. 5 (September/October 1968): 58–70.

Potter, Gary W., and Larry K. Gaines. "Country Comfort: Vice and Corruption in Rural Settings," *Journal of Contemporary Criminal Justice* (February 1992): 36–61.

Potter, Gary W., Larry K. Gaines, and Beth Holbrook. "Blowing Smoke: An Evaluation of Marijuana Eradication in Kentucky." *American Journal of Police* (1990): 97–116.

Powlas, Joe. *The Church with the Golden Roof.* Detroit: Harlo Press, 1988.

Pudup, Mary Beth. "Social Class and Economic Development in Southeastern Kentucky, 1820–1880." In *Appalachian Frontiers: Settlement, Society & Development in the Preindustrial Era*, edited by Robert D. Mitchell. Lexington: University Press of Kentucky, 1991.

_____. "The Limits of Subsistence: Agriculture and Industry in Central Appalachia." *Agricultural History* 64, no. 1 (1990): 61–89.

Pudup, Mary Beth, Dwight B. Billings, and Altina L. Waller, eds. *Appalachia in the Making: The Mountain South in the Nineteenth Century.* Chapel Hill: University of North Carolina Press, 1995.

Quadagno, Jill. *The Color of Welfare: How Racism Undermined the War on Poverty.* New York: Oxford University Press, 1994.

Reeves, Andrée E. *Congressional Committee Chairmen: Three Who Made an Evolution.* Lexington: University Press of Kentucky, 1993.

Reeves, T. Zane. *The Politics of the Peace Corps and VISTA.* Tuscaloosa: University of Alabama Press, 1988.

Remini, Robert V. *Henry Clay: Statesman for the Union.* New York: W.W. Norton, 1991.

Rennick, Robert M. "The Post Offices of Owsley County, Kentucky." *La Posta: A Journal of American Postal History* 35, no. 5 (2004): 56–64.

Revesv, Richard L. "Federalism and Environmental Regulation." *Harvard Law Review* 115, no. 2 (1997): 553–641.

Righter, Robert W. *The Battle Over Hetch Hetchy: America's Most Controversial Dam and the Birth of Modern Environmentalism.* New York: Oxford University Press, 2005.

Robinson, Michael C. "The Relationship between the Army Corps of Engineers and the Environmental Community." *Environmental Review* 13 (1989): 1–41.

Rogers, Michael. "TVA Population Removal: Attitudes and Expectations of the Dispossessed at the Norris and Cherokee Dam Sites." *Journal of East Tennessee History* 67 (1995): 89–105.

Rosen, Howard, and Martin Reuss, eds. *The Flood Control Challenge: Past, Present, and Future.* Chicago: Public Works Historical Society, 1988.

Rutherford, Glenn O. "The Saga of the Red River Gorge." *American Forests* (February 1972): 20–23.

Saloutos, Theodore. *The American Farmer and the New Deal.* Ames, IA: Iowa State University Press, 1982.

Salstrom, Paul. *Appalachia's Path to Dependency: Rethinking a Region's Economic History, 1730–1940.* Lexington: University Press of Kentucky, 1994.

Sarris, Jonathan Dean. *A Separate Civil War: Communities in Conflict in the Mountain South.* Charlottesville: University of Virginia Press, 2006.

Scarbrough, Linda. *Road, River, and Ol' Boy Politics: A Texas County's Path from Farm to Supersuburb.* Austin: Texas State Historical Association, 2005.

Schneiders, Robert Kelley. *Big Sky Rivers: The Yellowstone and the Upper Missouri.* Lawrence: University Press of Kansas, 2003.

_____. *Unruly River: Two Centuries of Change Along the Missouri.* Lawrence: University Press of Kansas, 1999.

Schoenbaum, Thomas J. *The New River Controversy.* Winston-Salem, NC: J.F. Blair, 1979.

Schulman, Robert. *John Sherman Cooper, the Global Kentuckian.* Lexington: University Press of Kentucky, 1976.

Schwarzweller, Harry K., James S. Brown, and J. J. Mangalam. *Mountain Families in Transition: A Case Study of Appalachian Migration.* University Park: Pennsylvania State University Press, 1971.

Scott, Shaunna L. *Two Sides to Everything: The Cultural Construction of Class Consciousness in Harlan County, Kentucky*. Albany: State University of New York Press, 1995.

Sellers, Charles. *The Market Revolution: Jacksonian America, 1815–1846*. New York: Oxford University Press, 1991.

Semple, Ellen Churchill. "The Anglo-Saxons of the Kentucky Mountains: A Study in Anthropogeography." *Geographic Journal* 17, no. 6 (1901): 588–623.

Shackleford, Nevyle. *The Romance of Lee County*. Beattyville, KY: The Beattyville Enterprise, 1947.

Shaffer, John W. *Clash of Loyalties: A Border County in the Civil War*. Morgantown: University of West Virginia Press, 2003.

Shallat, Todd. "Engineering Policy: The U.S. Army Corps of Engineers and the Historical Foundation of Power." *Public Historian* 11, no. 3 (1989): 7–27.

_____. *Structures in the Stream: Water, Science, and the Rise of the U.S. Army Corps of Engineers*. Austin: University of Texas Press, 1994.

Shannon, J.B., J.E. Reeves, H. Clyde Reeves, and Harry R. Lynn. *A Decade of Change in Kentucky Government and Politics*. Lexington: University of Kentucky Bureau of Government Research, 1943.

Shapiro, Henry D. *Appalachia on Our Mind: The Southern Mountains and Mountaineers in the American Consciousness, 1870–1920*. Chapel Hill: University of North Carolina Press, 1978.

Shifflett, Crandall A. *Coal Towns: Life, Work, and Culture in Company Towns of Southern Appalachia, 1880–1960*. Knoxville: University of Tennessee Press, 1995.

_____. *Patronage and Poverty in the Tobacco South: Louisa County, Virginia, 1860–1900*. Knoxville: University of Tennessee Press, 1982.

Shrake, Edwin. "Operation Build and Destroy." *Sports Illustrated* (1 April 1968): 46–49.

Simpson, John Warfield. *Dam!: Water, Power, Politics, and Preservation in Hetch Hetchy and Yosemite National Park*. New York: Pantheon Books, 2005.

Smith, John F. "The Salt-Making Industry of Clay County, Kentucky." *Filson Club History Quarterly* 1 (1927): 134–141.

Smith, Krista. "Slaveholders vs. Slaveholders: Divided Kentuckians in the Secession Crisis." *The Register of the Kentucky Historical Society* 97 (1999): 375–401.

Smith, Robert L. *Owsley County, Kentucky 1850 Census*. Cincinnati: Robert L. Smith, n.d.

_____. *Owsley County, Kentucky 1860 Census*. Cincinnati: Robert L. Smith, n.d.

_____. *Owsley County, Kentucky Tax Books 1844–1858*. Cincinnati: Robert L. Smith, n.d.

Snell, John W. *Red River Gorge: The Eloquent Landscape*. Morley, MO: Acclaim Press, 2006.

Sobel, Robert, ed. *Biographical Directory of the United States Executive Branch, 1774–1989*. Westport, CT: Greenwood Publishing Group, 1990.

Sproul, David Kent. "Environmentalism and the Kaiparowits Power Project, 1964–76." *Utah Historical Quarterly* 70, no. 4 (2002): 356–371.

Stewart, Kathleen. *A Space on the Side of the Road: Cultural Poetics in an "Other" America*. Princeton: Princeton University Press, 1996.

Stine, Jeffrey K. *Mixing the Waters: Environment, Politics, and the Building of the Tennessee-Tombigbee Waterway*. Akron: University of Akron Press, 1993.

Sullivan, Lynn P., and Susan C. Prezzano, eds. *Archaeology of the Appalachian Highlands*. Knoxville: University of Tennessee Press, 2001.

Tallant, Harold D. *Evil Necessity: Slavery and Political Culture in Antebellum Kentucky*. Lexington: University Press of Kentucky, 2003.

Thomas, Jerry Bruce. *An Appalachian New Deal: West Virginia in the Great Depression*. Lexington: University Press of Kentucky, 1998.

Tice, Karen, and Dwight Billings. "Appalachian Culture and Resistance." *Journal of Progressive Human Services* 2, no. 2 (1991): 1–18.

Tolnay, Stewart E., Robert M. Adelman, and Kyle D. Crowder. "Race, Regional Origin, and Residence in Northern Cities at the Beginning of the Great Migration." *American Sociological Review* 67, no. 3 (June 2002): 456–475.

Tomaskovic-Devey, Donald, and Vincent J. Roscigno. "Uneven Development and Local Inequality in the U.S. South: The

Role of Outside Investment, Landed Elites, and Racial Dynamics." *Sociological Forum* 12, no. 4 (December 1997): 565–597.

Trocano, Pat. *Lieutenant James McGuire, 1740–August 19, 1782: Reflections on my Fifth Great-grandfather and the Battle of Blue Licks.* Trocano Home Publishing, 1996.

Tunnell, Kenneth D. "The OxyContin Epidemic and Crime Panic in Rural Kentucky." *Contemporary Drug Problems* (Summer 2005): 225–258.

Turner, William H, and Edward J. Cabbell, eds. *Blacks in Appalachia.* Lexington: University Press of Kentucky, 1985.

Tursic, Phil. "Appalachia HIDTA Assesses Threat to Region." *Kentucky Law Enforcement News* (March 2005): 29–31.

Ulack, Richard, et al., eds. *Atlas of Kentucky.* Lexington: University Press of Kentucky, 1998.

Verhoeff, Mary. *Kentucky Mountain Transportation and Commerce 1750–1911: A Study in the Economic History of a Coal Field.* Louisville: John P. Morton, 1911.

_____. *Kentucky River Navigation.* Louisville: The Filson Club, 1917.

Vincent, George E. "A Retarded Frontier." *The American Journal of Sociology* 4 (1898): 1–20.

Waller, Altina L. *Feud: Hatfields, McCoys and Social Change in Appalachia.* Chapel Hill: University of North Carolina Press, 1988.

Wallerstein, Immanuel. *The Essential Wallerstein.* New York: New Press, 2000.

Walls, David S. "Internal Colony or Internal Periphery? A Critique of Current Models and an Alternative Formulation." In *Colonialism in Modern America: The Appalachian Case,* edited by Helen Lewis, Linda Johnson, and Donald Askins. Boone, NC: The Appalachian Consortium Press, 1978.

Waples, David A. *The Natural Gas Industry in Appalachia.* Jefferson, NC: McFarland, 2005.

Watson, Harry L. *Andrew Jackson vs. Henry Clay: Democracy and Development in Antebellum America.* New York: St. Martin's, 1998.

_____. *Liberty and Power: The Politics of Jacksonian America.* Updated edition. New York: Farrar, Straus, and Giroux, 2006.

Watson, Judge. *Eastern Kentucky, Economic and Cultural, 1900–1962.* Bartow, FL: Bartow Printing, 1993.

Weber, B.A., G.J. Duncan, and L.E. Whitener, eds. *Rural Dimensions of Welfare Reform: Welfare, Food Assistance, and Poverty in Rural America.* Kalamazoo, MI: Upjohn Institute, 2002.

Weingartner, Paul, Dwight B. Billings, and Kathleen Blee. "Agriculture in Preindustrial Appalachia: Subsistence Farming in Beech Creek, 1850–1880." *Appalachian Journal* 13 (1986): 154–170.

Weir, Margaret. *Politics and Jobs: The Boundaries of Employment Policy in the United States.* Princeton: Princeton University Press, 1992.

Weise, Robert S. *Grasping at Independence: Debt, Male Authority, and Mineral Rights in Appalachian Kentucky, 1850–1915.* Knoxville: University of Tennessee Press, 2001.

_____. "Remaking Red Bird: Isolation and the War on Poverty in a Rural Appalachian Locality." In *The Countryside in the Age of the Modern State: Political Histories of Rural America,* edited by Catherine McNicol Stock, and Robert D. Johnston. Ithaca: Cornell University Press, 2001.

Weller, Jack E. *Yesterday's People: Life in Contemporary Appalachia.* Lexington: University of Kentucky Press, 1965.

Wells, Diane, comp. *Roadside History: A Guide to Kentucky Highway Markers.* Frankfort: The Kentucky Historical Society, 2002.

Wharton, Mary Euginia. "Red River Dam Controversy." *AAAS Bulletin* (June 1969): n.p.

Whisnant, David E. *All That Is Native & Fine: The Politics of Culture in an American Region.* Chapel Hill: University of North Carolina Press, 1983.

_____. *Modernizing the Mountaineer: People, Power, and Planning in Appalachia.* Revised edition. Knoxville: University of Tennessee Press, 1994.

Wilentz, Sean. *The Rise of American Democracy: Jefferson to Lincoln.* New York: W.W. Norton, 2005.

Williams, John Alexander. *Appalachia: A History.* Chapel Hill: University of North Carolina Press, 2002.

Wilson, Jess. *When They Hanged the Fiddler and Other Stories from "It Happened*

Here" (Including Some Unpublished Works by the Author). Berea, KY: Kentucke Imprints, 1978.

Wilson, Jess D., ed. *Mountain Men in the Mexican War, 1847–1848: A Roster of Soldiers Enrolled for the Mexican War from the Eastern Kentucky Counties of Estill, Owsley, Clay, Laurel and Rockcastle*. McKee, KY: Jackson County Rural Electric Cooperative, 1975.

Wilson, Joyce. *This Was Yesterday: A Romantic History of Owsley County*. Ashland, KY: Economy Printers, 1977.

Wolfe, Margaret Ripley. "Eastern Kentucky and the War on Poverty: Grass-Roots Activism, Regional Politics, and Creative Federalism in the Appalachian South During the 1960s." *Ohio Valley History* 3, no. 1 (2003): 31–44.

_____. "Lifting Up His Eyes Unto the Hills: Harry M. Caudill and His Appalachia." *The Filson History Quarterly* 76, no. 1 (Winter 2002): 1–32.

Wolfle, Dael. "The Only Earth We Have." *Science* 159, no. 3811 (12 January 1968): 155.

Zarefsky, David. *President Johnson's War on Poverty: Rhetoric and History*. Tuscaloosa: University of Alabama Press, 1986.

UNPUBLISHED WORKS

Alexander, J. Trent. "Great Migrations: Race and Community in the Southern Exodus, 1917–1970." Ph.D. diss., Carnegie Mellon University, 2001.

Alexander, Sara E. "Conflict, Environmental Protection and Social Well-Being: The Exercise of Power in Red River Gorge." Ph.D. diss., University of Kentucky, 1987.

Allen, Jeffrey Brooke. "The Debate Over Slavery and Race in Ante-Bellum Kentucky, 1792–1850." Ph.D. diss., Northwestern University, 1973.

Andrews, Theodore Howard. "John F. Kennedy, Lyndon Johnson, and the Politics of Poverty, 1960–1967." Ph.D. diss., Stanford University, 1998.

Arnett, Douglas O'Neil. "Eastern Kentucky: The Politics of Dependence and Underdevelopment." Ph.D. diss., Duke University, 1978.

Bailey, Rebecca J. "Matewan Before the Massacre: Politics, Coal, and the Roots of Conflict in Mingo County, 1793–1920." Ph.D. diss., West Virginia University, 2001.

Bohannon, Keith S. "The Northeast Georgia Mountains During the Secession Crisis and Civil War." Ph.D. diss., Pennsylvania State University, 2001.

Boyd, John A. "Neutrality & Peace: Kentucky and the Secession Crisis of 1861." Ph.D. diss., University of Kentucky, 1999.

Burch, John Russell. "County Creation in Kentucky: Owsley and Lee Counties 1843–1870." M.A. thesis, University of Kentucky, 2003.

_____. "The Dammed: Imagining the American Dream in Appalachian Kentucky." Ph.D. diss., University of Kentucky, 2005.

Couto, Richard. "Poverty, Politics and Health Care: The Experience of One Appalachian County." Ph.D. diss., University of Kentucky, 1973.

Cowan, C. Wesley. "From Foraging to Incipient Food Production: Subsistence Change and Continuity on the Cumberland Plateau of Eastern Kentucky." Ph.D. diss., University of Michigan, 1985.

Cowan, Charles Wesley. "An Archaeological Survey and Assessment of the Proposed Red River Reservoir in Powell, Wolfe, and Menifee Counties, Kentucky." Tallahassee, FL: National Park Service, 1975.

Dunaway, Wilma A. "The Incorporation of Southern Appalachia into the Capitalist World-Economy, 1700–1860." Ph.D. diss., University of Tennessee, 1994.

Erwin, Mary Camille. "The Vicious Circle: A Study of the Effects of the Depression and New Deal Relief Programs in Eastern Kentucky." M.A. Thesis, University of Louisville, 1967.

Evens, Wayne Carl. "The Effects of Idea Systems on Social Policy: The Case of the Economic Opportunity Act of 1964." Ph.D. diss., University of Iowa, 1996.

Friend, Craig Thompson. "Inheriting Eden: The Creation of Society and Community in Early Kentucky, 1792–1812." Ph.D. diss., University of Kentucky, 1995.

Haeberle, Steven Howard. "The Appalachian Regional Commission: Evaluating and Experiment in Creative Federalism." Ph.D. diss., Duke University, 1981.

Hawkins, Robert D. "Social Control in the Eastern Kentucky Subculture of Violence." Ph.D. diss., Sam Houston State University, 1998.

Horton, Billy D. "The Appalachian Volunteers: A Case Study of Community Organization and Conflict." M.A. thesis, University of Kentucky, 1971.

Hyman, Diana Rachel. "Defenses of Solitude: Justice Douglas, the Right to Privacy, and the Preservation of the American Wilderness." Ph.D. diss, Harvard University, 2003.

Kiffmeyer, Thomas J. "From Self-Help to Sedition: The Appalachian Volunteers and the War on Poverty in Eastern Kentucky, 1964–1970." Ph.D. diss., University of Kentucky, 1998.

Laing, Craig R. "Mountain Aid: Geographic Assessment of the Appalachian Regional Commission's Social Programs." Ph.D. diss., University of Tennessee, 1997.

Mannion, Elgin. "The Method of Growth: Development Models and Income Distribution in Appalachian Kentucky from 1969 to 2003." Ph.D. diss., University of Kentucky, 2003.

Matvey, Joseph John. "Central Appalachia: Distortions in Development, 1750–1986." Ph.D. diss., University of Pittsburgh, 1987.

McClure, Virginia Clay. "The Settlement of the Kentucky Appalachian Highlands." Ph.D. diss., University of Kentucky, 1933.

Moore, Tyrel Gilce, Jr. "An Historical Geography of Economic Development in Appalachian Kentucky, 1800–1939." Ph.D. diss., University of Tennessee, 1984.

"Owsley County History." Manuscript in County Records File, Thomas D. Clark Library, Kentucky Historical Society, n.d.

Parker, Sara Gwenyth. "The Transformation of Cherokee Appalachia." Ph.D. diss., University of California, Berkeley, 1991.

Pearson, Byron Eugene. "People Above Scenery: The Struggle Over the Grand Canyon Dams, 1963–1968." Ph.D. diss., University of Arizona, 1998.

Rice, Leila Meier. "In the Trenches of the War on Poverty: The Local Implementation of the Community Action Program, 1964–1969." Ph.D. diss., Vanderbilt University, 1997.

Russell, Timothy McKnight. "Neutrality and Ideological Conflict in Kentucky During the First Year of the American Civil War." Ph.D. diss., University of New Mexico, 1989.

Schmitt, Edward Robert. "A Human Struggle: Robert Kennedy and the Problem of Poverty in America." Ph.D. diss., Marquette University, 2003.

Smith, Brian. "The Role of the Poor in the Poverty Program: The Origin and Development of Maximum Feasible Participation." M.A. thesis, Columbia University, 1966.

Smith, Charles Robert. "Anticipations of Change: A Socio-Economic Description of a Kentucky County Before Reservoir Construction." M.A. thesis, University of Kentucky, 2003.

Smoot, Richard C. "John Sherman Cooper: The Paradox of a Liberal Republican in Kentucky Politics." Ph.D. diss., University of Kentucky, 1988.

Sowards, Adam M. "'He's a Natural': Justice William O. Douglas and the American Environmental Tradition." Ph.D. diss., Arizona State University, 2001.

Steuernagel, Gertrude A. "American Liberalism: The Welfare State and the War on Poverty." Ph.D. diss., Kent State University, 1992.

Taul, Glen Edward. "Poverty, Development, and Government in Appalachia: Origins of the Appalachian Regional Commission." Ph.D. diss., University of Kentucky, 2001.

Weise, Robert Spencer. "Economy and Society in Appalachian Kentucky, 1850–1915." Ph.D. diss., University of Virginia, 1995.

Index

215